# AGAINST POSTMODERNISM

# AGAINST POSTMODERNISM

## A MARXIST CRITIQUE

ALEX CALLINICOS

St. Martin's Press

First published in the United States of America in 1990

Reprinted 1991, 1994, 1996, 1999

Printed in Great Britain

ISBN 0–312–04224–8 cloth
ISBN 0–312–04225–6 paper

*Library of Congress Cataloging-in-Publication Data*

Callinicos, Alex.
Against postmodernism.

1. Postmodernism — Controversial literature.
2. Philosophy, Marxist.    I. Title.
B831.2.C34     1990     190',9'049     89-70065
ISBN 0–312–04224–8
ISBN 0–312–04225–6 (pbk.)

What's the idea? to speak of progress to a world sinking into
the rigidity of death.

Walter Benjamin

Every age has disliked its own modernity; every age from the
first onwards has preferred the previous one to itself.

Walter Map

*To Max, in the hope that
he lives up to his name*

# CONTENTS

*Contents*

# PREFACE AND ACKNOWLEDGEMENTS

This book is an attempt to challenge the strange mixture of cultural and political pessimism and light-minded playfulness with which – in a more than usually farcical reprise of the apocalyptic mood at the end of the last century – much of the contemporary Western intelligentsia apparently intends to greet our own *fin de siècle*. At stake are more than philosophical and aesthetic issues. Fundamentally what is involved is whether classical Marxism – which most left-wing intellectuals now, like the New Right, regard as terribly old fashioned – can illuminate and contribute to improving our present condition. In trying to answer this question, however, I follow a tortuous path, employing the tools of philosophy and social theory to examine the claim that we are currently experiencing an epochal change in our social life – a claim which I reject as false.

I doubt if I would ever have written this book were it not for the promptings provided by various invitations to discuss what turned out to be its subject-matter: I am grateful especially to all those involved in the Cardiff Critical Theory Seminar, the journal *Theory, Culture & Society*, whose editors also very kindly allowed me to use (in chapter 3) parts of an article of mine which they published, the Critical Theory Colloquium at the University of Iowa, the Institute of Contemporary Arts in London, the British Sociological Association Theory Group Conference on postmodernism in January 1987, the seminar to which I read a paper at the Department of French at Birkbeck College, London, and the Political Theory Workshop at the University of York. I should also like to thank my colleagues in the Department of Politics at York for allowing me the time in which to write this book. Colin Gordon came up with the *bon mot* that became the title of chapter 1. The work of Perry Anderson, Peter Bürger, Frederic Jameson and Franco Moretti greatly clarified my under-standing of Modernism. And David Held was, once again, an encouraging, enthusiastic and helpful editor.

Russell Jacoby in his interesting (though flawed) book *The Last*

*Intellectuals* traces the postwar retreat of the American intelligentsia from public life into the academy. A roughly similar story could be told of their British counterparts. And no doubt the acknowledgements above make clear my own institutional location. But I am fortunate in being subject also to the discipline that comes from active involvement in socialist organization. I would therefore like, last of all, to thank my comrades in the Socialist Workers Party, both for the patience they show towards my speculative reveries, and for contributing so much to the understanding of contemporary capitalism that I try to develop in chapter 5 below.

# INTRODUCTION

Yet *another* book on postmodernism? What earthly justification could there be for contributing to the destruction of the world's dwindling forests in order to engage in debates which should surely have exhausted themselves long ago? My embarrassment in the face of this challenge is made all the more acute by the fact that at the origins of the present book lies that unworthy emotion, irritation. This feeling sprang from the way in which, in the course of the 1980s, the word 'postmodernism' seemed to slip into every imaginable theoretical discussion. I found myself invited to contribute to symposia, conferences, special issues of journals which all turned out to be about postmodernism. Since on more than one occasion I had thought them to be about something quite different this was a disconcerting experience.

It was not, however, an idiosyncratic one. The 1980s were a boom time for postmodernism. One of its principal propagandists, Ihab Hassan, could write in a collection published in 1987:

> Fastidious academics once shunned the word *postmodern* as they might shrink from the shadiest neologism. But now the term has become a shibboleth for tendencies in film, theatre, dance, music, art and architecture; in philosophy, theology, psychoanalysis and historiography; in new sciences, cybernetic technologies, and various cultural lifestyles. Indeed, postmodernism has now received the bureaucratic accolade of the National Endowment for the Humanities in the form of Summer Seminars for College Teachers; and beyond that, it has penetrated the discourse of late Marxist critics who, only a decade ago, dismissed the term as another instance of the dreck, fads and folderol of a consumer society.[1]

Hassan's claims are plainly concerned with the United States (or at most North America: postmodernism found some of its most extravagant enthusiasts in Canada). Nevertheless, the same intellectual trends made themselves felt in Britain. The notorious parochialism of the British academy ensured that the impact was greatest on the latter's periphery: those interested in the latest trends in the arts – a symposium on postmodernism at the Tate Gallery in October 1987 attracted 1,500 applicants for 200 places – or those on the intellectual liberal left, whose daily paper, the *Guardian*, devoted a series to the subject at the end of 1986 and whose favourite magazines, the *New Statesman* and *Marxism Today*, advertised various postmodernist themes. With local variations the term 'postmodernism' was also taken up elsewhere in the Western world.

But what did it mean? That was the question which came increasingly to agitate me as I confronted this proliferating discourse about postmodernism. Matters weren't helped by the fact that lead producers of the discourse such as Jean-François Lyotard and Charles Jencks offered definitions which were mutually inconsistent, internally contradictory and/or hopelessly vague. Nevertheless, it gradually became clear that postmodernism represented the convergence of three distinct cultural trends. The first involved certain changes in the arts over the previous couple of decades – in particular, the reaction against the International Style in architecture associated with such names as Robert Venturi and James Sterling which first brought the term 'Postmodern' into popular usage. (Throughout this book I use the word 'art' in a generic sense to refer not simply to painting and sculpture, but also to architecture, music, literature, drama etc. I also capitalize the names of artistic movements and styles such as Romanticism, Modernism and Surrealism. Consequently, the term 'postmodern' is sometimes capitalized and sometimes not: thus 'Postmodern architecture' but 'the social theory of postmodernity'.) This rejection of the functionalism and austerity prized by the Bauhaus, Mies van der Rohe and Gropius in favour of a heterogeneity of styles drawing especially on the past and on mass culture found its apparent counterparts elsewhere in the arts – in a return to figuration in painting, for example, and in the fiction of novelists such as Thomas Pynchon and Umberto Eco.[2] Secondly, however, a certain current in philosophy was thought to be giving conceptual expression to the themes explored by contemporary artists. This was a group of French theorists who came in the 1970s to be known in the English-speaking world by the shared label of 'poststructuralism' – in particular, Gilles Deleuze, Jacques Derrida and Michel Foucault. Despite their many disagreements, all three stressed the fragmentary, heterogeneous and plural character of reality, denied human thought the ability to arrive at any objective account of that reality and reduced the bearer of this thought, the subject, to an incoherent welter of sub- and trans-individual drives and desires. But, thirdly, art and philosophy seemed to reflect (somewhat at odds with poststructuralism's anti-realism) changes in the social world. A version of the transformations supposedly undergone by Western societies in the past quarter century was provided by the theory of postindustrial society developed by sociologists such as Daniel Bell and Alain Touraine. According to these theorists the developed world was experiencing the transition from one economy based on mass industrial production to one in which systematic theoretical research is the engine of growth – a change with enormous social, political and cultural implications.

Lyotard's book *The Postmodern Condition*, first published in 1979, enjoys a certain definitive status in discussion of postmodernism precisely because it weaves together Postmodern art, poststructuralist philosophy and the theory of postindustrial society into – perhaps not a seamless whole, but certainly one whose apparent coherence has impressed many. Lyotard defines the postmodern by contrast to the modern:

> I will use the term *modern* to designate any science that legitimates itself with reference to a metadiscourse ... making an explicit appeal to some grand narrative, such as the dialectics of Spirit, the hermeneutics of meaning, the emancipation of the rational or working subject, or the creation of wealth.

Hegel and Marx are plainly among the chief authors of such grand narratives which, Lyotard tells us, legitimate not simply theoretical discourses but also social institutions. By contrast, 'I define *postmodern* as incredulity toward metanarratives.' The denial which Lyotard holds to be characteristic of postmodernism – namely of the existence of any general pattern on which to base our conception of a true theory or a just society – are clearly related to the pluralism and anti-realism championed by poststructuralism. These philosophical positions find, however, according to Lyotard, some objective purchase by virtue of the fact that '[i]n the postindustrial and postmodern age', where 'knowledge has become the principal force of production', science itself fragments into a congerie of games, each seeking not deterministic laws but instabilities, and all legitimizing themselves, not by appeal to some grand narrative, but by paralogy, the violation of rules. To this shift in the character of theoretical discourse corresponds those forms of art which no longer seek coherence, totalization, integration into the whole.[3]

This analysis plainly has political implications. Lyotard who, as a member of the quasi-Trotskyist *Socialisme ou Barbarie* group in the 1950s had been committed to an anti-Stalinist version of Marxism,

had by the time of *The Postmodern Condition* come to reject the
objective of socialist revolution: 'there is no question here of propos-
ing a "pure" alternative to the system: we all know now, as the 1970s
come to a close, that an attempt at an alternative of that kind would
end up resembling the system it was meant to replace.'[4] 'We all' no
doubt refers to the consensus among the Parisian intelligentsia in the
wake of the *nouveaux philosophes*, who in the late 1970s articulated
the abandonment of Marxism by the disillusioned children of 1968.
Nevertheless, in the subsequent decade the themes of postmodernism
accorded well with the trend of opinion among many left-wing
intellectuals in the English-speaking world. Thus the arguments of
two leading 'Post-Marxists', Ernesto Laclau and Chantal Mouffe,
that socialists should abandon 'classism', the classical Marxist stress
upon the class struggle as the driving force of history and of the
working class as the agency of socialist change, could only be
reinforced by the idea that the Western world at least was entering a
'postmodern' epoch fundamentally different from the industrial capitalism of the nineteenth and twentieth centuries.[5]

The resulting fusion of postmodernism and Post-Marxism was well
expressed by the magazine *Marxism Today*, throughout the 1980s the
most forceful opponent of 'classism' on the British left, which not
long ago announced that we are living in 'New Times':

> Unless the Left can come to terms with those New Times, it must
> live on the sidelines ... At the heart of New Times is the shift from
> the old mass-production Fordist economy to a new, more flexible,
> post-Fordist order based on computers, information technology
> and robotics. But New Times are about much more than economic
> change. Our world is being remade. Mass production, the mass
> consumer, the big city, big-brother state, the sprawling housing
> estate, and the nation-state are in decline: flexibility, diversity,
> differentiation, mobility, communication, decentralization and in-
> ternationalization are in the ascendant. In the process our own
> identities, our sense of self, our own subjectivities are being
> transformed. We are in transition to a new era.[6]

This then is the terrain defined by talk of postmodernism – a
transformed social world which Postmodern art and poststructuralist
philosophy reflect, but in which they also participate, and which
requires a different kind of politics. Now I reject all this. I do not
believe that we live in 'New Times', in a 'postindustrial and postmodern age' fundamentally different from the capitalist mode of production globally dominant for the past two centuries. I deny the main
theses of poststructuralism, which seem to me in substance false. I

doubt very much that Postmodern art represents a qualitative break from the Modernism of the early twentieth century. Moreover, much of what is written in support of the idea that we live in a postmodern epoch seems to me of small calibre intellectually, usually superficial, often ignorant, sometimes incoherent.

I should, however, make a qualification to the judgement just passed. I do not believe that the work of the philosophers now known as poststructuralist can be dismissed in this way: wrong on fundamentals Deleuze, Derrida and Foucault may be, but they develop their ideas with considerable skill and sophistication, and offer partial insights of great value. But then it is not clear that they would necessarily endorse the idea of a postmodern age. Invited to comment on this idea not long before his death Foucault sardonically responded: 'What are we calling postmodernity? I'm not up to date?'[7] It is necessary to distinguish between the philosophical theories developed between the 1950s and the 1970s and subsequently grouped together under the heading of 'poststructuralism' and their appropriation in the past decade in support of the claim that a postmodern epoch is emerging. The running has been made in this latter development primarily by North American philosophers, critics and social theorists, with the help of a couple of Parisian figures, Lyotard and Jean Baudrillard, who appear, when set beside Deleuze, Derrida and Foucault, as the *epigoni* of poststructuralism.

A similar point can be made with respect to Postmodern art. It often seems as if the issue between postmodernists and their opponents turns on what one thinks of the merits or otherwise of recent writing, painting or architecture when compared with the Modernist masterworks of Joyce, Picasso or Mies.[8] But there is a prior question, which is independent of such judgements of value, and which is one of my main concerns in this book, namely whether one can indeed sharply distinguish between Modernism and Postmodernism as two separate epochs in the history of the arts. If, as I argue, one cannot, and if indeed the various claims for the existence or emergence of a postmodern era are false, as I further contend, then we are led to a further question: whence this proliferating discourse on postmodernity? Why is it that in the past decade so large a portion of the Western intelligentsia become convinced that both socio-economic system and cultural practices are undergoing a fundamental break from the recent past?

This book sets out to answer this question, as well as to refute the arguments advanced in support of the idea of such a break. It thus rather uneasily occupies a space defined by the convergence of philosophy, social theory and historical writing. Fortunately, there is an intellectual tradition which is characterized precisely by the synthesis it effects of these genres, namely the classical historical materialism of Marx himself, Engels, Lenin, Trotsky, Luxemburg and Gramsci. From the perspective of this tradition, the present book can be seen as continuing in a very minor key Marx's critique of religion, where he treats Christianity in particular not simply, as the Enlightenment had, as a set of false beliefs, but as the distorted expression of real needs denied by class society. Similarly, I seek here not simply to demonstrate the intellectual inadequacy of postmodernism, understood as the claim, justified by appeal to Postmodern art, poststructuralist philosophy, and the theory of postindustrial society, that we are entering a postmodern epoch, but to set it in historical context. Postmodernism, then, is best seen as a symptom.

The structure of the book reflects this strategy. Chapter 1 explores the main features of postmodernist discourse. It focuses especially on the peculiarly important status accorded in this discourse to Modernism, the way in which at once it is caricatured and its defining characteristics appropriated for Postmodern art, in order to create the impression of some recent and radical break in cultural experience. This leads in chapter 2 to an alternative account of Modernism. Drawing critically on the work of Perry Anderson, Peter Bürger and Franco Moretti, I argue that the great efflorescence of Modernist art at the beginning of the twentieth century must be seen in the context of a specific historical conjuncture which, in the wake of the October Revolution, gave rise to the radicalization of Modernism into such avant-garde movements as Constructivism and Surrealism challenging the institution of art itself as part of the struggle for broader social transformation. The defeat of socialist revolution was also that of the avant garde, and determined the subsequent history of Modernism, of which Postmodern art is merely a variation.

I then turn on chapter 3 to poststructuralism, best seen as, *inter alia*, the philosophical expression of *Modernism*, whose characteristic themes were indeed announced by Nietzsche, the central influence on Deleuze, Derrida and Foucault. I proceed to highlight what seem to be the main difficulties common to all these philosophers – their denial of any objectivity to discourse, their inability to ground the resistance to power which they claim to articulate, and their denial of any coherence or initiative to the human subject. I argue that Foucault's return in his last work to the Nietzschean idea of the subject inventing herself does not resolve these problems, and that Baudrillard's currently fashionable writing represents a vulgar caricature of what is interesting and novel in poststructuralism.

The most powerful recent critic of this tradition is Jürgen Habermas, especially in *The Philosophical Discourse of Modernity* (1985), surely one of the classic works of the decade. I argue in chapter 4 that Habermas's critique of postmodernism is seriously weakened by the essentially procedural conception of reason central to his theory of communicative action, which involves him in an implausible philosophy of language, an idealist theory of society, and an excessively uncritical account of modern liberal democracy. Only, I contend, classical historical materialism, reinforced by an account of language and thought that is naturalistic as well as communicative, can provide a secure basis for the defence of the 'radicalized Enlightenment' to which Habermas is committed.

Finally, in chapter 5, I engage with the social theory of postmodernity, not simply in the shape of the idea of postindustrial society, which is fairly easy to dismiss, but in the more cogent attempts by Marxists or *marxisants* such as Frederic Jameson, Scott Lash and John Urry to claim that a new 'multinational' or 'disorganized' phase of capitalism underlies the supposed emergence of Postmodern art. I argue that the changes these writers detect are, when not greatly exaggerated, either the consequences of much longer-term trends or specific to the particular, and highly unstable economic conjuncture of the 1980s. Consideration of this conjuncture then leads naturally to a discussion of the roots of postmodernism itself, which I argue are to be found in the combination of the disillusioned aftermath of 1968 throughout the Western world and the opportunities for an 'overconsumptionist' lifestyle offered upper white-collar strata by capitalism in the Reagan-Thatcher era.

This argument leads to political conclusions consonant with the intellectual commitments already stated. For not least among the purposes of this book is the reaffirmation of the revolutionary socialist tradition against the apostles of 'New Times'. How well I have backed up this reaffirmation with good arguments I leave it to my readers to judge. But the attempt to do so provides an answer – satisfactory to me at least – to the demand to justify writing this book.

Its tone is predominantly critical, as the foregoing summary should have made clear. My concern here is to demonstrate the erroneous nature of others' views, not to expound my own. Nevertheless, implicit throughout the book, and intermittently explicit, are fragments of a rival account of the issues on which the debate about postmodernism has focused attention – for example, the nature of modernity and of Modern art (chapter 2), and the properties of rationality (chapter 4). Inevitably, this account lacks a sustained argument in its support; perhaps my criticisms of postmodernism, if effective, will act as a recommendation for my own views. Some of the argumentation missing here is provided in another book, *Making History*, in which I try to develop a theory of structure and agency, a necessary counterweight to the antihumanism of Deleuze, Derrida and Foucault. In the end, however, the arguments with which this book – and especially chapter 5 – engage resolve themselves into the more general debate over whether classical Marxism is still capable of providing theoretical and political guidance through the contemporary world, a debate whose resolution will not take place in discourse but on the terrain of politics itself.

# 1
# THE JARGON OF POSTMODERNITY

> We live, I regret to say, in an age of surfaces.
> *Oscar Wilde*

## 1.1 THE ENLIGHTENMENT AND ALL THAT

'Postmodernity' and revolution: the subject of this book may be summed up by these two words apparently with little in common. In fact, they share at least one feature: both lack a referent in the social world. But the two words fail to refer in quite different ways. Socialist revolution is the outcome of historical processes at work throughout the present century which have produced a series of major social and political convulsions, and on one occasion – Russia in October 1917 – the actual emergence, albeit short lived, of a workers' state. The absence of successful socialist revolution is a contingent historical fact. Postmodernity by contrast is merely a theoretical construct, of interest primarily as a symptom of the current mood of the Western intelligentsia (hence the quotation marks around 'postmodernity' above which should be treated as invisibly surrounding every other occurrence of the word in this book). Postmodernity and revolution are, however, connected. Not only does belief in a postmodern epoch generally go along with rejection of socialist revolution as either feasible or desirable, but it is the perceived failure of revolution which has helped to gain widespread acceptance of this belief.

Lyotard treats the rejection of revolution as an instance of a more general phenomenon constitutive of the postmodern, namely the collapse of the 'grand narratives'. These he associates especially with the Enlightenment, that is, with those primarily French and Scottish thinkers of the eighteenth century who sought to extend the methods of theoretical inquiry they believed to be characteristic of the seven-teenth-century scientific revolution from the explanation of the physical to that of the social world as part of a broader attempt by human beings to gain rational control of their environment. The philosophy of history which tended to issue from this approach is well expressed by the title of Condorcet's famous essay, *Sketch of the Progress of the Human Mind*: in the evolution of society can be traced the progressive improvement of the human condition. Lyotard plainly regards Hegel and Marx as, in this respect at least, the successors of the *philosophes*.

But now, he claims, the entire Enlightenment project has foundered:

> This idea of progress as possible, probable or necessary was rooted in the certainty that the development of the arts, technology, knowledge and liberty would be profitable to mankind as a whole.
>
> After two centuries, we are more sensitive to signs that signify the contrary. Neither economic nor political liberalism, nor the various Marxisms, emerge from the sanguinary last two centuries free from the suspicion of crimes against mankind ... What kind of thought is able to sublate (*Aufheben*) Auschwitz in a general (either empirical or speculative) process towards a universal emancipation?[1]

Lyotard calls this thought 'trivial'; a better word would be 'old'. What Georg Lukács called 'Romantic anti-capitalism' had already emerged by the end of the eighteenth century to challenge the Enlightenment and the bourgeois social order which it appeared to sanction in the name of an idealized precapitalist past.[2] Hegel and Marx can be seen as responding to the Romantic critique of the Enlightenment, seeking to integrate it into a more complex understanding of historical development than that offered by Condorcet and the other *philosophes*. Rejection of the Enlightenment, frequently claiming inspiration from Nietzsche, was notoriously a staple of *fin-de-siècle* European thought. Perhaps the most celebrated (and complex) recent example of this tradition is Max Horkheimer's and Theodor Adorno's *Dialectic of Enlightenment* (1944), where the urge to dominate nature, sanctioned by the *philosophes*, culminates in the 'totally administered world' of late capitalism, in which the repressed returns in the barbarous and irrational form of fascism.

'Incredulity towards metanarratives' seems therefore to be at least as old as the Enlightenment which was so productive of grand narratives in the first place. The *fin-de-siècle* recognition of what Sorel called the illusions of progress seems especially embarrassing for those who want to associate distinctively Postmodern art with this incredulity. For the leading figures of the heroic era of Modernism at the beginning of the century generally rejected the notion of historical progress. Thus T. S. Eliot in his famous 1923 review of *Ulysses* describes Joyce's use of myth as 'simply a way of controlling, of ordering, of giving a shape and a significance to the immense panorama of futility and anarchy that is contemporary history'.[3] Frank Kermode argues that what he calls 'the sense of an ending', the feeling of being at the end of an epoch, 'the mood of end-dominated crisis' is 'endemic to what we call modernism'.[4]

Nevertheless an apocalyptic conception of postmodernity as the site of the final catastrophe of Western civilization is fairly commonplace. Thus Arthur Kroker and David Cooke write: 'Ours is a *fin-de-millenium* consciousness, which, existing at the end of history in the twilight time of ultramodernism (of technology) and hyperprimitivism (of public moods), uncovers a great arc of disintegration and decay against the background radiation of parody, kitsch, and burnout.'[5] But postmodernists tend not simply to claim this apocalyptic consciousness (quite a common feature of Western thought, according to Kermode, since the Middle Ages) for their own,[6] but to counterpose it to Modernism, which tends to be conceived as itself an example of the Enlightenment. Thus Linda Hutcheon ascribes to Modernism '[f]aith in the rational, scientific mastery of reality' – precisely what was distinctive to the Enlightenment project.[7]

Russell Berman points out that both postmodernists and defenders of the Enlightenment project such as Habermas

> assert that the concepts of modernity and modernism which are at stake correspond to the cultural formations of humanism that have prevailed in the West since the Renaissance or at least the nineteenth century. Hence the apparent similarity of contemporary polemics to the confrontation between the Enlightenment and its Romantic opposition, so often repeated during the past two centuries. The consequence of this epochal definition of modernity is the relative denigration of the aesthetic revolution at the end of the nineteenth century and the beginning of the twentieth century and the emergence of what is commonly known as 'modern art' or 'modernist literature' in contrast to the traditional and conventional forms of the preceding decades.[8]

We shall return to this lack of historical specificity in section 1.4 below, but let us first consider the other side of this assimilation of Modernist *art* to the Enlightenment, namely the appropriation of features of Modernism in order to give Postmodern art its distinctive identity.

## 1.2  THE EVISCERATION OF MODERNISM

Compare these two passages:

> In the multidimensional and slippery space of Postmodernism anything goes with anything, like a game without rules. Floating images such as those we see in the painting of David Salle maintain no relationship with anything at all, and meaning becomes detachable like the keys on a key ring. Dissociated and decontextualized, they slide past one another failing to link up into a coherent sequence. Their fluctuating but not reciprocal interactions are unable to fix meaning.[9]

> [T]he nature of our epoch is multiplicity and indeterminacy. It can only rest on *das Gleitende* [the moving, the slipping, the sliding], and is aware that what other generations believed to be firm is in fact *das Gleitende*.[10]

The first passage comes from a talk given by the art critic Suzy Gablik in Los Angeles in 1987, the second was written by the poet Hugo von Hofmannsthal in 1905. Both depict the world as plural and polysemic, but for Gablik such a view is distinctive to Postmodern art. A conception of reality of ultimately Nietzschean provenance which was fairly widespread among the intelligentsia of *Mitteleuropa* at the end of the last century and which is often present in the work of major Modernist figures such as Hofmannsthal is presented as peculiarly *Post*modernist.

But this kind of appropriation of Modernist motifs is absolutely typical of accounts of Postmodernist art. The force of this point can only be established by considering first the nature of Modernism itself. Eugene Lunn offers an excellent definition:

'1  *Aesthetic Self-Consciousness or Self-Reflexiveness.*' The process of producing the work of art becomes the focus of the work itself: Proust, of course, provided the definitive example in *A la recherche du temps perdu.*
'2  *Simultaneity, Juxtaposition, or "Montage".*' The work loses its organic form and becomes an assemblage of fragments, often drawn from different discourses or cultural media. Cubist and Surrealist collages come to mind, along with the practice of cinematic montage developed by Eisenstein, Vertov and other revolutionary Russian film-makers.
'3  *Paradox, Ambiguity, and Uncertainty.*' The world itself ceases to have a coherent, rationally ascertainable structure, and

becomes, as Hofmannsthal says, multiple and indeterminate. Klimt's great paintings 'Philosophy', 'Medicine' and 'Jurisprudence', commissioned for the University of Vienna but rejected because of the scandal their dark and ambiguous images represented to Enlightenment thought, exemplify this vision.
'4 *"Dehumanization" and the Demise of the Integrated Individual Subject or Personality.'* Rimbaud's famous declaration '*JE est un autre*' ('*I* am another') finds its echoes in the literary explorations of the unconscious inaugurated by Joyce and pursued by the Surrealists.[11]

Oddly enough, the authors of two of the most interesting recent discussions of Modernism, Perry Anderson and Franco Moretti, both deny that there is any relatively unified set of artistic practices which can be captured by a definition such as Lunn's. Anderson writes: 'Modern*ism* as a notion is the emptiest of cultural categories. Unlike Gothic, Renaissance, Baroque, Mannerist, Romantic, or Neoclassical, it designates no describable object in its own right at all; it is completely lacking in positive content.'[12] Anderson perhaps places excessive faith in the traditional categories of art history, terms whose origins are often arbitrary and use uncertain and shifting.[13] Moretti is rather more concrete in the way he expresses his scepticism about the label 'Modernism':

'Modernism' is a portmanteau word that perhaps should not be used too often. But I don't think I would classify Brecht as a modernist ... I just cannot think of a meaningful category that could include, say, surrealism, *Ulysses*, and something by Brecht. I can't think what the common attributes of such a concept could be. The objects are too dissimilar.[14]

But in fact Brecht's plays can be seen quite plausibly to fall under the 'common attributes' of Lunn's definition: the alienation (*Verfremdung*) effect is intended precisely to make the audience realize that they are in a theatre and not eavesdropping on real life; Brecht explicitly gives montage as a defining feature of his epic theatre; the plays are constructed in part to deny the spectator the satisfaction of an unequivocal meaning; and the narratives they unfold no longer treat the individual subject as the sovereign and coherent author of events. This is not to deny the considerable variations within Modernism: one of the merits of Lunn's account is the contrast it draws between the confident rationalism of Cubism in France before 1914, and, on the one hand, the 'langorous aestheticism' of Vienna, and, on the other, the 'nervous, agitated and suffering' art produced by German Expressionism.[15] Nor is it to ignore the very important differences within Modernism concerning the status of art itself – a matter to which I shall return below and in chapter 2. Nevertheless, Lunn's definition does, in my view, capture the distinctive features of the art which emerged across Europe at the end of the nineteenth century.

The advantages of having some such conception of Modernism become plain when one considers the definitions offered of Postmodernism, for example by Charles Jencks: 'To this day I would define Postmodernism as ... *double-coding: the combination of Modern techniques with something else (usually traditional building) in order for architecture to communicate with the public and a concerned minority, usually other architects.*'[16] This definition gets its purchase from the attempts by architects over the last couple of decades to get away from the elongated slabs characteristic of the International Style, with which architectural Modernism is identified. But if (as it is intended to be) it is taken as a *general* characterization of Postmodern art,[17] then it is hopelessly inadequate. 'Double-coding' – what Lunn calls 'Simultaneity, Juxtaposition, or "Montage"' – is a defining feature of Modernism. Thus Peter Ackroyd writes of *The Waste Land*:

> Eliot found his own voice by first reproducing that of others – as if it was only through his reading of, and response to, literature that he could find anything to hold onto, anything 'real'. That is why *Ulysses* struck him so forcibly, in a way no other novel ever did. Joyce had created a world which exists only in, and through, the multiple uses of language – through voices, through parodies of style ... Joyce had a historical consciousness of language and thus of the relativity of any one 'style'. The whole course of Eliot's development would lead him to share such a consciousness ... In the closing sequence of *The Waste Land* itself he creates a montage of lines from Dante, Kyd, Gérard de Nerval, the *Pervigilium Veneris* and Sanskrit ... There is no 'truth' to be found, only a number of styles and interpretations – one laid upon another in an endless and apparently meaningless process.[18]

Eliot is a particularly relevant example to take in the light of Jenck's claim that Postmodernism represents a 'return to the larger Western tradition' after Modernism's 'fetish of discontinuity'.[19] For one of Eliot's main preoccupations – expressed, for example, in 'Tradition and the individual talent' – was the relationship of both continuity and discontinuity between his own work and the broader European tradition:

> the historical sense compels a man to write not merely with his own generation in his bones, but with a feeling that the whole literature of Europe from Homer and within it the whole literature of his own country has a simultaneous existence and composes a simultaneous order. This historical sense, which is a sense of the timeless as well as of the temporal and of the timeless and the temporal together, is what makes a writer traditional. And it is at the same time what makes a writer most acutely conscious of his place in time, of his own contemporaneity.[20]

Eliot is in no sense exceptional among the major Modernists in this concern for placing himself with respect to 'the larger Western tradition', as any acquaintance with the work, say, of Joyce or Schönberg or Picasso will confirm. It is, therefore, difficult to be persuaded by Linda Hutcheon's claim that 'postmodernism goes beyond self-reflexivity to situate discourse in a broader context.'[21] She uses what she calls 'historiographic metafiction', a number of contemporary novels, in order to illustrate this thesis, but the examples she gives – Salman Rushdie's *Midnight's Children*, John Fowles's *The French Lieutenant's Woman*, Julian Barnes's *Flaubert's Parrot* and E.L. Doctorow's *Ragtime* among others – seem fairly heterogeneous, and united chiefly by their use, for various ends and in different modes, of the Modernist fictional devices pioneered by Conrad, Proust, Joyce, Woolf and others at the beginning of the century.

Hutcheon's argument is one among a number of manoeuvres used to deal with the embarrassing fact that both the definitions given and the examples cited of Postmodern art place it most plausibly as a continuation of and not a break from the *fin-de-siècle* Modernist revolution. Another popular move is to treat Modernism as essentially elitist. Thus Hutcheon talks of '[t]he obscurity and hermeticism of modernism',[22] while even Andreas Huyssen (who is usually above such things) tells us that 'the most significant trends within postmodernism have challenged modernism's relentless hostility to mass culture.'[23] Taken as claims about the internal construction of Modernist art these are far too strong. Even the forbiddingly mandarin Eliot loved the London music hall and sought to integrate its rhythms into some of his poetry, especially *Sweeney Agonistes*.[24] Stravinsky wrote not only *Le Sacre du printemps* but also *L'Histoire du soldat*, which draws heavily on ragtime. If directed at the great Modernists' Aestheticism, their tendency to view art as refuge from 'the immense panorama of futility and anarchy that is contemporary history', the accusation of elitism does strike home, but even here those committed to the idea of a radically novel Postmodern art must confront the development of avant-garde movements such as Dadaism, Constructivism and Surrealism which deployed Modernist techniques to overcome the separation between art and life as part of a broader struggle to revolutionize society itself. This is a question which I consider in the next chapter: however, the arguments presented so far seem to me sufficient to cast doubt on the claims made for the novelty of Postmodern art.

## 1.3   THE SEARCH FOR PRECURSORS

There are nevertheless considerably more subtle attempts to establish the existence of a distinctively Postmodern art than any considered so far. These conceive Postmodernism as a tendency within Modernism itself. Such an approach clearly involves a retreat from, or the rejection of the idea that Modernism and Postmodernism can be correlated in any very strong sense with distinctive stages of social development – say, respectively, industrial and postindustrial society.

Confusingly enough Lyotard, who helped to get the hare of a new, postmodern epoch running in the first place, also argues that treating the '"post-" in the term "postmodernist" ... in the sense of a simple succession, of a diachrony of periods, each of them clearly identifiable' is 'totally modern ... Since we are beginning something completely new, we have to re-set the hands of the clock at zero.' But the idea of a total break with tradition 'is, rather, a manner of forgetting or repressing the past. That's to say of repeating it. Not overcoming it.'[25]

If Postmodernism isn't a movement beyond Modernism, what is it? 'It is undoubtedly a part of the modern', Lyotard replies.[26] To develop his point he draws here on Kant's conception, elaborated in the *Critique of Judgement* as part of his aesthetics, of the sublime, which 'is to be found in an object even devoid of form, so far as it immediately involves, or its presence provokes, a representation of *limitlessness*, yet a superadded thought of its totality.' The particular philosophical significance of the sublime is that it offers us an experience of nature 'in its chaos, or in its wildest and most irregular disorder and desolation', which, 'provided it gives signs of magnitude and power', leads us to formulate ideas of pure reason, in particular that of the physical world as a unified and purposive order, which, according to Kant, cannot be found in sense-experience. The feeling, therefore, of the sublime is a form of aesthetic experience which breaks the boundaries of the sensuous. And, 'though the imagination, no doubt, finds nothing beyond the sensible world to which it can lay hold, still this thrusting aside of the sensible barriers gives it a feeling of being unbounded and this removal is thus a presentation of the infinite.' Kant suggests that there may be 'no more sublime passage' than the Mosaic ban on graven images.[27]

The essential for Lyotard is less the religio-metaphysical connotations of the sublime for Kant but rather 'the incommensurability of reality to concept which is implied in the Kantian philosophy of the sublime.' He emphasizes, not the 'superadded thought of . . . totality' which Kant says is inherent in the feeling of the sublime, but rather our inability to experience this totality. Lyotard distinguishes between two different attitudes towards 'the sublime relation between the presentable and the conceivable', the Modern and the Postmodern:

> modern aesthetics is an aesthetic of the sublime, though a nostalgic one. It allows the unpresentable to be put forward only as the missing contents; but the form, because of its recognizable consistency, continues to offer to the reader or viewer matter for solace or pleasure . . . The postmodern would be that which, in the modern, puts forward the unpresentable in presentation itself; that which denies itself the solace of good forms, the consensus of a good taste which would make it possible to share collectively the nostalgia for the unattainable; that which searches for new presentations, not in order to enjoy them but in order to impart a stronger sense of the unpresentable.[28]

Postmodern art therefore differs from Modernism in the attitude it takes up towards our inability to experience the world as a coherent and harmonious whole. Modernism reacts to 'the immense panorama of futility and anarchy that is contemporary history' by looking back nostalgically to a time before our sense of totality was lost, as Eliot does when he claims that in the Metaphysical poets of the seventeenth century there was 'a direct sensuous apprehension of thought, or a recreation of thought into feeling', which disappeared after the 'dissociation of sensibility' already evident in Milton and Dryden.[29] Postmodernism, by contrast, ceases to look back. It focuses instead 'on the power of the faculty to conceive, on its "inhumanity" so to speak (it was the quality Apollinaire demanded of modern artists)' and 'on the increase of being and jubilation which result from the invention of new rules of the game, be it pictorial, artistic, or any other'.[30]

This conception of Postmodernism effectively abandons the

attempt to ascribe to it structural characteristics such as 'double-coding' in order to differentiate it from Modernism. Indeed, as Frederic Jameson observes, Lyotard's argument has 'something of the celebration of modernism as its first ideologues projected it – a constant and ever more dynamic revolution in the languages, forms and tastes of art'.[31] Similarly Jencks complains that 'Lyotard continues in his writings to confuse Post-Modernism with the latest avant-gardism, that is Late Modernism.'[32] Jencks has in mind in particular some of the Minimalist art of the 1960s and 1970s, and indeed it does seem that Lyotard is inclined to favour such work, as is suggested by the exhibition, *Les Immatériaux*, which he organized at the Pompidou Centre. The main thrust of Lyotard's argument, however, involves the claim that Postmodernism is a tendency within Modernism characterized by its refusal to mourn, and indeed its willingness to celebrate our inability to experience reality as an ordered and integrated totality. Minimalist art may fall under this definition, but a perhaps more interesting question concerns the exemplars of Postmodernism during the heroic era of Modernism at the beginning of the century.

Lyotard offers one rather unconvincing example. He argues that Proust's work is plainly Modernist, since although 'the hero is no longer a character but the inner consciousness of time, . . . the unity of the book, the odyssey of that consciousness, even if it is deferred from chapter to chapter, is not seriously challenged.' By contrast 'Joyce allows the unpresentable to become perceptible in his writing itself, in the signifier. The whole range of available narrative and even stylistic operators is put into play without concern for the unity of the whole, and new operators are tried.'[33] But surely, despite the variety of styles and voices present in *Ulysses*, an implicit coherence is achieved through Joyce's use of myth? And is not this order even more evidently at work in *Finnegans Wake* in the cyclical pattern traced by both the book and history?[34]

Joyce is placed firmly in the Modernist camp by Jameson in his brilliant study of Wyndam Lewis, the most sustained attempt to show Postmodernist impulses at work within Modernism. Lewis's significance for Jameson lies in his rejection of the 'impressionistic aesthetic' characteristic of 'Anglo-American modernism'. Pound, Eliot, Joyce, Lawrence and Yeats all pursued 'strategies of inwardness, which set out to reappropriate an alienated universe by transforming it into personal styles and private languages'. Nothing could be more different than 'the prodigious force with which Wyndam Lewis propagates his bristling mechanical sentences and hammers the world into a forbidding cubist surface', the relentless externality of his style, in which the human, the physical and the mechanical are shattered and assimilated to each other. In a daring and imaginative move for a Marxist to take, Jameson argues that the writing of Lewis – fascist, sexist, racist, elitist – must be seen, precisely because of its distinctive formal 'expressionism', as a particularly powerful 'protest against the reified experience of an alienated social life, in which, against its own will, it remains formally and ideologically locked'.[35]

The difficulty lies not so much with Jameson's reading of Lewis, which is essentially a particularly bold example of what Frank Kermode calls the 'discrepancy theory', in accord with which Marxist criticism seeks to uncover in texts an unconscious meaning often at odds with their author's intentions,[36] but with the picture of mainstream Modernism which he contrasts with Lewis's writing. Modernism on this account is especially concerned with the time of private, subjective experience, what Bergson called *durée*, time as the individual person lives it, at once fragmented and operating at quite different rhythms from the homogeneous and linear 'objective' time of modern society.[37] Perhaps this will do when applied to Proust, but it fits Lewis's great English-speaking contemporaries rather badly. To take (yet again) the case of Eliot, we saw above that he conceived the entire European tradition as composing 'a simultaneous order' with his own writing. Indeed, it has been argued more generally that literary Modernism is characterized precisely by the *spatialization* of writing, the juxtaposition of fragmentary images torn out of any temporal sequence.[38] In 'Tradition and the individual talent' Eliot also makes the celebrated claim that '[p]oetry is not a turning loose of emotion, but an escape from emotion; it is not the expression of personality, but an escape from personality.'[39] Such statements seem to fit poems like *The Waste Land* better than the claim that they represent a 'strategy of inwardness', a retreat into the 'inner consciousness of time'. Eliot approvingly described *Ulysses* as a return to Classicism that uses the materials provided by modern life rather than rely on a sterile academicism; interestingly Lewis claimed that the 'Men of 1914', by which he meant Eliot, Pound, Joyce and himself, represented 'an attempt to get away from romantic into classical art' comparable to Picasso's revolution in painting.[40]

Jameson, the author after all of a book called *The Political Unconscious*, might argue that such professions by Eliot and others of a commitment to an impersonal, spatialized art very different from the 'impressionist aesthetic' which he ascribes to them are less important than what is revealed by the formal construction of their work. But without entering into such a formal analysis, it is worth observing how much less plausible Jameson's interpretation becomes when applied to the broader currents of Modernism beyond the English-speaking world. Where, for example, does Expressionism fit in – a highly subjective kind of art which nevertheless *externalized* inner anguish, projecting it on to and thereby distorting the objective environment of the personality? Or Cubism, which systematically dismantled the objects of common-sense experience, spreading out before the viewer their internal structure and external relationships?[41] Or the *Neue Sachlichkeit* of Weimar Germany, which reacted against the extravagances of Expressionism in favour of cool, matter-of-fact (*sachlich*), sometimes avowedly Neo-Classical art, but combined this with a critical, if not revolutionary attitude towards existing society – an art whose greatest achievement was perhaps Brecht's 'theatre for a scientific age'?[42]

More generally, Jameson's attempt to counterpose Lewis's 'expressionism' with the 'impressionistic aesthetic' supposedly typical of Modernism occludes what is best understood as a dialectical relationship between interiority and exteriority. The exploration of the peculiar rhythms of subjective experience is undoubtedly one of the major themes of Modernist writing: think of Proust, Woolf, Joyce. The paradox is that the deeper one probes beyond even fragmentary inner consciousness into the unconscious, the more one threatens to crack the subject open, and to confront the external forces which traverse and constitute the ego.

This is the trajectory taken by Freud: the unravelling of unconscious desires led him face to face with history – not simply the history of the individual subject, but the historical processes which produced the social institutions, above all the family, subtending the odyssey of the self. Deleuze and Guattari argue that Freud's fault was that he did not take the process far enough, relying instead on the mythologized history which rendered the bourgeois family eternal.[43] However that may be, the point stands that the logic of depth psychology, the exploration of inner consciousness, is to disintegrate the subject, and display its fragments as directly related to the social and natural environment supposedly external to the self. One can see this logic at work, for example, in two of the great figures of Viennese Modernism, Klimt and Kokoschka. Klimt's paintings are suffused with an inner unease and pervasive eroticism which are still held in control in a harmonious, indeed stylized relationship of the parts to the whole; in Kokoschka the tensions which Klimt was still able more or less to manage have exploded, distorting and disorganizing the subjects of his paintings, which are traversed by an anarchic psychic energy.[44]

One might argue that Postmodernism is nothing but the outcome of this dialectic of interiority and exteriority, an art of the surface, the depthless, even the immediate. Thus Scott Lash proposes that we see Postmodernism as 'a figural, as distinct from discursive, regime of signification. To signify via figures rather than words is to signify iconically. Images or other figures which signify iconically do so through their resemblance to the referent.' Consequently Postmodern art involves 'de-differentiation', so that, on the one hand, the signified (meaning) tends 'to wither away and the signifier to function as a referent', and, on the other hand, 'the referent functions as a signifier'. Contemporary film (*Blue Velvet*) and criticism (Susan Sontag's attack on interpretation) provide Lash with examples of this essentially Imagist art, but, like Lyotard, he sees Postmodernism as immanent within Modernism, particularly in the shape of Surrealism, which 'understood reality to be composed of signifying elements. Thus Naville enthused that we should get pleasure from the streets of the city in which kiosks, autos and lights were in a sense already representations, and Breton spoke of the world itself as "automatic writing".'[45]

One obvious difficulty with this analysis is that it offers no account of how Postmodernism thus understood differs from those arts – for example, painting and cinema – which are necessarily iconic. John Berger has claimed recently that painting is distinguished by the way it 'offers palpable, instantaneous, unswerving, continuous, physical presence. It is the most immediately sensuous of the arts.'[46] It is at least arguable that one of the main thrusts of Modernist painting is to release this immediate sensuous charge inherent in painting from both aesthetic ideologies of form and representation and broader social ideologies subordinating art to organized religion and the state. One can see the resulting sense of liberation at work, for example, in Matisse's paintings. The attempt to achieve something like the same effect in poetry was a crucial impulse in the Modernist literary revolution: Pound called Imagism the 'sort of poetry where painting or sculpture seems as if it were "just coming over into speech"'.[47] If the figural is the defining characteristic of Postmodernism, then the latter is a far more pervasive feature of Modernism than Lash appears to believe.

Matters are not much improved if we focus on Surrealism, as Lash does. It is quite true that the Surrealists had a magical conception of reality according to which chance events in the daily life of the city offered occasions of what Walter Benjamin called 'profane illumination'. In this sense reality did indeed function for them as a signifier. But by the mid-1920s what had originally been a primarily Aestheticist project intended to realize Rimbaud's injunction that '[t]he poet makes himself a *seer* by a long, prodigious and rational *disordering of all the senses*' had developed into a broader political commitment to social revolution which led most leading Surrealists to join the Communist Party (in most cases rather briefly) and Breton to a life-long involvement in the anti-Stalinist left. '"Transform the world", Marx said; "change life", Rimbaud said – these two watchwords are for us one and the same', Breton told the Congress of Writers for the Defence of Culture in 1935.[48]

This conjoining of political and aesthetic revolution makes it difficult to see the Surrealists as precursors of Postmodernism. For most accounts of Postmodern art tend to emphasize its rejection of revolutionary political change. Lyotard associates 'the nostalgia of the whole and one, . . . the reconciliation of the concept and the sensible, of the transparent and the communicable experience' with 'terror, . . . the fantasy to seize reality'.[49] The thought is presumably the traditional liberal one that any attempt at total social change will lead straight to the Gulag. One consideration behind the frequent claims made for Postmodern 'wit' and 'irony' seems to be that the collapse of belief in the possibility or desirability of global political transformation leaves us with nothing better to do than playfully to parody what we can no longer take seriously. Parody is, however, so pervasively present in the great Modernists – Eliot and Joyce, for example – that any attempt to claim it exclusively for Postmodernism just seems implausible; indeed in chapter 2 we shall consider Franco Moretti's claim that irony is a constitutive feature of Modernism. Jameson suggests that matters have gone a stage further – that while Modernist parody retains some conception of a norm from which one is deviating, Postmodernism is distinguished by pastiche, the 'neutral practice of mimicry, without any of parody's ulterior motives, amputated of the satiric impulse, devoid of laughter and of any conviction that alongside the abnormal tongue you have momentarily borrowed, some healthy linguistic normality still exists.'[50]

How can Surrealism, which united Rimbaldian artistic experimentation with Marxist revolutionary socialism, be plausibly regarded as a precursor of Postmodernism, which sees revolution as, at best a joke, at worst a disaster? Lash doesn't help matters by drawing on Benjamin's discussion of post-auratic art. Benjamin used the term 'aura' in order to capture the properties of uniqueness and unapproachability which he argues are characteristic of the traditional work of art. '[T]he unique value of the "authentic" work of art has its basis in ritual', he claims, 'the location of its original use value.' The aura preserves this 'ritual function' even after the decline of organized religion in the shape of the 'secular cult of beauty, developed during the Renaissance' and the 'negative theology' of art involved in nineteenth-century Aestheticism (*l'art pour l'art*). The contemporary development of the mass reproduction of art by mechanical means reaching its climax in cinema, however, causes the aura to decay, both by destroying the uniqueness of images and by altering their mode of consumption – the reception of the work of art is no longer a matter of individual absorption in the image, but – above all in the film theatre – is 'consummated by a collectivity in a state of distraction'.[51]

Now Lash claims that Modernism is typically auratic, Postmodernism post-auratic, the latter shattering the organic unity of the work of art 'through pastiche, collage, allegory and so on'.[52] Lash doesn't explain how Postmodernism's use of collage and the like distinguishes it from a paradigmatically Modernist movement like Cubism. More to the point, his argument involves a serious misunderstanding of Benjamin's account of post-auratic art. Benjamin argued that decay of the aura achieved by mass media such as cinema was the explicit objective of avant-garde movements such as Dada. 'What they intended and achieved was a relentless destruction of the aura of their creations ... Dadaistic activities actually assured a rather vehement distraction by making works of art the centre of scandal.' But the kinds of shock effects sought by the Dadaists with their meaningless poems and assaults on their audiences are achieved on a much larger scale by film, whose rapid succession of shots interrupts the spectator's consciousness, preventing her from sinking into a state of absorbed contemplation.[53]

The significance of the resulting changes in the mode of reception was for Benjamin political. The decline of the aura means that art is no longer 'based on ritual' but 'begins to be based on another practice – politics'. 'Reception in a state of distraction' allows the audience to adopt a more detached and critical attitude: 'The public is an examiner, but an absent-minded one.'[54] This new mode of reception, Benjamin believed, would lead the mass consumers of mechanically reproduced art to adopt a critical stance not merely towards what they saw but towards the capitalist society that produced it. Adorno argued that this belief involved a naive technological determinism, detaching the new physical means of mass reproduction from the bourgeois social relations of their use.[55] Whatever one thinks of this, Benjamin was certainly right to detect a political dynamic at work within avant-garde movements' attempts to alter the mode of reception of art. This is true even of the Dadaists, who were not the apolitical jokers depicted by postmodernists eager to appropriate them. The Berlin group in particular emerged in a context defined by the First World War, the Russian Revolution of October 1917 and the German Revolution of November 1918. Its leading figures – Richard Huelsenbeck, Wieland Herzefelde, John Heartfield, George Grosz – saw themselves, like the Surrealists a few years later, as political as well as aesthetic revolutionaries, and were sympathizers or members of the German Communist Party. 'Dada is German Bolshevism', Huelsenbeck said.[56] Grosz – whose savage assaults on the German bourgeoisie in works like *The Face of the Ruling Class* have permanently fixed our image of the Weimar republic – later wrote: 'I came to believe, however fleetingly, that art divorced from political struggle was pointless. My own art would be my rifle, my sword; all brushes and pens not dedicated to the great fight for freedom were no more use than empty straws.'[57]

The relationship between the Modernist avant garde and revolutionary politics is in fact complex and problematic, as we shall see in chapter 2. Nevertheless, Benjamin's chief example of artistic practice consciously directed at achieving the same effects as are produced in cinema – Brecht's epic theatre – represents perhaps the most sustained attempt to unite aesthetic Modernism and revolutionary Marxism. Thus Benjamin argues that the 'forms of epic theatre correspond to the new technical forms – cinema and radio'. Brecht's aim, he says, is to create an audience that is relaxed rather than absorbed, so that 'instead of identifying itself with the hero' it will 'learn to be astonished at the circumstances within which he has his being.' Brechtian alienation, the 'making strange' of social conditions we normally take for granted, produces a detached audience involved in a process of active discovery rather than fixed in a passive condition of identification with actors whose participation in a piece of fiction the conventions of theatrical Naturalism seek to conceal.[58] Benjamin's adoption of epic theatre as a prime example of post-auratic art, however, does not sit well with Lash's argument, since Lash cites Sontag's rejection of Brecht's 'theatre of dialogue' for Artaud's 'theatre of the senses' as a key instance of the shift towards Postmodernism. There have, in fact, been some attempts to claim Brecht for Postmodernism,[59] but these are highly implausible. Brecht's emphasis on epic theatre as 'theatre for instruction', directed towards 'an audience of the scientific age', concerned to encourage its consumers to reflect on, and develop a rational, critical understanding of the world, is so plainly intended to achieve a theatre of *enlightenment* that it is hard to imagine his plays fitting easily into a Postmodernist canon.[60] Lash's attempt to use Benjamin's aesthetics to characterize Postmodern art does therefore seem rather to confirm Andreas Huyssen's sardonic comment: 'Given the ravenous eclecticism of postmodernism, it has recently become fashionable to include Adorno and Benjamin in the canon of postmodernism *avant la lettre* – truly a case of the critical text writing itself without the interference of any historical consciousness whatsoever.'[61]


## 1.4   THE ABOLITION OF DIFFERENCE

The abiding impression left by the various claims made for Postmodern art surveyed in the preceding pages is their contradictory character. Postmodernism corresponds to a new historical stage of social development (Lyotard) or it doesn't (Lyotard again). Postmodern art is a continuation of (Lyotard), or a break from (Jencks) Modernism. Joyce is a Modernist (Jameson) or a Postmodernist (Lyotard). Postmodernism turns its back on social revolution, but then practitioners and advocates of a revolutionary art like Breton and Benjamin are claimed as precursors. No wonder that Kermode calls Postmodernism 'another of those period descriptions that help you to take a view of the past suitable to whatever it is you want to do.'[62]

What runs through all the various – mutually and often internally inconsistent – accounts of Postmodernism is the idea that recent aesthetic changes (however characteristized) are symptomatic of a broader, radical novelty, a sea-change in Western civilization. A little before the postmodern boom got into full swing Daniel Bell noted the widespread 'sense of an ending' among the Western intelligentsia 'symbolized . . . in the widespread use of the word *post* . . . to define, as a combined form, the age into which we are moving'. Bell illustrated this proliferation of 'posts-' by listing the following examples: post-capitalist, post-bourgeois, post-modern, post-civilized, post-collectivist, post-Puritan, post-Protestant, post-Christian, post-literature, post-traditional, post-historical, post-market society, post-organization society, post-economic, post-scarcity, post-welfare, post-liberal, post-industrial . . .[63]

For postmodernists the decisive break is usually with the Enlightenment, with which, as we saw in section 1.1 above, Modernism tends to be identified. Sometimes this involves the most astonishing claims, such as the following: 'Modernism in philosophy goes back a long way: Bacon, Galileo, Descartes – pillars of the modernist conception of the fashionable, the new and the innovative'[64] – a statement so ignorant as almost to invite one's admiration. How can thinkers committed to a representational epistemology most fully articulated by Locke in which the sensory qualities of objects are signs of their rationally ascertainable inner structure be assimilated an artistic movement whose products affronted common-sense expectations often in the belief that the scientific knowledge of reality was neither possible or even desirable? The point of such assertions seems to be less their factual content, which is slight, than the attempt to establish the novelty of Postmodernism, usually characterized in terms borrowed from Modernism, by treating the latter as merely the latest exemplar of Western rationalism.

This operation tends to involve conceiving Postmodernism's break with the Enlightenment in apocalyptic terms, so that it becomes the revelation of the fundamental flaw inherent in European civilization for centuries if not millenia. Perhaps the silliest example of this mode of thinking is provided by Kroker and Cook, who claim that 'since Augustine nothing has changed in the deep, structural code of Western experience', so that *De Trinitate* offers 'special insight into the modern project, at the very moment of its inception and from inside out'. Indeed, not simply the 'modern project' but the 'postmodern scene ... begins in the fourth century ... everything since the Augustinian refusal has been nothing but a fantastic and grisly implosion of experience as Western culture itself runs under the signs of passive and suicidal nihilism'. The apocalyptic 'sense of an ending' which postmodernism supposedly articulates loses any historical specificity, becoming instead the chronic condition of Western civilization since the fall of Rome. Here indeed is the night Hegel spoke of when criticizing Schelling, in which all cows are black, in which Augustine, Kant, Marx, Nietzsche, Parsons, Foucault, Barthes and Baudrillard have all been analysing the same 'postmodern scene'.[65]

Kroker's and Cook's vacuous parlour nihilism is in fact the *reductio ad absurdum* of a style of thinking with rather more distinguished antecedents. Both Nietzsche and Heidegger see Western metaphysics as founded upon a constitutive fault traversing its entire history – respectively Plato's reduction of the plurality of reality to phenomenal manifestations of the essential realm of the Forms, and the oblivion at the time of the Presocratics of the originary ontological difference between Being and beings. The subsequent history of European thought consists of variations on and elaborations of this founding error, which reaches its climax in the philosophy of self-constituting subjectivity founded by Descartes and thereby serves to legitimize the rationalized domination of both nature and humanity characteristic of modernity. Habermas highlights the contradiction which Nietzsche and Heidegger, as well as their successors – notably Foucault and Derrida – face in using the tools of rationality – philosophical argument and historical analysis – in order to carry out the critique of reason as such.[66] Although we shall return to this question in chapter 3 below, more relevant for present purposes is the way in which so sweeping a dismissal of Western civilization as founded since antiquity upon error encourages precisely the kind of dissolution of historical differences into repetitions of this original sin which we saw above to be typical of postmodernism.

As it happens, this tendency of the Nietzscheo-Heideggerian tradition, so embarrassing for self-proclaimed philosophers of difference, has been subjected to the most probing of critiques by Hans Blumenberg. Blumenberg's particular concern is with the 'secularization thesis', the treatment of modern beliefs, institutions, and practices as secularized versions of Christian motifs, and specifically with the theory, elaborated by Karl Löwith, that the Enlightenment conception of historical progress was merely the translation into pseudo-scientific vocabulary of the Christian notion of divine providence. As Blumenberg observes, the 'secularization of Christianity that produces modernity becomes for Löwith a comparatively unimportant differentiation' compared to the earlier 'turning away from the pagan cosmos of antiquity' with its cyclical conception of time which Judaism and Christianity perform by conceiving human history as the unfolding of God's plan of salvation. It is impossible here to do justice to the wealth of historical knowledge which Blumenberg displays in order to demonstrate the distinctive character of modern thought and the qualitative break which it represents with respect to Christian theology. He traces the origins of this break to the nominalist critique of Aristotelian metaphysics in the later Middle Ages, which in particular disenchanted the physical world, expelling from it any hint of divine purpose and reducing it to the purely contingent result of God's exercise of his will. The nominalist denial of any worldly intimation of divine order, intended to highlight the absolute perfection and power of the 'hidden God' (*deus absconditus*), had the paradoxical effect of creating a space within which took shape what for Blumenberg is the distinctively modern attitude of 'self-assertion': 'The more indifferent and ruthless nature seemed to be with respect to man, the less it could be a matter of indifference to him, and the more ruthlessly he had to materialize, for his mastering grasp, even that was pregiven to him as nature.' Nature could no longer be contemplated as a hierarchy of purposes by the 'blissful onlooker' inherited by mediaeval scholasticism from Plato and Aristotle. The nominalist 'postulate that man had to behave as though God were dead . . . induces a restless taking stock of the world which can be designated as the motive power of the age of science'. Curiosity ceases to be the vice it was for Christian theology and becomes systematized in the methodical interference in nature characteristic of

Galilean science. The scholastic conception of the world as a finite and definitively knowable order is supplanted by 'the reality-concept of the open context, which anticipates reality as the always incomplete result of a realization, as dependability constituting itself successively, as never definitive and absolutely granted consistency'. This conception of reality as open and incomplete in turn underlies the Enlightenment conception of progress which, unlike Christian eschatology, does not focus on 'an event breaking into history . . . that transcends as is heterogeneous to it', but 'extrapolates from a structure present in every moment to a future that is immanent in history'. Thus 'the idea of progress is . . . the continuous self-justification of the present by means of the future that it gives itself, before the past, with which it compares itself.'[67]

Blumenberg provides a rich and powerful critique of the style of thinking inaugurated by Nietzsche and continued by Heidegger, one in which, according to Löwith's secularization thesis, 'things must remain the same as they were made' by 'Christianity's intervention in European history (and through European history in world history)', 'so that even a post-Christian atheism is actually an intra-Christian mode of expression of negative theology, and a materialism is the continuation of the Incarnation by other means'.[68] But Blumenberg's preoccupation with the distinctive character of modernity also highlights the question implicit in this whole chapter. Postmodernism in its various manifestations defines itself by contrast with Modernist art and more generally with the 'modern age' which we have supposedly now left behind us. The main thrust of this chapter has been negative – to demonstrate both the weight attached by postmodernists to Postmodern art and their inability to come up with a plausible and coherent account of its distinguishing characteristics. The reader might, however, quite reasonably demand a positive account of the nature of modernity and of the Modernist art which is presumably its critical reflex. I attempt to meet this demand in chapter 2, and to do so in a way that, unlike the postmodernist theories critically surveyed in this chapter, gives its proper due to the historical specificity of the phenomena under examination.

# 2
# MODERNISM AND CAPITALISM

Lucidity came to me when I at last succumbed to the vertigo of the modern.

*Louis Aragon*

## 2.1 THE VERTIGO OF THE MODERN

What is modernity? Baudelaire is often thought to have definitively answered this question when he wrote: 'Modernity is that which is ephemeral, fugitive, contingent upon the occasion'.[1] The context of this remark, the essay 'The painter of modern life', makes it clear that it reflects Baudelaire's specific concern to characterize an art which discovers the eternal *in* the transitory as opposed to an abstract and academic cult of timeless beauty. Nevertheless, his definition seems to capture an experience particular to the past two centuries summed up by David Frisby as 'the newness of the present'.[2]

Correlative to, and indeed productive of this experience is a different kind of modernity, conceived this time as a distinct stage in the historical development of human society. Modern society represents a radical break from the static nature of traditional societies. No longer is humanity's relation to nature governed by the repetitive cycle of agricultural production. Instead, particularly with the onset of the Industrial Revolution, modern societies are characterized by their efforts systematically to control and to transform their physical environment. Constant technical innovations, transmitted via the expanding world market, unleash a process of rapid change which soon embraces the entire planet. Tradition-bound social relations, cultural practices and religious beliefs find themselves swept away in the ensuing maelstrom of change. Marx's famous description of capitalism in the *Communist Manifesto* provides the classic statement of the unceasing, dynamic process of development intrinsic to modernity.

> Constant revolutionizing of production, uninterrupted disturbance of all social conditions, everlasting uncertainty and agitation distinguish the bourgeois epoch from all earlier ones. All fixed, fast-frozen relations, with their train of ancient and venerable prejudices and opinions, are swept away, all new-formed ones become antiquated before they can ossify. All that is solid melts into air, all that is holy is profaned, and man is at last compelled to face with sober senses, his real conditions of life, and his relations with his kind.[3]

What could be more natural than to see Modernist art as an aesthetic response to the experience of modernity's permanent revolution? Consider the claims Marinetti makes for his art in the first *Futurist Manifesto* (1909):

> We will sing of great crowds engaged in work, pleasure, or revolt: we will sing of the many-coloured and polyphonic tides of revolution in modern capital cities: we will sing of the clangour and the heat of nights in the shipyards and the docks blazing with violent devouring smoking snakes; of factories hanging from the clouds by the twisted threads of their smoke trails.[4]

Marinetti's almost cinematic style calls to mind Vertov's celebration of the energies released by the October Revolution in *The Man with a Movie Camera*. But even those Modernists who are doubtful of modernity's promise can still be seen as responding to the social changes they were experiencing. Modernism, it has often been observed, is an art of the city – above all, of the Paris of Baudelaire and Rimbaud, of the Cubists and the Surrealists, but also of Eliot's London, Brecht's Berlin, Kafka's Prague, Dos Passos's New York, Musil's Vienna[5]. In his famous essay 'The metropolis and mental life' Georg Simmel argued that the modern city produces a particular kind of experience involving 'the *intensification of nervous stimulation* which results from the swift and uninterrupted change of outer and inner stimuli'. The unceasing flood of new impressions to which the citizens of the great metropolis are subjected encourages them to adopt a dissociated 'blasé attitude', the refusal to register any further changes, while the fear of anonymity, of being reduced to a cipher, encourages both a 'sensitivity to differences' and the adoption of 'the most tendentious peculiarities, that is, the specifically metropolitan extravagances of mannerism, caprice and preciousness'.[6] That Modernism is a response to the 'Unreal City' of modern life is a theme explored above all by Benjamin in the *Passagen-Werk*, his great unfinished study of Baudelaire's Paris. The belief that the new urban and industrial world required also a new kind of art, very different from Romantic nature-worship, is nowhere more clearly expressed than by the painter David Bomberg in the catalogue of his 1914 show: 'I APPEAL to a *Sense of Force* ... I am *searching for an intenser* expression ... I look upon *Nature*, while I live in a *steel city*. Where decoration happens, it is accidental. My object is the *construction of pure Form*.'[7]

The idea that the experience of modernity acts as a middle term between the dynamic process of socio-economic development central to the history of the past two centuries – of modernization – and cultural Modernism is developed most fully by Marshall Berman in his well-known book *All That Is Solid Melts Into Air*:

> There is a mode of vital experience – experience of space and time, of the self and others, of life's possibilities and perils – that is shared by men and women all over the world today. I will call this experience 'modernity'. To be modern is to find ourselves in an environment that promises us adventure, power, joy, growth, transformation of the ourselves and the world – and, at the same time, that threatens to destroy everything we have, everything we know, everything we are. Modern environments and experiences cut across all boundaries of geography and ethnicity, of class and nationality, of religion and ideology: in this sense, modernity can be said to unite all mankind. But it is a paradoxical unity, a unity of disunity: it pours us into a maelstrom of perpetual disintegration and renewal, of struggle and contradiction, of ambiguity and anguish. To be modern is to be part of a universe in which, as Marx said, 'all that is solid melts into air'.[8]

Berman's thesis has been subject to searching though sympathetic criticism by Perry Anderson in an essay I discuss in section 2.2 below. Though I find Anderson's arguments convincing, Berman's central claim – developed in a series of rich and subtle analyses of particular cases from Goethe to Bely – concerning the peculiar contradiction of modern experience seems to me essentially correct. The dynamism of the social world offers the promise of happiness – and of disaster. What is much less clear is whether concepts such as those of modernity and modernization are adequate to characterize and account for this contradiction.

For one thing these concepts have philosophical antecedents in Enlightenment thought. Habermas writes that 'the secular concept of modernity expresses the conviction that the future has begun: it is the epoch that lives for the future, that opens itself up to the novelty of the future.'[9] This orientation on the future presupposes the formulation of what Hans Blumenberg calls 'the reality-concept of the open context' developed in particular by the thinkers of the seventeenth-century scientific revolution, who thereby broke from the ancient and mediaeval conception of a closed and finite world. The 'reality-concept' of modern (i.e. post-Renaissance) philosophy, Blumenberg says, 'legitimizes the quality of the new, of the surprising and unfamiliar element, as both a theoretical and aesthetic quality'.[10] This valorization of the new is part of a broader shift. No longer can beliefs, institutions and practices be justified by their derivation from traditional models and principles. 'Modernity can and will no longer borrow the criteria by which it takes its orientation from the models supplied by another epoch', Habermas argues: *'it has to create its own normativity out of itself.'*[11]

This conception of modernity as oriented to the future not the past and as self-legitimizing can be seen as the means by which some intellectuals in seventeenth- and eighteenth-century Europe sought to make sense of the unfamiliar but remarkably successful theoretical beliefs and procedures involved in the new physics, as well as of what seemed like analogous changes in other cultural spheres, in particular the *querelle des anciens et des modernes* in the arts. The concept became, however, embedded in a philosophy of history once the *philosophes* began to argue that the kind of intellectual innovation made respectable by Newton was the motor of general social progress – a belief which requires conceiving the unfolding of time as recording not the decay of a fallen world or the eternal cyclical repetition of the same or even the operations of the divine will but rather the steady improvement of the human condition thanks to the development and dissemination of scientific knowledge. The notion of enlightenment did not simply provide this philosophy of history with a name: it offered both an explanation and a measure of the extent of human progress, while its absence accounted for the obstacles to change, particularly in the shape of the clergy, the social agency by which the masses are held in the night of superstition.

Modernity came to be conceived of as the society in which the Enlightenment project is realized, in which the scientific understanding of the human and physical worlds regulates social interaction.[12] Saint-Simon, influenced by Condorcet's theory of history, thought of the industrial society whose emergence he anticipated in precisely these terms. The great social theorists of the turn of the nineteenth century did not share Condorcet's and Saint-Simon's optimism about the future, but all saw contemporary society as shaped by the practical application of the kinds of concepts and theoretical procedures involved in the seventeenth-century scientific revolution. Various vocabularies – Weber's distinction between traditional and rational-bureaucratic forms of domination, Durkheim's between mechanical and organic solidarity, Tönnies's between *Gemeinschaft* and *Gesellschaft* – were used to draw a broad contrast between two fundamentally different forms of social organization, separated above all by the dissolving and dynamizing effect of modern scientific rationality and its practical realizations.

Weber's theory of rationalization – perhaps the centrepiece of non-Marxist social theory – provided the most important single account of the constitution of modernity. Modernization involves, in the first place, the differentiation of originally unitary social practices, in particular, of the capitalist economy and the modern state. 'Only in Western societies', Habermas writes, 'does the differentiation of these two, complementarily interrelated subsystems lead so far that modernization can distinguish itself from its initial constellation and continue in a self-regulating way.' Secondly, this process of differentiation involves the institutionalization of a specific kind of action, what Weber calls purposive-rational (*zweckrational*), or instrumentally rational action, which is oriented to selecting the most effective means to achieving some pregiven goal. The rationalization of social life consists for Weber in the increasing regulation of conduct by instrumental rationality rather than by traditional norms and values, a process which is accompanied by the more ever more widespread use of the methods of post-Galilean science to determine the most efficacious course of action available to individuals in pursuit of their goals. Weber analysed what Habermas calls 'the *rationalization of worldviews*', on the one hand the disenchantment of the world, the expulsion of purpose from nature, and on the other the differentiation of a once unitary culture into distinct spheres (science, art, morality), each governed by the same formal rationality. The key to understanding the process of modernization is 'the transposition of cultural rationalization into societal rationalization', for example, the process whereby the Calvinist conception of life as a vocation encouraged the institutionalization of instrumentally rational economic action.[13]

Weber did not, of course, regard the process of modernization thus characterized with much enthusiasm, both because of the subjective nature of *Zweckrationalität*, which could offer no objective criteria for selecting the goals of action, as opposed to the means to achieve some already determined goal, and because the outcome of its institutionalization seemed to be the imprisonment of humanity in the 'iron cage' of bureaucratic structures which, while formally rational, offered little in the way of either freedom or meaning. These doubts played little part in the version of Weber's theory used by postwar sociologists of modernization in the English-speaking world such as Talcott Parsons. As Habermas notes, this 'theory of modernization ... dissociates "modernity" from its modern European origins and stylizes it into a spatio-temporally neutral model for processes of social development in general'.[14] Parsons conceived modernization as an evolutionary process in which social systems, governed by a ' "law of inertia" of social process' orienting them towards stability, are prompted by disruptive exogenous and endogenous factors to undergo a process of structural differentiation.[15] Differentiation – in particular the emergence of an autonomous market economy – in turn makes possible the 'adaptive upgrading' of the social system, the enhancement of society's ability to control its environment, above all through the Industrial Revolution. But the process of differentiation both requires and is consequent upon a change in the prevailing pattern of values, the replacement of those characteristic of traditional society, the 'Particularistic-Ascriptive Pattern', combining specific loyalties with the occupation of social roles by virtue of such mechanisms as inheritance, with the 'Universalistic-Achievement Pattern' prevalent in modern society, where agents come to make increasingly general value-commitments and to be allocated to positions on the basis of their performance. 'The main direction of modern societal development', Parsons argues, 'is towards an essentially new pattern of stratification', in which 'legitimate inequality' is based no longer on ascription, but on the functions performed by members of society within the highly differentiated system of roles required by industrialization.[16]

The plainly apologetic overtones which Parsons imparted to the theory of modernization gave pause even to those sharing broadly the same problematic. Thus Habermas complains that Parsons establishes an '*analytic* relation between a high level of system complexity on the one hand and, on the other, universalistic forms of social integration and an individualism institutionalized in a noncoercive manner' which prevents him addressing 'the pathologies that emerge in the modern age'.[17] Habermas, as we shall see in chapter 4, seeks to remedy these faults by subsuming the theory of modernization within a broader account of communicative rationality. Quite independently of the criticisms I make of that account in chapter 4, there seem to me good reasons for abandoning the problematic of modernization. In the first place, drawing the contrast between traditional and modern society leads only too easily to an ahistorical parody of the range, diversity and complexity of social formations prior to the Industrial Revolution. Weber's strong historical sense, deployed to great effect in his discussion of different forms of domination in *Economy and Society*, was undermined by an epistemology which made a virtue of stylization and caricature, and by his preoccupation with the problem of rationalization. Secondly, the theory of rationalization itself, particularly once banalized in the form of Parsons' 'pattern-variables', involves an idealist theory of social change, in which alterations in belief underly historical transformations. Technological change tends to be thought of as the materialization of theoretical discoveries, social conflict as the consequence of 'strains' produced by some disequilibrium within the prevailing value-system.

Finally, the theory of modernization in the functionalist and evolutionist form which Parsons gave it, is implicitly teleological, treating the most 'developed' existing society, the United States, as the goal towards which, not simply its counterparts elsewhere in the Western bloc, but also the 'less developed' societies of the Third World will increasingly tend. As John Taylor put it

> since the functionalist theory of change establishes – through *ex post facto* generalization – an evolutionary correlation between industrialization and differentiation, it can only resolve the problem of future possible directions of change in Third World societies by referring them to a *particular end-state*, namely that attained by the contemporarily *most differentiated* social systems. On the basis of its evolutionary postulates, a universal historical path towards greater differentiation emerges, which all social systems *must necessarily follow*, if they are to industrialize ... Consequently, the 'Europocentric bias' evident in functionalist theories of modernization is not – as some authors have suggested – simply a reflection of the ideological interests of particular theorists, but a *necessary effect* of the theory in which they operate.[18]

Historical materialism, which analyses the phenomena with which Weber, Parsons and Habermas are concerned primarily under the concept of the capitalist mode of production, offers in my view a superior theoretical perspective to the problematic of modernization. Thus, in the first place, the concept of mode of production, a specific combination of productive forces (labour-power, means of production) and of production relations (relations of effective control over the productive forces), permits careful discrimination between different kinds of social formation, including those – the slave, feudal and tributary modes of production – which precede the development of capitalism. Some of the best contemporary Marxist historical writing has been concerned with precapitalist social formations. Secondly, the Marxist theory of social change is materialist, according explanatory primacy to the structural contradictions which develop between the forces and relations of production and to the class struggle which emerges from exploitive production relations. Thirdly, historical materialism is a non-teleological theory of social evolution: not only does it deny that capitalism is the final stage of historical development, but communism, the classless society which Marx believed would be the outcome of socialist revolution, is not the inevitable consequence of the contradictions of capitalism, since an alternative exists, what Marx called 'the mutual ruination of the contending classes', Rosa Luxemburg 'barbarism'.[19]

The superiority of historical materialism as social theory does not imply that there is no place for the vocabulary of modernity. Terms such as 'modernization' may serve descriptively to characterize the changes involved in the development of industrial capitalism. Furthermore, these changes do involve a radically novel mode of living by comparison with all precapitalist social formations, for example, with respect to the active and transformative relation between humanity and nature characteristic of capitalism, the development of qualitatively new forms of urban life, and the emergence of a homogeneous and linear conception of time.[20] Fernand Braudel argues that the concept of civilization, of 'an order, bringing together thousands of cultural possessions effectively different from, and at first sight even foreign to, each other – goods, that range from those of the spirit and the intellect to the tools and objects of everyday life', is 'a category of history, a necessary classification'.[21] Perhaps we should think of modernity as the kind of civilization formed by the development and global dominance of the capitalist mode of production.

It is as an *explanation* of the changes preoccupying modernization theorists that historical materialism claims our attention. The defining characteristics of capitalist relations of production – the transformation of labour-power into a commodity and the control of the means of production by competing capitals – are responsible for a tendency for the productive forces to develop rapidly. Competing capitals seek to undercut their rivals by introducing cost-cutting technological innovations, while the subjection of workers to the labour-market allows capitalists to develop systematic incentives designed to enhance labour productivity.[22] Hence the emphasis laid by Marx in the *Manifesto* on the dynamism of capitalism, its accomplishment of 'wonders far surpassing Egyptian pyramids, Roman aqueducts, and Gothic cathedrals': 'The bourgeoisie cannot exist without constantly

revolutionizing the instruments of production, and thereby the relations of production, and with them the whole relations of society.'[23]

Marx did not, of course, restrict himself to celebrating the productive achievements of capitalism. He described what he believed to be
the capitalist modernization of India under British rule, which he
argued was historically necessary, as an instance of a kind of progress
which 'resemble[s] the hideous pagan idol, who will not drink the
nectar but from the skulls of the slain'.[24] Historical development is
for Marx a contradictory and not a unilinear process. His most
interesting discussion of the two-sided character of modernization
highlighted by Berman comes in the *Grundrisse*. Here Marx cham-
pions capitalism against its Romantic critics. He stresses

> the great civilizing influence of capital; its production of a stage of
> society in comparison to which all earlier ones appear as mere *local
> developments* of humanity and as *nature-idolatry*. For the first
> time, nature becomes purely an object for mankind, purely a matter
> of utility; ceases to be recognized as a power for itself; and the
> theoretical discovery of its autonomous laws appears merely as a
> ruse so as to subjugate it under human needs, whether as an object
> of human consumption or as a means of production. In accord with
> this tendency, capital drives beyond national barriers and pre-
> judices as much as beyond nature worship, as well as all traditional,
> confined, complacent, encrusted satisfactions of present needs, and
> reproductions of old ways of life.[25]

Similarly, Marx argues that

> the old view, in which the human being appears as the aim of
> production, regardless of his limited national, religious, political
> character, seems to be very lofty when contrasted with the modern
> world, where production appears as the aim of mankind and
> wealth as the aim of production. In fact, however, when the limited
> bourgeois form is stripped away, what is wealth other than the
> universality of individual needs, capacities, pleasures, productive
> forces etc., created through universal exchange?[26]

Marx nevertheless recognizes the force of the Romantic critique of
capitalism:

> In bourgeois economics – and in the epoch of production to which
> it corresponds – this complete working-out of the human content
> appears as a complete emptying out, this universal objectification as
> total alienation, and the tearing down of all limited, one-sided aims
> as sacrifice of the human end-in-itself to an entirely external end.

This is why the childish world of antiquity appears on one side as loftier. On the other side, it really is loftier in all matters where closed shapes, forms and given limits are sought for. It is satisfaction from a limited standpoint; while the modern gives no satisfaction; or, where it appears satisfied with itself, it is vulgar.

However,

[i]t is as ridiculous to yearn for a return to that original fullness as it is to believe that with this complete emptiness history has come to a standstill. The bourgeois viewpoint has never advanced beyond this antithesis between itself and this romantic viewpoint, and therefore the latter will accompany it as legitimate antithesis up to its blessed end.[27]

One of the most interesting ideas Marx develops in these passages is that the liberal defence and the Romantic critique of capitalism are complementary and correlative perspectives, each partial and un-ilateral, the one merely celebrating the development of the productive forces under capitalism, the other denouncing the 'complete emptiness' of bourgeois society in the name of a lost, and indeed fictional 'original fullness'. Marx is able to transcend both perspectives because he focuses on the contradiction between the expansion of human productive powers which capitalism makes possible and the 'limited bourgeois form' in which this expansion takes place, resting as it does upon the exploitation of wage-labour and an anarchic process of competitive accumulation. This contradiction gives rise to chronic economic crises signalling the need to replace capitalism with a communist society in which the fulfilment of human needs made possible by the prior development of the productive forces is finally realized. Marx can see beyond both liberal and Romantic viewpoints because he is oriented on capitalism's 'blessed end', the revolutionary outcome of the contradictory process of development whose climax is the '[c]onstant revolutionizing of production, uninterrupted disturbance of all social conditions, everlasting and uncertainty' of 'the bourgeois epoch'.

## 2.2   THE MODERNIST CONJUNCTURE

The analytical priority of Marx's theory of the capitalist mode of production over the conceptual vocabulary of modernization under-lies one of Anderson's two main criticisms of Berman's *All That Is Solid Melts Into Air*. Anderson argues that the 'adjectives "constant", "uninterrupted" and "everlasting"' which Berman uses in order to characterize the restless dynamism of modernity 'denote a *homogeneous* historical time in which each moment is perpetually different from every other moment by virtue of being *next*, but – by the same token – each moment is eternally the *same* as an interchangeable unit in a process of infinite recurrence. Extracted from the totality of Marx's theory of capitalist development, this emphasis very quickly and easily yields the paradigm of modernization proper.' By contrast, 'Marx's own conception of the historical time of the capitalist mode of production as a whole was quite different from this: it was of a complex and *differential* temporality in which episodes or eras were discontinuous from each other and heterogeneous within themselves'. This criticism implies that a more specific historical context for Modernism is required than modernization *tout court*. Analogously, Anderson argues that Berman's conception of Modernism itself is far too undifferentiated. Thus, 'modernism, as a specific set of aesthetic forms, is generally dated precisely *from* the twentieth century, is indeed typically construed by contrast with realist and other classical forms of the nineteenth, eighteenth, or earlier centuries. Virtually all of the actual literary texts analysed so well by Berman – whether Goethe or Baudelaire, Pushkin or Dostoevsky – precede modernism proper in this usual sense of the word.'[28]

Anderson is (mistakenly, as we saw in 1.2 above) sceptical about whether even 'modernism proper' represents a coherent set of movements sharing a common identity, but the '*decisive* currents of "modernism"' which he identifies – '[s]ymbolism, expressionism, cubism, futurism or constructivism, surrealism' – suggests a focus on the end of the nineteenth century in line with, for example, Malcolm Bradbury's and James McFarlane's proposal that we treat the period 1890–1930 as *the* Modernist era.[29] Anderson proceeds to offer 'a *conjunctural* explanation of the aesthetic practices and doctrines subsequently grouped together as "modernist"':

In my view, 'modernism' can best be understood as a cultural force-field 'triangulated' by three decisive co-ordinates. The first of these is ... the codification of a highly formalized *academicism* in the visual and other arts, which was institutionalized within official regimes of state and society still massively pervaded, often dominated, by aristocratic or landowning classes that were in one sense 'superseded' no doubt, but in others were still setting the political and cultural tone in country after country of pre-First World War Europe ... The second co-ordinate is then a logical complement of the first: the still incipient, hence essentially *novel*, emergence

within these societies of the key technologies or inventions of the
second industrial revolution; that is telephone, radio, automobiles,
aircraft, and so on . . . [Thirdly,] the imaginative proximity of social
revolution. The extent of hope or apprehension that the prospect of
such revolution arouses varies widely, but over most of Europe it
was 'in the air' during the Belle Époque itself.[30]

Anderson argues that 'the persistence of the anciens régimes, and
the academicism consonant with them, provided a critical range of
cultural values *against which* insurgent forms of art could measure
themselves but also *in terms of which* they could partly articulate
themselves.' But while some Modernists – Pound and Eliot, for
example – used 'the tradition' of European high culture to distance
themselves for a present they despised, 'the energies and attractions of
a new machine age were a powerful imaginative stimulus' to others –
the Cubists, Futurists, and Constructivists.

Finally, the haze of social revolution drifting across the horizon of
this epoch gave it much of its apocalyptic light for those currents of
modernism most unremittingly and violently radical in their rejection of the social order as a whole, of which the most significant
was certainly German expressionism. European modernism in the
first years of this century thus flowered in the space between a still
usable classical past, a still indeterminate technical present, and a
still unpredictable political future. Or, put another way, it arose at
the intersection between a semi-aristocratic ruling order, a semi-
industrialized capitalist economy, and a semi-emergent, or semi-
insurgent, labour movement.[31]

Although I find this analysis largely convincing, let me first state
one major reservation about Anderson's argument. It concerns his
characterization of *fin-de-siècle* European society, derived, as Anderson acknowledges, from what he calls 'Arno Mayer's recent and
fundamental work, *The Persistence of the Old Regime*'.[32] Mayer's
interpretation of Europe on the eve of the Great War centres on the
claim that

[d]own to 1914 Europe was pre-eminently pre-industrial and
pre-bourgeois, its civil societies being deeply grounded in economies of labour-intensive agriculture, consumer manufacture and
petty commerce. Admittedly, industrial capitalism and its class
formations, notably the bourgeoisie and the factory proletariat,
made vast strides, especially after 1890. But they were in no
position to challenge or supplant the tenacious structures of the
pre-existent order.[33]

Agriculture remained the principal sector of the European economy, underpinning the political dominance of the aristocracy and more generally of the landed classes across the continent – a state of affairs reflected in the monarchical character of every major state except France. The bourgeoisie, politically subordinate, adapted itself to the *anciens régimes*: instead of seeking to overthrow the old monarchies, rising industrial and financial magnates took on the colour of their surroundings, seeking to ape the lifestyle and buy into the landed estates of their aristocratic betters. No wonder, then, that the education system, especially in its emphasis on the Greek and Latin classics, still transmitted the values of Europe's agrarian notables, and that '[i]n form, content and style the artefacts of high culture continued to be anchored and swathed in conventions that relayed and celebrated traditions supportive of the old order.'[34]

Mayer's analysis offers a distinctive perspective on the dynamics of the crisis whose culmination was the First World War, itself the opening episode of 'the Thirty Years War of the general crisis of the twentieth century'. The motor of this crisis was the increasingly reactionary stance of the European ruling classes from the 1890s onwards, which found expression not simply in the widely noted polarization of official politics and rise of ultra-conservative mass parties, but in the popularity of Nietzsche and Social Darwinism. By 1900 'the governing elites' had become 'Europe's most formidable *class dangereuse*'. Consequently, '[i]f a crisis arose in Europe after the turn of the century, it was fuelled not by insurgent popular forces against the established order but by resurgent ultra-conservatives bend on bracing it.' The 'rupture of the international system into two rigid blocs ... was more effect than cause' of this wave of reaction. 'The Great War', therefore, 'was an expression of the decline and fall of the old order fighting to prolong its life rather than of the explosive rise of industrial capitalism bent on imposing its primacy.' Nor did the collapse of the Central European monarchies in 1917–18 settle matters: 'It would take two World Wars and the Holocaust ... to finally dislodge the feudal and aristocratic presumption from Europe's civil and political societies.'[35]

This analysis of *fin-de-siècle* Europe can be questioned on various grounds. In the first place, the thesis of persisting aristocratic domination is highly controversial. Anderson is himself the author of an interpretation of English history which focuses on the supposedly supine character of the industrial bourgeoisie in the face of a landed aristocracy whose hegemony has been continued into the twentieth century in the shape of the City of London, and Mayer's argument can indeed be seen as a generalization of this thesis to Europe as a whole; however, Anderson's arguments have been subjected to searching and, in my view, devastating criticism.[36] A version of the same approach, which conceives German society prior to 1945 as peculiarly 'pre-modern', has also received a powerful challenge recently from David Blackbourn and Geoff Eley, who argue that after 1871 the German state, although still staffed primarily by the agrarian *Junker* class, operated in the interests of industrial capital.[37]

More generally, Eric Hobsbawm argues that we should see the nineteenth century, not as that of 'the persistence of the *ancien régime*', but rather as that of 'the triumph and transformation of capitalism in the historically specific forms of bourgeois society in its liberal version'. While the bulk of the bourgeoisie, basking in the prosperity characteristic at least in urban life of the second half of the century, developed a distinctive 'less formal, more genuinely private and privatized lifestyle', big capital 'had no great difficulty in organizing itself as an elite, since it could use methods very similar to those used by aristocracies, or even – as in Great Britain – the actual mechanisms of aristocracy'. The haut-bourgeois adoption of aris-tocratic lifestyle was not 'simply an abdication of bourgeois before old aristocratic values'. Thus the essentially novel use of 'socialization through elite (or any) schools ... assimilated aristocratic values to a moral system designed for a bourgeois society and its public service.'[38] Mayer himself notes that secondary education throughout nineteenth-century Europe was characterized by an *increased* stress on the classics – a trend which one might plausibly represent as an attempt to integrate (to borrow Matthew Arnold's terms) bourgeois 'Philistines' and aristocratic 'Barbarians' into a common ruling class rather then to subordinate one group to the other.[39]

One reason for dwelling on the question of whether *fin-de-siècle* Europe was an aristocratic order or a bourgeois society is that the answer one gives is likely to determine one's assessment of the 'Thirty Years War' of 1914–45. For Mayer, the torments of Europe in these years (transmitted to the rest of the world thanks to imperialism) were a consequence of the conflict between the *anciens régimes* and emergent industrial capitalism, with the former playing the active role. One might then see the two World Wars and the social convulsions surrounding them (Russia 1905 and 1917, Germany 1918, 1933 and 1945, China 1925–7 and 1949, etc.) as, in terms of their objective consequences rather than the intentions of the actors involved, a process of modernization which swept away the 'feudal and aristocratic' obstacles to capitalist development. The bourgeois era proper would on this account have begun in Europe only after 1945. The apologetic connotations of this analysis should be reasonably clear: capitalism emerges from the horrors of the first half of the century absolved of responsibility, which lies instead at the door of the forces of European reaction pledged to defend the aristocratic past. So cleaned up a version of capitalism is likely to be conceptualized in essentially neo-liberal terms, as a market economy in which perfect competition prevails; military competition between states – of course as much a fixture on the global scene after as it was before 1945 – tends correlatively, to be treated as autonomous of the capitalist mode of production. The idea of the belated modernization of Europe after 1945 is related to the question, discussed in chapter 5, of whether or not the world is entering a new phase of socio-economic development. Let us note for the present that the classical Marxist tradition of Lenin, Luxemberg, Hilferding and Bukharin, continued (in this respect at least) by Hobsbawm, by contrast locates the origins of the 'Thirty Years War' in the increasingly serious contradictions of *fin-de-siècle* capitalism, and in particular in the growing concentration of economic power, most notably in rising industrial economies such as Germany and the US, in the hands of large corporations, the connected tendency of not simply banking and industrial capital but also the state and private capital to fuse into a single national complex of interests, and the consequent transformation of market competition between firms into military rivalries among the Great Powers.[40]

Explaining the eruption of military and social conflict after 1900 in terms of contradictions internal to the capitalist mode of production does not imply that the survivals of the agrarian order on which Mayer concentrates can be ignored. But they have to be seen in the context of the progressive restructuring of European social formations to reflect the predominance of capital. Moreover, what Norman Stone, generalizing from George Dangerfield's famous study of Britain under the Campbell-Bannerman and Asquith governments of 1906–14, suggests we think of as 'the strange death of liberal Europe' before 1914 can best be seen as the consequence of the destabilizing impact of the development of industrial capitalism in the last third of the nineteenth century.[41] The uneven and incomplete nature of this development added to the dislocating and disruptive impact of industrialization. Here the most illuminating perspective is provided by Trotsky's concept of uneven and combined development, whose origins lie in his attempt, after the 1905 Revolution, to characterize the crisis of Tsarist society: the combination of a predominantly feudal rural order with pockets of industrial capitalism based on very advanced plant imported from the West made Russia peculiarly vulnerable to social convulsions liable to challenge bourgeoisie and autocracy alike.[42] Mayer, by focusing on the survivals of the *anciens régimes*, ignores their *contradictory* relationship with the capitalist transformations underway, whose consequence was to radicalize social conflict by linking – not simply in Russia, but in Germany and Italy, for example – demands for the removal of aristocratic privilege (e.g., agrarian reform, universal suffrage) which would, in Marxian terms, 'complete the bourgeois revolution', with anti-capitalist struggles by the industrial working class. Mayer ignores the escalation of social conflict in Europe immediately prior to 1914 – from Russia after the Lena goldfields massacre of 1912 to Britain during the great 'Labour Unrest' of 1910–14, although it is against the backdrop of successive waves of intense class struggle that the ultra-conservative reaction takes shape, making intelligible cries like that of the pan-German leader Heinrich Class: 'I long for the holy, redeeming war.'[43] The *grande peur* of the European ruling classes at the turn of the century, treated by Mayer as an independent variable, is best seen as a response to the destabilizing consequences of capitalist development.

This stress, *contra* Mayer, on the contradictory unity of the *anciens régimes* and the industrial capitalist order, inflects Anderson's analysis of the historical context of Modernism rather than refutes it. Indeed, in the light of my criticisms it becomes easier to clarify the anomalous status of England: as Anderson observes, 'beachhead for Eliot or Pound, offshore to Joyce, it produced no virtually significant native movement of a modernist type in the first decades of this century – unlike Germany or Italy, France or Russia, Holland or America.'[44] Once we see – as Anderson even now in his historical writing only grudgingly and inconsistently acknowledges – that the English landowners were, in Edward Thompson's words, 'a superbly successful and self-confident capitalist class' long before the Industrial Revolution, then we can understand the respect in which British society was exceptional by comparison with the Continent. A thoroughly bourgeois society even before its relatively gradual but massive industrialization, Britain by the late nineteenth century did not offer the sharp contrast between old and new provided by the comparatively sudden onset of industrial capitalism in genuinely *ancien régime* orders such as Prussia, Russia and Austria-Hungary. The decisive contribution to English-speaking Modernism made by American emigrés is no less easy to explain from this perspective than the relatively slight role of natives of Britain: Eliot, Pound and Lewis are characterized by an acute awareness of the contrast between the traditional European high culture they assimilated and the prodigious social transformations wrought by capitalist industrialization – changes which, of course, which were taken to their farthest extreme in the land of Henry Ford.

That, despite these qualifications, Andersons' delineation of the conjuncture within which Modernism took shape is essentially correct can be illustrated by considering one most important case — Vienna. Vienna, the city where, one is tempted to say, the twentieth century was invented. The sheer range of cultural innovation which Vienna produced during the decisive Modernist period of 1890–1930 is quite astonishing: in painting, Klimt, Kokoschka and Schiele; in architecture and design, Wagner, Olbrich, Loos and Hoffman; in literature, Schnitzler, Hofmannsthal, Kraus, Musil, Broch, Trakl and Werfel; in philosophy and physics, Mach, Boltzmann, Mauthner, Wittgenstein, Schlick, Neurath and Popper; in political economy, Menger, Böhm-Bawerk, Hilferding and Schumpeter; in music, Schönberg, Webern and Berg; in film, Stroheim, Sternberg, Lang and Preminger. And, of course, pervading our whole view of *fin-de-siècle* Vienna is the giant figure of Freud. This dazzling culture is surely a test case for any general account of Modernism.[45]

Such an account must confront attempts to treat Viennese Modernism as exceptional, of a different kind from its counterparts elsewhere in Europe, perhaps even an anticipation of Postmodernism. Thus Claudio Magris claims that 'Austrian civilization aspires at once to a baroque totality which transcends history and a postmodern dispersion. Austrian heroes are epigones and precursors, at once pre- and postmodern. Certainly they lack the energetic and progressivist synthesis of the modern hero, but it is this which makes them figures of lack and of absence, the faces of our destiny.'[46] Jean Clair develops the argument further, distinguishing the Modernism of the Vienna Secession from the avant-garde movements elsewhere in Europe – Dadaism, Surrealism, Constructivism: 'If the avant-garde . . . springs from an aspiration toward the future, the secessionist modernity springs from an anxiety about the past. The one projects a foundation, the other contests a tradition. The first participates not in the myth of revolution and of *innovatio*, but in the myth of a regeneration, and of *renovatio*.' That this contrast is informed by a political animus redolent more of the Paris of the *nouveaux philosophes* than of the Vienna of Freud and Schönberg is made clear when Clair says that 'those illustrations where one sees Trotsky [exiled in Vienna before the First World War] converse with the great minds of the place' represent for him 'the horror of the modern world which sees the hangmen fraternize with their victims'.[47]

We shall consider the nature of avant-garde movements in the next section: nevertheless, without denying the specificity of Viennese Modernism, nothing that Magris and Clair say about its sceptical attitude towards modernity, orientation on the past and emphasis on absence and lack distinguishes it from, say, Eliot or Proust. Nor is it sufficient to regard *fin-de-siècle* Vienna as the site of a rebellion against the Enlightenment cult of reason. It is undoubtedly true that nowhere was a sense of the inadequacies of the kind of progress towards which the *philosophes* looked forward more vividly express- ed than in Vienna between the 1890s and the 1930s. But there were other tendencies at work. Thus the Vienna Circle can be seen not simply as engaged in a technical philosophical exercise – the formula- tion of the epistemological and semantic doctrines of logical positiv- ism – but as a defence of the Enlightenment against the various forms of irrationalism that were only too visible a feature of postwar Vienna and which found expression in the clerical fascism of Dollfuss as well as in Nazism. Ernest Nagel, writing in 1936, described a lecture by Schlick, given 'in a city foundering economically, at a time when social reaction was in the saddle', as 'a potential intellectual explo- sive. I wondered how much longer such doctrines would be tolerated in Vienna.'[48] Not for long, as Schlick's assassination showed, but the Vienna Circle's commitment to the defence of reason was continued, despite his criticisms of logical positivism, by Popper. Even Freud, the thinker who did more than any other to dethrone the self-certain subject of Cartesian rationalism, remained committed to achieving a scientific understanding of the unconscious processes he had unco- vered. Finally, to suppose that Vienna was immune from the fears and hopes raised by an unpredictable political future is, of course, absurd. Karl Lueger's mayorship of Vienna before 1914 provided Hitler with his model of mass antisemitic politics; the city was one of the main centres of European social democracy, among whose chief intellectual ornaments were the Austro-Marxists – Rudolph Hilferding, Otto Bauer, Max Adler, Karl Renner and others. Bauer in particular was put to the test by a succession of postwar upheavals – the 1918 Revolution, the police massacre of 15 July 1927 and Dollfuss's suppression of the Austrian labour movement in February 1934, when Europe witnessed in the working-class quarters of Vienna the first mass armed resistance to fascism.[49]

Far from being exceptional, Vienna at the turn of the century highlighted in intensified form the constellation of elements which contributed to the emergence of Modernism. It was the capital of Musil's Kakania – of the baroquely constructed *kaiserlich und könglich* Dual Monarchy of Franz Joseph, the most absurd of all the *anciens régimes*; but it was also – unlike London and Paris, but like Berlin and St Petersburg – a great manufacturing centre, among whose population of 2,000,000 there were 375,000 industrial workers.[50] The resulting social tensions were exacerbated by the polyglot character of Vienna's inhabitants who were drawn from all the subject peoples of the empire – Germans, Czechs, Poles, Jews, Magyars, Croats, Serbs, Slovenes, Rumanians, Italians. By the 1890s the mass movements thrown up by these changes – Christian democracy, Pan-Germanism, Slavic nationalism, social democracy – threatened to upend the liberal constitutional régime established after Austria's defeat by Prussia in 1866.

Carl Schorske in his brilliant studies of *fin-de-siècle* Vienna suggests that we should see the city's incredible cultural efflorescence in the context of the crisis of the liberal bourgeoisie which was that régime's main social prop. 'Two basic social facts distinguish the Austrian from the French and English bourgeoisie: it did not succeed either in destroying or in fully fusing with aristocracy; and because of its weakness, it remained both dependent upon and deeply loyal to the emperor as a remote but necessary father-protector.'[51] The outsider status of the bourgeoisie was reinforced by the larger proportion of Jews within its ranks – 80 per cent of bankers were Jewish, as was the great steelmaster Karl Wittgenstein, the philosopher's father.[52] The cultural fusion of aristocracy and bourgeoisie was complicated by the fact that Habsburg art was that of the Catholic Counter-Reformation, 'a sensuous, plastic culture . . . The Austrian bour-geoisie, rooted in the liberal culture of reason and law, thus confronted an older aristocratic culture of feeling and grace.' The process of assimilation nevertheless attempted by the liberal bourgeoisie reached its climax at the turn of the century, when it signified a withdrawal from politics in the face of the rise of the antisemitic right, the labour movement and Slavic nationalism. 'The life of art became a substitute for the life of action. Indeed, as civic action proved increasingly futile, art became almost a religion, the source of meaning and the food of the soul.' The Baroque tradition, however, fused with a specifically liberal-individualist stress on 'the cultivation of the self'. Thus, by the 1890s,

> [i]n its attempt at assimilation into the pre-existing aristocratic culture of grace, the educated bourgeoisie had appropriated the aesthetic sensibility, but in a secularized, distorted highly individu-ated form. Narcissism and a hypertrophy of the life of feeling were the consequence. The threat of the political mass movements lent new intensity to this already present trend by weakening the traditional liberal confidence in its own legacy of rationality, moral law, and progress. Art became transformed from an ornament to an essence, from an expression of value to a source of value.[53]

We shall consider one of the main examples Schorske gives in support of this thesis – Klimt's art – in the next section. It should, however, be clear in any case that Schorske's interpretation of Viennese culture is consistent with Anderson's general claim that Modernism emerged in 'the space between a still usable classical past, a still indeterminate technical present, and a still unpredictable political future'. Schorske's discussions of *fin-de-siècle* Vienna are also noteworthy in stressing the way in which the *political* frustrations of Austrian liberalism were sublimated not only, for example, in the art of the Secession, but also in Freudian psychoanalysis.[54] This raises the broader question of the politics of Modernism, to which I now turn.


## 2.3   THE RISE AND FALL OF THE AVANT-GARDE

In a brief but remarkable essay Franco Moretti has recently warned against the tendency of contemporary Marxist criticism to become 'little more than a left-wing "Apology for Modernism"', treating its devices as inherently subversive of the existing social order. Moretti argues that the characteristic Modernist stress on ambiguity expresses 'an aesthetic-ironic attitude whose best definition still lies in an old formula – "willing suspension of disbelief" – which shows how much of the modernist imagination – where nothing is unbelievable – has its source in romantic irony'.[55] In order adequately to characterize Romanticism Moretti appeals to one of the most remarkable figures of the modern European right, the brilliant but sinister Carl Schmitt. 'Romanticism is subjectified occasionalism,' Schmitt says. '... the romantic subject treats the world as an occasion and opportunity for his romantic productivity.' Any sense of the world itself and of the subject's transactions with that world being governed by objective, causal relationships is lost. 'The romantic withdraws from reality ... He ironically avoids the constraints of objectivity and guards himself against being committed to anything. The reservation of all infinite possibilities lies in irony.' Consequently, 'everything – society and history, the cosmos and humanity – serves only the productivity of the romantic ego ... every event is transformed into a fantastic and dreamlike ambiguity, and every object can become anything.'[56]

Schmitt argues that this aestheticization of the relationship between individual and reality was possible 'only in a bourgeois world', where 'it is left to the private individual to be his own priest', but also 'his own poet, his own philosopher, his own king, and his own master-builder in the cathedral of his own personality.'[57] Moretti takes this explanation a step further. Modernism is 'a crucial component of that great symbolic transformation that has taken place in modern Western societies: the meaning of life is sought no more in the realm of public life, politics, and work; instead, it has migrated into the world of consumption and private life.' The 'unending day-dreams' of Modernism 'owe their very existence to the bored and blind indifference of our public life.' Modernism's 'unbelievable range of political choices can be explained only by its basic political indifference'.[58]

It might be objected to this view of Modernism that it ignores the often unacknowledged or at least concealed and allusive presence of politics in Modernist texts: thus Colin MacCabe has shown the importance of the Irish Revolution for an understanding of Joyce's writing.[59] This is, I think, to miss the point. Frederic Jameson has argued for 'the priority of the political interpretation of literary texts', for integrating them into 'the unity of a single great collective story', the history of class struggle. 'It is in detecting the traces of that uninterrupted narrative, in restoring to the surface of the text the repressed and buried reality of this fundamental text, that the doctrine of a political unconscious finds its function and its necessity.'[60] But the political, according to Jameson, is precisely *unconscious*, requiring a practice of interpretation to uncover it. It is quite consistent with Moretti's thesis that Modernism's primarily aesthetic relation to the world may be a distorted expression of 'the repressed and buried reality' of class struggle.

That Modernism tends to involve precisely the kind of aesthetic withdrawal from reality described by Schmitt and Moretti can be shown by numerous examples: I shall give but two. One of Klimt's greatest works is his 'Beethoven Frieze', painted for the 1902 exhibition at the Secession building in Vienna in honour of Max Klinger's statue of the composer. Schorske contrasts the frieze with the grim view of politics in Klimt's earlier 'Jurisprudence', which had offered 'the frightening spectacle of the law as ruthless punishment, consuming its victims'. Now Klimt took as his theme Beethoven's Ninth, but transformed the revolutionary Promethianism of the symphony, and of Schiller's 'Ode to Joy' into 'a manifestation of narcissistic regression and utopian bliss ... Where politics had brought defeat and suffering, art provided escape and comfort.' In the first two panels Klimt contrasted the 'Longing for Happiness' with 'The Hostile Forces'; in the climactic third panel, 'The Longing for Happiness Finds Surcease in Poetry', a couple embraces. Its inspiration was Schiller's phrase, 'The kiss to the whole world'. But, '[f]or Schiller and for Beethoven, the kiss was political, the kiss of the brotherhood of man – "Be embraced, ye millions" was Schiller's universalistic injunction. Beethoven introduces the line through male voices only, *Andante maestoso*, with all strength and dignity of fraternal fervour. For Klimt, the sentiment is not heroic but purely erotic. More remarkable still, the kiss and embrace takes place in a womb.' Schorske calls the frieze Klimt's 'fullest statement of the ideal of art as a refuge from modern life. In "Beethoven", the dreamer's utopia, wholly abstracted from that life's historical concreteness, is itself imprisonment in the womb, a fulfilment through regression.'[61]

If Klimt's retreat into art supports Schorske's general interpretation of Viennese culture, my second example may seem more surprising, since it is a novel set amidst political upheaval. Andrei Bely's *Petersburg* was placed by Nabokov alongside *Ulysses*, *Metamorphosis* and the first half of *À la recherche du temps perdu* as one of 'the greatest masterpieces of twentieth-century prose'.[62] It is the story of how, during the climax of the 1905 Revolution, a young *intelligent*, Nikolai Apollonovich Ableukhov, one of the alienated 'superfluous men' whose dilemmas form the main theme of the classical Russian novel, grapples with the mission assigned him by a terrorist group to blow up his father, a seniot Tsarist bureaucrat. *Petersburg* is, however, much more than this – above all, a portrait steeped in literary tradition and teeming with Modernist devices, of the great city itself, a city buzzing with revolutionary tumults, haunted by the ghosts of the past symbolized by the great bronze statue of Peter the Great to which Pushkin devoted 'The Bronze Horseman'. For Marshall Berman, *Petersburg* is a key Modernist text.[63] One may readily acknowledge the novel's greatness – in particular, its vivid cinematic style, which jump-cuts from scene to scene – and still be struck by the extent to which it marks a retreat from the political concerns of the great nineteenth-century Realists – of Tolstoy, Dostoevsky and Turgenev. Bely vividly evokes the atmosphere of Petersburg in October 1905, a city convulsed by the great general strike which gave birth to the first *soviet*. But these mass struggles – Bely revealingly dismisses the crowd, whether of bowler-hatted commuters or revolutionary proletarians, as 'a human myriapod' – form merely a backdrop against which individuals, in particular Ableukhov *père et fils* and the revolutionary *intelligent* Dudkin, pursue their destiny. Nikolai Apollonovich, obsessed by the bomb with which he has been charged to kill his father, is recognizably the descendant of Raskolnikov and the other anti-heroes of Dostoevsky's novels. But whereas their personal dilemmas dramatize the exploration of political and metaphysical arguments central to Dostoevsky's art, Nikolai Apollonovich bobs along the flow of events like a cork, the passive witness even of his own private drama, including the activation and detonation of the bomb. Ethical and political choices have faded by comparison with the intensity of mere experience; in the end Nikolai Apollonovich flees Russia, the world of living history, to become an archaeologist in North Africa, content to examine the remains of the remote past. *Petersburg* is a novel which dramatizes the 'spell of indecision' which, Moretti claims, captured Modernism.

This reading of Modernism, which underlines its adoption of an aesthetic relation to reality and treatment of art as a refuge, does not imply that Modernist works of art never express political commitments. What is, however, striking is how variable these commitments are. Eugene Lunn's four defining characteristics of Modernism – reflexivity, montage, ambiguity and dehumanization (see section 1.2) – have co-existed with a wide range of political stances, from the revolutionary socialism of Brecht, Eisenstein and Mayakovsky to the fascism of Pound, Lewis and Céline. This contrast is well known, but Jeffrey Herf has in a fascinating recent study pointed to the phenomenon of 'reactionary modernism' in Weimar and Nazi Germany, of 'nationalists who turned the romantic anticapitalism of the German Right away from backward-looking pastoralism, pointing instead to the outlines of a beautiful new order replacing the formless chaos due to capitalism in a united, technologically advanced nation'. Perhaps the most striking example Herf gives is that of Ernst Jünger. Jünger celebrated the *Fronterlebnis* (front experience) in the trenches of the First World War because the mechanized destruction involved (captured in the disgusting image of 'a turbine filled with blood') was an anticipation of a society in which it would be understood that *'technology and nature are not opposites'*, that technology is *'the embodiment of an icy will'*, a society in which class antagonisms would be overcome, worker and capitalist united in a community committed to realizing through military expansion the will to power given visible form by the machinery of mass production and destruction. What is astonishing about Jünger is the way in which the images not merely of modern warfare but of the twentieth-century metropolis – 'in the big city, between automobiles and electric signs, in political mass meetings, in the motorized tempo of work and leisure, in the middle of the bustle of the modern Babylon' – are treated as illustrations of the *Lebensphilosophie* which had previously dismissed them as symptoms of decadence.[64]

Benjamin had Jünger especially in mind when he argued that the 'logical result of fascism is the introduction of aesthetics into political life'. But he also said that the kind of aestheticization of politics involved in Marinetti's declaration 'War is beautiful' is 'the consummation of *"l'art pour l'art"*'.[65] Here Benjamin touches on a theme developed much further by Peter Bürger. Bürger argues that art emerges in the late eighteenth century as a distinct institution, whose separate status is rationalized by the thesis of the autonomy of art from other social practices, a thesis articulated theoretically thanks to the virtually simultaneous emergence of philosophical aesthetics. The 'art institution' is a product of bourgeois society. Not only is the work of art liberated from its previous subordination to cultic ritual and its production transformed from a collaborative, artisanal into an individual practice – changes already under way under the absolute monarchies – but its mode of reception becomes individual, as opposed to the collective consumption of the mediaeval congregation or early-modern court. However, in the course of the nineteenth century, as bourgeois domination is consolidated, the autonomous status of the 'art institution' is relfected in the content of the works themselves. Themes such as that central to the Realist novel as 'the relationship between individual and society' are 'overshadowed by the ever-increasing concentration the makers of art bring to the medium itself'. This tendency reaches its climax in *fin-de-siècle* Aestheticism, 'where art becomes the content of life'.[66]

Benjamin described the Aestheticism of Mallarmé and other artists at the turn of the century 'a negative theology in the form of the idea of "pure" art which not only denied any social function of art but also any categorizing by subject matter.'[67] This stance had a precursor well known to him, Baudelaire, from whom dandyism is 'the last gleam of heroism in times of decadence', a challenge to 'the rising tide of democracy, overwhelming and levelling everything'. The dandy asserts 'the aristocratic superiority of his personality', practising, with 'spirituality and stoicism', 'a sort of cult of oneself'.[68] Foucault comments: 'Modern man, for Baudelaire, . . . is the man who tries to invent himself.' He summarizes Baudelaire's conception of modernity:

This ironic heroization of the present, this transfiguring play of freedom with reality, this ascetic elaboration of the self – Baudelaire does not imagine that these have any place in society itself, or in the body politic. They can only be produced in another, a different place, which Baudelaire calls art.[69]

It is precisely these attitudes which Modernism makes the very content of art, with its self-reflexiveness and ambiguity. Benjamin argued that Baudelaire's dandyism was a response to the commodification of social life in the modern city: 'The non-conformists rebel against the surrender of art to the market. They rally round the banner of *l'art pour l'art* . . . The rites with which it is celebrated are the counterpart of the distractions which transfigure the commodity.'[70] It is plausible to follow Moretti in relating the emergence of Modernism to the transformation of nineteenth-century urban life analysed, among others, by Richard Sennett, as a result of which individuals' primary emotional investment came to be in the private sphere of personal relations, while the public sphere withered into, at best, a means of self-expression, changes inseparable from the progressive penetration of social relations by the market on which Benjamin laid such stress (see also section 5.4 below).[71]

Is not the general tendency to this analysis similar to Lukács's celebrated denunciation of Modernism as 'aesthetically appealing, but decadent'? Modernism, he argues, is merely a late variant of Naturalism, whose replacement of Realism was a consequence of the transformation of the nineteenth-century bourgeoisie from a revolutionary into a reactionary class.[72] No. In the first place, the interpretation of Modernism outlined in this and the previous section rejects what Anderson calls Lukács's '*evolutionism*' that is, 'time differs from one epoch to another, but *within* each epoch all sectors of social reality move in synchrony with one another, such that decline at one level must be reflected in descent at every other.'[73] While Modernism's propensity to treat reality as an occasion for aesthetic experience may have arisen from the historical processes sketched out in the foregoing three paragraphs, its emergence is intelligible only in the context of the specific conjuncture discussed in section 2.2 above. Secondly, to highlight the fact that Modernism shares with Romanticism 'subjectified occasionalism' is not thereby to pass a negative aesthetic judgement on the works of art grouped together under the former label. Brecht's polemic against the extreme formalism which led Lukács to deny merit to any work not conforming to a hypostatized model derived from nineteenth-century Realism retains all its force today.[74]

Thirdly, it is at least arguable that Modernist art expresses a protest against the capitalist society which it is, in complex ways, related. The most extreme version of this claim is made, of course, by Adorno:

> The modernity of art lies in its mimetic relation to a petrified and alienated reality. This, and not the denial of that reality, is what makes art speak. One consequence is that modern art does not tolerate anything that smacks of innocuous compromise. Baudelaire ... neither reproduced reinfication nor railed against it. Instead, he protested against it indirectly through experience of its archetypes, using artistic form as a medium of such an experience. It is this that enables him to rise to a level of art high above late-romantic sentimentalism. His strength as a writer lies in the

ability to syncopate the overwhelming objectivity of the commodi-
ty-form, which absorbs into itself all human residues, with the
objectivity of the work as such, which is prior to the living subject.
Here the absolute work of art merges with the absolute
commodity.[75]

For Adorno it is the 'absoluteness' of the Modernist work, its
abstract, depersonalized, visibly constructed character which allows it
to criticize, by allusion, a social world dominated by commodity
fetishism, in which social relations are transformed into relations
between things. But there is another, more emphatic sense in which
Modernism issues in political critique. Bürger argued that what is
distinctive about the avant-garde movements of the early twentieth
century – Dadaism, early Surrealism, post-revolutionary Russian
Constructivism – is their 'attack on the status of art in bourgeois
society. What is negated is not an earlier form of art (a style) but art as
an institution that is unassociated with the life-praxis of men':

> The avant-gardistes proposed the sublation of art – sublation of art
> in the Hegelian sense: art was not to be simply destroyed, but
> transferred to the praxis of life, where it would be preserved, albeit
> in a changed form. The avant-gardistes thus adopted an essential
> element of Aestheticism. Aestheticism had made the distance from
> the praxis of life the content of works. The praxis of life to which
> Aestheticism refers and which it negates is the means-end rational-
> ity of the bourgeois everyday. Now, it is not the aim of the
> avant-gardistes to integrate art into *this* praxis. On the contrary,
> they assent to the Aestheticists' rejection of the world and its
> means-end rationality. What distinguishes them from the latter is
> the attempt to organize a new life-praxis from a basis in art.[76]

According to Bürger, then, *l'art pour l'art* and avant-garde movements such as Surrealism represent different ways of rejecting
bourgeois society, one retreating into a reflexive exploration of the
'art institution' itself, the other seeking to resolve art back into the
social world as part of the struggle to revolutionize that world. The
slogan of the avant garde was thus given by Breton when he declared:
'"Transform the world," Marx said; "change life," Rimbaud said –
these two watchwords are for us one and the same' (see section 1.3
above). Bürger in drawing this contrast between Aestheticism and the
avant garde, does not discuss Modernism as such, indeed forbearing
to use the very category. That this is a weakness of an otherwise most
illuminating analysis is made clear when we consider Bürger's discussion of the 'nonorganic work of art'. In order to characterize the

avant garde's break with any conception of the work of art as a
harmonious, organic totality Bürger draws on Benjamin's extraordinary study of the Baroque *Trauerspiel*. Benjamin, who notes the
similarities between the Baroque and Expressionism, argues that the
former involves the use of allegory, which is characterized by 'the
primacy of the thing over the personal, the fragment over the total': a
melancholic view of the world as fallen, doomed to death and decay,
leads the Baroque playwright to aim at 'significantly dividing a living
entity into the *disiecta membra* of allegory'.[77]
   Similarly, according to Bürger,

> [t]he organic work of art seeks to make unrecognizable the fact that
> it has been made. The opposite is true of the avant-gardiste work: it
> proclaims itself an artificial construct, an artifact. To this extent,
> montage may be considered to be the fundamental principle of
> avant-gardiste art. The 'fitted' (*montierte*) work calls attention to
> the fact that it is made up of reality-fragments; it breaks through
> the appearance (*Schein*) of totality. Paradoxically, the avant-
> gardiste intention to destroy art as an institution is thus realized in
> the work of art itself. The intention to revolutionize life by
> returning art to its praxis turns into a revolutionizing of art.[78]

   The turning point in the development of the avant-gardiste technique of montage came, according to Bürger, with Cubism, 'that
movement in modern painting which most consciously destroyed the
representational system that had prevailed since the Renaissance'.
The revolutionary character of Cubism lay in its techniques of
composition, and in particular in the creation of collages incorporating portions extracted from everyday life – scraps of newspaper, for
example – in the paintings. 'The insertion of reality-fragments into
the work of art fundamentally transforms that work', Bürger argues.
'The artist not only renounces shaping a whole, but gives the painting
a different status, since parts of it no longer have the relationship to
reality characteristic of the organic work of art. They are no longer
signs pointing to reality, they *are* reality.' By undermining the
traditional view of the work of art as a self-contained ideal world
mirroring the real world beyond it, Cubism also challenged the notion
of art as an autonomous institution distinct from the rest of social life.
But – as Bürger concedes – this challenge to the 'art institution' was
only implicit in Cubism: a painting by Picasso or Braque is still 'an
aesthetic object'.[79] The point could be generalized: techniques analogous to montage can be discovered in Modernists who are clearly
committed to the Aestheticist concept of art as a refuge from alienated
social life – the interweaving of different voices in Joyce's fiction and

Eliot's early poetry is an example we discussed in section 1.2 above.

Modernism therefore prepared the way for the avant garde. It took over a conception of art first developed by classical German idealism and central to Romanticism, in which aesthetic experience represents a higher form of consciousness than the merely discursive understanding provided by scientific knowledge. Art thus conceived is a refusal of 'the means-end rationality of the bourgeois everyday', a retreat from a social world pervaded by commodity fetishism. But such an art can have, of necessity, one object – itself. An aesthetic practice which aspires to escape the fragmentation of social life is driven to focus on its own processes of creation precisely because they seem to rise above this fragmentation (although the very existence of art as a differentiated and autonomous institution is itself a consequence of the transformations in social relations against which Modernism rebels). By reflexively taking itself as its own object, however, Modernism makes possible a critique of the isolated status of art, and the aspiration to overcome the social alienation to which *l'art pour l'art* is a response by resolving art back into a transformed 'life-praxis' – for example, the Surrealist attempt at a synthesis of Marx and Rimbaud. Modernism is a necessary condition of the avant garde also in a second sense. The technical innovations characteristic of Modernism – montage above all – distinguish it from earlier attempts such as Romanticism to develop what Benjamin called a 'theology of art'. By disassembling the organic work of art, by openly displaying their creations as agglomerations of discrete fragments, the Cubists and the great literary Modernists sought to respond to what Eliot called 'the immense panorama of futility and anarchy that is contemporary history'. They thus opened the door to a conception of art as continuous with and participating in – rather than a refuge from – a social world whose fusion with aesthetic practices would be central to its transformation.

That Bürger is right nevertheless to insist on the distinctive character of the avant-garde as movements seeking to abolish the separation between art and life seems to me unquestionable. Bürger himself concentrates primarily on Surrealism, although its inclusion among avant-garde movements has, mistakenly I think, been challenged.[80] There are in any case other major movements of which perhaps the most important was Russian Constructivism. The main technical innovations of this movement, a tendency towards increasing abstraction, and the dynamical representation of a world transformed by humanity using machines in order to conquer nature, were made in the years immediately prior to and during the First World War by a number of major figures – Malevich, Goncharova, Tatlin,

Popova, Exter, Rosanova, Rodchenko, Larionov. But these artists occupied a small and isolated *Bohème*; their Dada-like cabarets and extravagant dress (Mayakovsky favoured a bright yellow blouse) flaunted their defiance of the bourgeois world. Camilla Gray comments: 'In their antics and public clowning, one can detect an intuitive, naive attempt to restore the artist's place in ordinary life, to allow him to become, as they themselves so profoundly felt the need to be, an active citizen.'[81] The opportunity to reunite art and life came after the Revolution of October 1917. Most of the pre-revolutionary Modernists enthusiastically identified with the Bolshevik régime. Malevich claimed that 'Cubism and Futurism were the revolutionary forms in art foreshadowing the revolution in political and economic life of 1917.' And now the two revolutions, aesthetic and political, would be united by the sublation of art in a transformed social life. Mayakovsky declared in November 1918: 'We do not need a dead mausoleum of art where dead works are worshipped, but a living factory of the human spirit – in the streets, in the tramways, in the factories, workshops and workers' homes.'[82] And for a few brief years, in his and other artists' propaganda activities for the Revolution, in the great public pageants they organized, in the theatre of Meyerhold and Tretiakov, in projects such as Tatlin's planned 'Monument to the Third International', in the films of Eisenstein and Vertov, there seemed to be some correspondence between this aspiration and social reality.

The significance of Russian Constructivism is that is shows that the radicalization of Modernism into avant garde was not simply the working through of a logic intrinsic to *fin-de-siècle* Aestheticism; it depended upon political conditions, and in particular on the October Revolution, which made concrete the vision of a social transformation through which art and life could be re-united. The same pattern, in which aesthetic innovation and revolutionary politics were fused thanks to the hopes raised by October 1917, can be seen elsewhere in Europe, and especially in Weimar Germany, itself the product of a revolution which threatened to spread Bolshevism to the heartlands of Western capitalism. Bruno Taut wrote in the manifesto of the Arbeitsrat für Kunst, founded immediately after the Revolution of November 1918: 'Art and people must form an entity. Art shall no longer be a luxury for the few, but should be enjoyed and experienced by the broad masses. The aim is the alliance of the arts under the wing of a great architecture.' The central role of architecture in restoring, on a socialist basis, the kind of integrated culture achieved by the Middle Ages was underlined by Walter Gropius, writing at the same time: 'Painters, sculptors, break down the barriers around

architecture and become co-builders and comrades-in-arms towards
act's ultimate goal: the creative idea of the Cathedral of the Future,
which will once more encompass everything in one form –
architecture and sculpture and painting.' This aspiration to build the
'Cathedral of Socialism' as a *Gesamtkunstwerk* was continued during
the Weimar years at the Bauhaus under the direction, successively, of
Gropius, Hannes Meyer and Mies van der Rohe.[83] The vigour with
which Tom Wolfe pursues Modern architecture in *From Bauhaus to
Our House* seems to derive, at least in part, from a McCarthyite fury
provoked by the discovery that downtown America is designed along
lines largely first devised by a bunch of Reds.

The case of Weimar Germany is of more general interest for an
understanding of Modernism. If *fin-de-siècle* Vienna was the city
where the twentieth century was invented, then Berlin between 1918
and 1933 was the city where all the contradictions of the century
were visible in the most dramatic form. Capital of a republic founded
on military defeat and which foundered amidst the Great Depression,
centre of at once the most advanced industrial capitalism in Europe
and of a landed aristocracy formed by the traditions of Prussian
Absolutism, a city polarized by social tensions, shaken by the anger of
rebellious workers, pauperized petty bourgeois and unemployed
lumpenproletarians, the battleground of Communists, Social Demo-
crats, Monarchists and the ultimately victorious Nazis, Berlin was
also a key Modernist centre. This was not simply because of the
significance of the local avant garde – of figures such as Grosz,
Heartfield, Brecht, Eisler, Hindemith, Piscator and others. The great
rehousing programmes implemented by the Social Democratic city
administration allowed radical architects such as Taut, Gropius and
Mies to apply Modernist principles to the design of working-class
apartment blocks. And Weimar Germany was the main conduit
through which the influence of the Russian avant garde reached the
West. The treaty of Rapallo of April 1922 between the two pariah-
states of the Versailles peace restored some of the strong links
between Russia and Germany that had existed before the Revolution.
These connections were cultural as well as economic and military.
Kandinsky had been a central figure in the Expressionist *Blaue Reiter*
group in Munich before the war. After the Rapallo thaw El Lissitzky,
Mayakovsky, Ilya Ehrenburg and others visited Germany, spreading
the influence of Constructivism westwards. It was its enthusiastic
reception in Berlin which first brought Eisenstein's *Battleship Potem-
kin* to international attention. And, as the Weimar welfare state
disintegrated under the impact of world slump at the end of the
1920s, Modernist architects such as Taut and Meyer emigrated to the

Soviet Union to participate in the vast construction programmes required by the First Five-Year Plan.

John Willett captures the particular quality of the Berlin avant garde in his important study of the *Neue Sachlichkeit*, the distinctive cultural style of Weimar Germany in its brief period of stability between 1923 and 1928,

> a new realism that sought methods of dealing both with real subjects and with real human needs, a sharply critical view of existing society and individuals, and a determination to master new media and discover new collective approaches to the communication of artistic concepts. The constructive vision in question will be found applied in various fields – first in 'pure' art in two or three dimensions, then in photography, the cinema, architecture, various forms of design and the theatre – often according to principles derived, far more significantly than before 1914, from the rapidly developing technological sphere: that is, not so much from the outward appearance of machines so much as from the kind of thinking that underlies their design and operation. The critical vision comes out of Dada and the disillusionments of the war and of the German Revolution; it is in effect a cooler and more sceptical counterpart to the optimistic humanitarianism of the Expressionists in the years 1916–19, and as this began deflating it moved into the gap, to become known under the slightly misleading title of The New Objectivity.[84]

*Neue Sachlichkeit* art adopted a cool, impersonal tone. This did not imply the adoption of a neutral stance. Brecht wrote in 1927: 'It strikes me that those plays of this period that are of any use spring from their authors' astonishment at the things that happen in life. Our wish to put them straight, to create precedents and found a tradition of overcoming difficulties, gives rise to the plays of a period that will be filled with the rush of humanity to the big cities.'[85] It was an art pervaded by a sense of the modern metropolis in general and of Berlin in particular. The city's modernity dominated, for example, Walter Ruttman's and Carl Meyer's 1927 documentary film, *Berlin – the Symphony of a Great City*, a modernity on whose horizon loomed the shadow of *Amerikanismus*, humanity's future, a vast, dynamic, anonymous, industrial civilisation. Techniques such as post-revolutionary Russian 'factography', reportage modelled on the documentary style of John Reed's *Ten Days That Shook The World*, and the montage of the Cubists, Joyce and Eisenstein were used to capture the ambiguity of the metropolis, both promise and threat, and to draw the social contrasts on which these artists' revolutionary politics led them to concentrate.

But if Weimar Germany saw the development of one of the most important avant-garde movements, it was also the scene where the hopes of all these movements were dashed. The defeat of the German Revolution, only finally accomplished after the suppression of the abortive Communist insurrection of October 1923, unleashed two counter-revolutionary processes: on the one hand, the consolidation, under the pressure of a hostile international environment, of a bureaucratic state-capitalist regime in the USSR; on the other, in the climate of social crisis created by the Great Depression, the victory of fascism in Germany.[86] Between them Stalinism and Nazism destroyed the avant garde. This was most obviously true in the sense that the two regimes set out administratively to suppress what one called 'bourgeois formalism', the other *Kulturbolchewismus*. With the First Five-Year Plan the comparative tolerance of artistic experimentation characteristic of the USSR in the 1920s came to an end: during the period of voluntarist enthusiasm which historians now call the 'cultural revolution' of 1928–31 the naive enthusiasts of 'proletarian culture' were allowed free rein, before in their turn being knocked on the head and replaced by the apparatchiks of 'Socialist Realism'.[87] 'The love boat of life has shattered on the rocks of philistinism', wrote Mayakovsky in his last poem before his suicide in 1930. Meyerhold and Tretiakov along with many other artists perished in the Gulag. Those who survived did so with difficulty – most of Eisenstein's film projects were still-born. The Nazi conquest of power sent a flood of artists out of Germany, part of the massive emigration of the intelligentsia of Central Europe that is so important to an understanding of the Anglophone cultures which absorbed most of these exiles.

The disaster of Stalinism and fascism killed off the avant-garde movements in another, more fundamental respect. It deprived them of the anticipated social revolution essential to the integration of art and life which they sought. The postwar stabilization of capitalism left the few still committed to avant-garde objectives beached: the tortuous path followed by Brecht, moving from a Hollywood rendered uninhabitable by McCarthyism to a Stalinist East Germany to which he gave an only qualified endorsement, illustrates the dilemma of the revolutionary artist in an apparently pacified, but far from reconciled world.

The shipwreck of the avant garde dramatized the more general exhaustion of Modernism. Moretti observes that the 'extraordinary concentration of literary masterpieces around the First World War . . . constituted the last *literary season* of Western culture. Within a few years European literature gave its utmost and seemed on the verge of opening new and boundless horizons: instead, it died. A few isolated icebergs, and many imitators: but nothing comparable to the past.'[88] Wyndham Lewis said something similar in 1937. Referring to 'the men of 1914' – Eliot, Pound, Joyce and himself – he wrote: '*We are the first men of a Future that has not materialized.* We belong to a "great age" that has not "come off".' His explanation was that '[i]f you ... fix your attention on any art ... you will be forced to the conclusion that in every instance "commercialism", as we say, is most efficiently destroying it or has effectively destroyed it.'[89]

The commodification of social life is part also of Anderson's account of the disintegration of the Modernist conjuncture after 1945:

> It was the Second World War that destroyed all three of the historical coordinates I have discussed and therewith cut off the vitality of modernism. After 1945, the old semiaristocratic or agrarian order and its appurtenances were finished, in every country. Bourgeois democracy was finally universalized. With that, certain critical links with a precapitalist past were snapped. At the same time, Fordism arrived in force. Mass production and consumption transformed the West European economies along North American lines. There could no longer be the smallest doubt as to what kind of society this technology would consolidate: an oppressively stable, monolithically industrial, capitalist civilization was now in place ... Finally, the image or hope of revolution faded away in the West. The onset of the Cold War, and the Sovietization of Eastern Europe, cancelled any realistic prospect of a socialist overthrow of advanced capitalism for a whole historical period. The ambiguity of aristocracy, the absurdity of academicism, the gaiety of the first cars or movies, the palpability of the socialist alternative, were now all gone. In their place there now reigned a routinized, bureaucratic economy of universal commodity production, in which 'mass consumption' and 'mass culture' had become virtually interchangeable terms.[90]

I explore the cultural implications of these changes in chapter 5. First, however, I consider some of the forms in which the case for and against modernity has been subjected to philosophical scrutiny.

# 3

# THE APORIAS OF
# POSTSTRUCTURALISM

I have it from her ladyship's own maid . . . that it was her intention
to start you almost immediately upon Nietzsche. You would not
enjoy Nietzsche, sir. He is fundamentally unsound.

*P. G. Wodehouse*

## 3.1   THE OWL OF MINERVA TAKES WING AT DAWN:
### NIETZSCHE

Marx, Nietzsche, and Saint-Simon may plausibly be regarded as the
founders of the three most influential ways of thinking about
modernity. All three take the Enlightenment as their starting-point, all
three have a distinctive conception of the modern epoch inaugurated
by the dual industrial and political revolutions at the end of the
eighteenth century. Saint-Simon inherited Condorcet's conception of
history as the 'progress of the human mind'. He saw this progress
taking concrete shape in industrial society, where scientific knowledge
would become the basis of social power and class antagonisms
disappear. Marx and Nietzsche are also both recognizable children of
the Enlightenment. Both Marxian *Ideologiekritik* and Nietzschean
genealogy continued the *philosophes'* attempts to trace the social
roots of ideologies.[1] Neither Marx or Nietzsche, however, shared the
Enlightenment view of history as continuous progress. Marx of
course saw bourgeois society, not as the actualization of reason, but
as the latest version of class exploitation, distinguished chiefly by its
technological dynamism and by its nurturing of the proletariat, the
social force with the capacity to abolish class society itself (see section
2.1 above). Nietzsche also unravelled an historical succession of
forms of domination, but denied the possibility of a nonexploitive
society. Even scientific reason, which Marx had turned against the
bourgeoisie to decode the laws of motion of capitalism, became for

Nietzsche an embodiment of the will to power intrinsic to organic life itself. Saint-Simon lives on in the theorists of 'industrial' and 'postindustrial' society – Parsons, Aron, Bell, Touraine and the like. The name of Marx's progeny is legion. Weber was the most important social thinker influenced by Nietzsche, but the latter's thought has enjoyed a remarkable recrudescence in postwar France, in the group of thinkers now usually labelled as poststructuralist – Foucault, Derrida and Deleuze in particular. It is on their ideas – central to any discussion of postmodernism – that I concentrate in this chapter.

Habermas argues that the triple response to modernity outlined above originates in the collapse of Hegel's system. For it was Hegel who 'inaugurated the discourse of modernity', whose theme is 'the self-critical reassurance of modernity'. Hegel grasped the distinctive problem of modernity, its need for *self*-justification, given the collapse of traditional norms and models consequent on the seventeenth-century revolution (see section 2.1 above). For Hegel, modernity is distinguished by the manner in which 'religious life, state and society as well as science, morality and art are transformed into so many embodiments of the principle of subjectivity.' But he conceives subjectivity as 'a structure of self-relation' identical not with finite individual persons but with the Absolute whose self-development underlies human history: modernity is the age where the Absolute attains self-consciousness through the agency of finite subjects. As Habermas puts it, 'as absolute knowledge, reason assumes a form so overwhelming that it not only solves the problem of a self-reassurance of modernity, but solves it *too well*.' The conscious human action that is the stuff of history becomes, by virtue of the ruse of reason, the means by which, independently of the intentions of the actors, the Absolute achieves its ends. Nevertheless, Hegel set the mould of subsequent discussion of modernity:

The relation of history to reason remains constitutive for the discourse of modernity – for better or worse. Whoever participates in this discourse (and nothing about this discourse has changed to our own day) makes a distinct use of the expressions 'reason' and 'rationality'. They are used neither in accord with the game rules of ontology to characterize God or being as a whole: nor in accord with the game rules of empiricists to characterize individual subjects capable of knowledge and action. Reason is valid neither as something ready-made, as an objective teleology in nature or history, nor as a mere subjective faculty. Instead the patterns looked for in historical events yield uncoded indications of unfinished, uninterrupted and misguided processes of self-formation that transcend the subjective consciousness of the individual.[2]

Habermas argues that the collapse of Hegel's attempt to discover reason in history originated in the Young Hegelians' critique of the Absolute as effectively sanctioning continued exploitation and oppression. '[W]e remain contemparies of the Young Hegelians', not simply in rejecting absolute idealism, but in following one of three paths away from it:

> The *Left Hegelian* critique, turned toward the practical and aroused for revolution, aimed at mobilizing the historically accumulated potential of reason (awaiting release) against its mutilation, against its one-sided rationalization of the bourgeois world. The *Right Hegelians* followed Hegel in the conviction that the substance of state and religion would compensate for the restlessness of bourgeois society, as soon as the subjectivity of the revolutionary consciousness that incited restlessness yielded to objective insight into the rationality of the status quo ... Finally, *Nietzsche* wanted to unmask the dramaturgy of the entire stage-piece in which both − revolutionary hope and the reaction to it − enter on the scene. He removed the dialectical thorn from a critique of a reason centred on the subject and shrivelled into purposive rationality; and he related to reason as a whole to the way the Young Hegelians related to its sublimations: Reason is *nothing else* than power, than the will to power, which it so radiantly conceals.[3]

Marx of course took the first path; Habermas cites various contemporary German neo-conservatives − Hans Freyer, Joachim Ritter et al. − as exemplars of Right Hegelianism, but a social theorist such as Parsons seems to be a more important example of this kind of 'affirmative attitude toward social modernity'.[4] Nietzsche's thought is undoubtedly central to contemporary discussions of modernity and postmodernity. Those who detect the emergence of a postmodern epoch typically repeat arguments first developed by Nietzsche. The principal Nietzschean theses invoked in contemporary discussion are perhaps the following:

1 The individual subject, far from being the self-certain foundation of modernity, is a fiction, a historically contingent construct beneath whose apparent unity throbs a welter of conflicting unconscious drives;
2 The plural nature of the self is merely one instance of the inherently multiple and heterogeneous character of reality itself: running through the whole of nature, including the human world, is what Nietzsche called the 'will to power', the disposition of different power-centres to engage in a perpetual struggle

for domination whose outcomes alter both the relationships fundamentally constitutive of reality and the identities of the parties to those relationships;

3 The will to power is operative within human history: political and military struggles, social and economic transformations, moral and aesthetic revolutions – all are comprehensible only in the context of the unending conflicts from which successive forms of domination arise;

4 Nor is thought itself exempt from this struggle: modern scientific rationality is a particularly successful variant of the will to power, its urge to dominate nature originating in Plato's claim that thought can uncover the inner structure of an antecedently existing, and indeed unchanging reality; the only attitude appropriate to the seething heterogeneity of the actual world is perspectivism, which recognizes every thought as an interpretation, valid only within a conceptual framework the grounds for whose acceptance lie not in any supposed correspondence with reality, but in the purpose, construable ultimately in terms of the will to power, which it serves.[5]

I discuss contemporary versions of these claims in the following sections. It is, however, worth noting first the extent to which Nietzsche was a precursor of Modernism. As Habermas observes,

he is the first to conceptualize the attitude of aesthetic modernity before avant-garde consciousness assumed objective shape in the literature, painting, and music of the twentieth century – and could be elaborated [by Adorno] into an *Aesthetic Theory*. In the upgrading of the transitory, in the celebration of the dynamic, in the glorification of the current and new, there is expressed an aesthetically motivated time-consciousness and a longing for an unspoiled, inward presence.[6]

Similarly, in an important recent study Alexander Nehemas highlights 'Nietzsche's aestheticism, his essential reliance on artistic models for understanding the world and life and for evaluating people and actions. This aestheticism springs from his effort to bring style into the centre of his own thought and to repeat once more what he took to be the great achievement of the Greeks and the Romans, to make of "the grand style no longer mere art but ... reality, truth, *life*".'[7]

Nietzsche's Aestheticism is not simply reflected in the importance he attaches to art, great though that is: 'Art and nothing but art: It is the great means of making life possible, the great seduction to life, the great stimulant to life.' It is also that the nature of aesthetic experience contains *in nuce* the form of understanding proper to the world itself. Thus Nietzsche speaks of '[t]he world as a work of art that gives birth to itself'.[8] Richard Schacht suggests that this remark implies that 'the world possesses the sort of ambiguity characteristic of works of art. One of their more significant features is that, while they are by no means formless, they are commonly "rich", defying simply and univocal analysis.'[9] Conceiving the world as a work of art contributes to the idea that it is inherently plural, a view which in turn supports the claim that an indefinite number of mutually inconsistent perspectives offering equally valid interpretations of its nature. The kinship between the pluralism and perspectivism expressed in this conception of the world and the sense of what Hofmannsthal called *das Gleitende*, the unstable, mobile, indeterminate, so important for Modernism is obvious. Similarly, the dialectic of interiority and exteriority which I argued in section 1.3 above to be an important feature of Modernist art finds its anticipation in such anti-Platonist passages as the following: 'Oh, those Greeks! They knew how to live. What is required for that is to stop courageously at the surface, the fold, the skin, to adore appearance, to believe in forms, tones, words, in the whole Olympus of appearance. Those Greeks were superficial – *out of profundity*.'[10]

There is another respect in which Nietzsche can be said to have anticipated Modernism, and that is in the importance he attaches to the notion of self-creation. We saw, in section 2.3 above, that Baudelaire described dandyism as 'a sort of cult of oneself', leading Foucault to comment that '[m]odern man, for Baudelaire, . . . is the man who tries to invent himself.' Now compare Nietzsche on the kind of person which his revaluation of all values seeks to promote: 'We, however, *want to become those we are* – human beings who are new, unique, incomparable, who give themselves laws, who create themselves.'[11] Nietzsche describes Goethe, 'the last German for whom I feel reverence', thus: 'What he aspired to was *totality*; . . . he disciplined himself to a whole, he *created* himself.'[12] But above all Nietzsche regarded himself as a self-creation. He writes in *Ecce Homo*, whose subtitle is *How One Becomes What One Is*:

> For the task of a *revaluation of all values* more capacities may have been needed than have ever dwelt together in a single individual – above all, even contrary capacities that had to be kept from disturbing, destroying one another. An order of rank among these

capacities; distance; the art of separating without setting against one another; to mix nothing, to 'reconcile' nothing; a tremendous variety that is nevertheless the opposite of chaos – that was the precondition, the long, secret work and artistry of my instinct.[13]

Thus although Nietzsche denies that there is any necessary unity of the self, indeed denies that there is any necessity for human beings to be selves in the sense in which the self can be created, he nevertheless attaches great importance to the idea that some at least can 'invent themselves' through a process of self-mastery. Self-creation is to make a work of art of oneself. Nehemas suggests that we should think of *À la recherche du temps perdu* as a model of what is involved. At the end of the novel we discover that the meaning of the narrator's life is simply the process of its unfolding, which he seeks to capture by beginning to write the book we have just finished. Similarly, '[t]o become what one is . . . is to identify oneself with all one's actions, to see that everything one does (what one becomes) is what one is. In the ideal case it is also to fit all this into a coherent whole and to want to be what one is: it is to give style to one's character; to be, we might say, becoming.' Nietzsche's own writings exemplify this conception by constructing a character who has created himself – Nietzsche himself, the hero of *Ecce Homo*. Thus, Nehemas concludes, Nietzsche's 'passion for self-reference combines with his urge for self-fashioning to make him the first Modernist at the same time that he is the last Romantic'.[14]

Nietzsche's overall stance is perhaps best understood as a variant of Romantic anticapitalism, which is defined by Robert Sayre and Michael Löwy as '*opposition to capitalism in the name of pre-capitalist values*'.[15] Nietzsche rejected contemporary bourgeois civilization as decadent: 'we, we moderns, with our anxious care for ourselves and love of our neighbour, with our virtues of work, of unpretentiousness, of fair play, of scientificality – acquisitive, economical, machine-minded – appear as a *weak* age.'[16] Inasmuch as any society offered a model of the kind of values he advocated it was classical Greece, among whose characteristics was an aristocratic culture of self-creation: 'A leisure class whose members make things difficult for themselves and exercise much self-overcoming. The power of form, the will to give form to oneself.'[17] It is not hard, in the light of the analysis sketched out in the previous chapter, to understand how such a system of ideas, in many respects a philosophical articulation of the main themes of Modernism, should have emerged during the *Gründerzeit*, the period after German unification in 1871 when Junkerdom and industrial capitalism fused in a peculiarly complacent, authoritarian and materialistic mould. I consider in the following section why these ideas should have enjoyed such a revival in postwar France.

## 3.2   TWO KINDS OF POSTSTRUCTURALISM

'Poststructuralism' is in fact a term first used in the United States to refer to two distinct but related strands of thought. The first Richard Rorty felicitously names 'textualism', and described as the heir of German classical idealism. But, he writes, '[w]hereas nineteenth-century idealism wanted to substitute one sort of science (philosophy) for another (natural science) as the centre for culture, textualism wants to place literature at the centre, and to treat both science and philosophy as, at best, literary genres.'[18] 'Textualism' in my usage refers chiefly to Jacques Derrida and his mainly North American followers, of whom perhaps the most celebrated (or perhaps one should say notorious since the posthumous discovery of his wartime pro-Nazi writings) is the late Paul de Man. Rorty does not distinguish this line of thought from a second form of poststructuralism. Here the master-category is Michel Foucault's 'power-knowledge'. The difference between Foucauldian genealogy and textualism is brought out by Foucault's definition of the *dispositif*, or apparatus, constitutive of the social body as 'a thoroughly heterogeneous ensemble consisting of discourses, institutions, architectural forms, regulatory decisions, laws, administrative measures, scientific statements, philosophical, moral and philanthropic propositions – in short, the said and the unsaid.'[19] Distinctive of this 'worldly' poststructuralism, as Edward Said calls it, is its articulation of 'the said and the unsaid', of the discursive and the nondiscursive.[20] This method is evident not simply in the succession of historical texts in which Foucault sought to reconstruct the genealogy of modernity, but also in the work of Gilles Deleuze, Félix Guattari, and Jacques Donzelot among others. Textualism, however, denies us the possibility of ever escaping the discursive. '*Il n'y a pas de hors-texte*' – '*There is no outside-text*', as Derrida famously put it.[21]

The debt owed by both variants of poststructuralism to Nietzsche is overwhelming. Deleuze adumbrated many principal themes of his own thought in *Nietzsche et la Philosophie* (1962). Derrida has acknowledged Nietzsche's influence in various texts.[22] Foucault went the furthest, declaring 'I am simply a Nietzschean' not long before his death, and giving two key expositions of his own method in the form of readings of Nietzsche.[23] The filiations between poststructuralism and Modernism are, however, less often observed, though, as Andreas Huyssen argues, 'poststructuralism is much closer to modernism than is usually assumed by the advocates of postmodernism.' Indeed, Huyssen goes on to make the stronger claim that 'poststructuralism is primarily a discourse of and about modernism.'[24]

Certainly the importance of Modernism for both variants of poststructuralism seems undeniable. Once again, Foucault provides the clearest evidence. Perhaps the most striking passage comes not in those texts explicitly devoted to Modernist artists such as Magritte and Raymond Roussel but in the preface of *Les Mots et les choses*. Foucault begins by citing a wonderful passage from Borges about '"a certain Chinese encyclopaedia" in which it is written that "animals are divided into: (a) belonging to the Emperor, (b) embalmed, (c) tame, (d) sucking pigs, (e) sirens, (f) fabulous, (g) stray dogs, (h) included in the present classification, (i) frenzied, (j) innumerable, (k) drawn with a very fine camelhair brush, (l) *et cetera*, (m) having just broken the water pitcher, (n) that from a long way off look like flies"'. Foucault reflects on the arbitrariness of all classifications and on the conditions of possibility (what he calls the 'historical *a priori*') which allow one to think of such disparate objects as members of the same set of categories. In doing so, he calls up another startling combination, 'the umbrella and the sewing-machine on the operating table'.[25] This image is, of course, used by Lautréamont to capture the beauty of his hero, 'Mervyn, that son of a fair England': 'He is as handsome . . . as the chance juxtaposition of a sewing-machine and an umbrella on a dissecting table!'[26] Prized by the Surrealists, it is, as Moretti observes, 'a small classic of the modernist imagination', which 'ironically negates any idea of "totality" and any hierarchy of meanings, leaving the field free for a virtually unlimited interpretive play'.[27]

Foucault's invocation of Lautréamont dramatizes the extent to which his thought is informed by a Modernist sensibility. When, later in the same book, Foucault attempts to capture the specificity of modernity, he argues that it involves 'the appearance of language as a multiple profusion', as 'an enigmatic multiplicity that must be mastered' rather than the transparent grid of representation which it had been conceived as in the classical era (the seventeenth and eighteenth centuries), an event that he associates especially with the names of Nietzsche and Mallarmé. The most important consequence of this change is to subvert the subject, to undermine the central position to which it had been allocated since Descartes: 'the question of language', Foucault says, 'seems to lay siege on every side to the figure of man'. The significance of literary Modernism – the examples

Foucault lists are Artaud, Roussel, the Surrealists, Kafka, Bataille and Blanchot – is that '[f]rom within language experienced and traversed as language, in the play of its possibilities extended to their furthest point, what emerges is that man "has come to an end"' – a claim repeated in the famous concluding sentence of *Les Mots et les choses*, where Foucault speculated that the changes he had described meant that 'man would be erased, like a face drawn in sand at the edge of the sea.'[28]

Foucault thus seems to be exploring questions first philosophically articulated by Nietzsche but which he regards as having been explored in the greatest depth by certain Modernist writers. The centrality of aesthetics for Foucault is underlined by the fact that he first read Nietzsche in 1953 'because of Bataille and Bataille because of Blanchot'.[29] The Aestheticism of the textualist strand of poststructuralism founded by Derrida is, if anything, more marked. Christopher Norris argues that 'Derrida's influence came as such a liberating force' for American critics because '[h]is work provided a whole new set of powerful strategies which placed the literary critic, not simply on a footing with the philosopher, but in a complex relationship (or rivalry) with him, whereby philosophical claims were open to rhetorical questioning or *deconstruction*. Paul de Man has described this process of thought in which "literature turns out to be the main topic of philosophy and the model of the kind of truth to which it aspires".'[30] Rorty expresses the same thought when he says that textualism treats science and philosophy as 'literary genres'. As Habermas observes, 'Derrida proceeds by a critique of style, in that he finds something like indirect communications, by which the text denies its manifest content, in the rhetorical surplus of meaning inherent in the literary strata of texts that present themselves as nonliterary.' The effect is an *'aestheticizing of language'*: the practice of deconstruction denies theoretical texts their apparent cognitive content, reducing them to an array of rhetorical devices and thereby effacing any difference between them and explicitly literary texts.[31]

This erasure of the distinction between philosophy and literature leads Derrida to write books some of which – *Glas*, for example, in their punning, allusive style, their endless unravelling of the meanings of words, their reflexive absorption in exposing their own rhetorical nature, resemble nothing more than Modernist works of art. But this is merely an extreme case of a feature common by to all the main representatives of what Luc Ferry and Alain Renaut call '"68 thought" or, if you will permit the expression, ... "French philosophy of the 68 years", ... a constellation of works chronologically near to May, and, above all, whose authors were recognized, most often explicitly, as having contributed to inspiring the movement.' This current of thought, broader than poststructuralism as defined here since it embraced figures such as the founding fathers of structuralism, Lévi-Strauss and Lacan, as well as Althusser, who shared a common anti-humanism, a common demotion of the subject to a secondary and subordinate status. It also possessed, Ferry and Renaut note, a distinctive style, '*the cult of paradox and, if not the refusal of clarity, at least the insistent demand for complexity*'.[32] This style first developed by Lacan, whose influence is evident in the sometimes wilful obscurity of Althusser's writings of the 1960s, bears an obvious kinship to the literary practices of Modernism. It seems as if the effort to deny the subject its self-certain unity and dislodge it from the throne on which Descartes had placed it required a self-consciously difficult style, which relied as much on indirection and allusion as it did on explicit assertion and consecutive argument.

But why should a philosophical current so akin to Modernism in preoccupations and style arise in postwar France? Part of the answer is hinted at in a highly suggestive passage where Anderson suggests that the 'cinema of Jean-Luc Godard, in the 1960s', represented one of the few exceptions to the general decline of Modernism consequent on the disappearance of the historical conjuncture which produced it:

> As the Fourth Republic belatedly passed into the Fifth, and rural and provincial France was suddenly transformed by a Gaullist industrialization appropriating the newest technologies, something like a brief afterglow of the earlier conjuncture that produced the classical innovatory art of the century flared into life again. Godard's cinema was marked in its way by all three of the co-ordinates described earlier. Suffused with quotation and allusion to a high cultural past, Eliot-style; equivocal celebrant of the automobile and the airport, the camera and the carbine, Leger-style; expectant of revolutionary tempests from the East, Nizan-style.[33]

It is tempting to generalize from this observation, and to argue that the experience of uneven and combined development in postwar France – of rapid industrialization within a contested, increasingly authoritarian political framework, in a society where the existence of a mass Communist Party helped both to legitimize Marxism among the intelligentsia and, by its blind Stalinism, to encourage more critical forms of thought – encouraged the survival of a Modernist sensibility, of which Godard's films were the most important artistic expression, but which also informed, in the ways outlined, the ideas of a generation of philosophers most of whom began writing in the two decades after 1945. But even if we broadly accept this argument, there remain other considerations, concerned with the internal development of French thought, which need to be taken into account.

Vincent Descombes, in his critical survey of postwar French thought, makes the following suggestion: 'We can see in the recent evolution of philosophy in France the passage of the generation of the "three Hs", as one said after 1945, to the generation of the three "masters of suspicion", as one will say in 1960. The three Hs are Hegel, Husserl, Heidegger, and the three masters of suspicion are Marx, Nietzsche and Freud.'[34] The shift, roughly speaking, is that from the constitutive role which Husserlian phenomenology – a crucial influence on the major Parisian figures of the immediate postwar era, Sartre and Merleau-Ponty – assigns to the subject, and the constituted status to which it is demoted by '68 thought', whether the constituting role is now assumed by the forces and relations of production, the unconscious, or the will to power.

Now while Descombes's formulation does capture the changes involved in the emergence of poststructuralism, it cannot be emphasized sufficiently that one of the 'three Hs' remains a decisive influence on '68 thought', namely Heidegger. Derrida's work situates itself quite explicitly as a continuation of Heidegger's thought. Foucault said not long before his death: 'Heidegger has always been for me the essential philosopher.'[35] Even Althusser's writing bears the mark of Heidegger's influence.[36] The significance of Heidegger for French anti-humanism lay in what Habermas calls 'the lack of ambiguity with which he places subject-centred reason on trial', 'delineating the modern dominance of the subject in terms of a history of metaphysics.'[37] The trajectory of Western thought according to Heidegger is that of the progressive forgetfulness of Being expressed most clearly by the centrality given the subject by post-Cartesian philosophy and culminating in the triumph of an instrumental rationality systematically reducing the world to the raw material of subjective needs – a conceptual framework from which no philosophy, including Heidegger's own, can escape and which can be subverted only by allusive reference to the ontological difference between Being and beings whose concealment is constitutive of metaphysics.

Such a critique of the subject was made attractive to the founders of French anti-humanism by perceived defects of Husserlian phenomenology. Foucault recalled that 'throughout the period from 1945 to 1955 ... the young French university ... tried to wed Marxism and phenomenology.' This project, one of the main preoccupations of Sartre and Merleau-Ponty, foundered, however, on 'the problem of language': 'it was clear that phenomenology was no match for structural analysis in accounting for the effects of meaning that could be produced by a structure of a linguistic type, in which the subject (in the phenomenological sense) did not intervene to confer meaning.'[38] Saussure's structural linguistics, which conceived language as a system of differences, accorded the subject only at best a secondary role in the production of meaning; yet it offered a paradigm whose power to account for more than language strictly understood was apparently demonstrated by the use to which it was put by Lévi-Strauss in anthropology and by Lacan in psychoanalysis. *Post*structuralism, which built on but radicalized these innovations, may indeed be seen as the result of the encounter of Nietzsche, Heidegger and Saussure.

Poststructuralism, particularly in the shape of its two most influential representatives, Derrida and Foucault, has been the object of detailed, and, in my view, quite conclusive criticism, most notably by Habermas in *The Philosophical Discourse of Modernity* and by Peter Dews in *Logics of Disintegration*. Rather than simply repeat what these two admirable books say, or what I have myself said elsewhere, I concentrate in the remainder of this chapter on the main aporias of poststructuralism, the flaws in this body of thought which expose defects intrinsic to its very construction.[39] The three principal weaknesses concern rationality, resistance and the subject.

## 3.3  APORIA 1: RATIONALITY

Derrida more than any other poststructuralist exploited the philosophical resources provided by Saussure's theory of language, in particular to resolve the dilemmas of Husserlian phenomenology. The most significant feature in this respect of Saussure's conception of language as a system of differences is that it involves an anti-realist theory of meaning, one which brackets the question of reference, that is, of the relationship between linguistic expressions and the extradiscursive objects which they denote. For Saussure the crucial distinction is not that between word and object, but that between signifier (word) and signified (concept). Furthermore, '[t]he important thing in the word is ... the phonic differences which make it possible to distinguish this word from all others, for differences carry signification.' Not only '[i]n language there are only differences', but 'in language there are only differences *without positive terms*. Whether we take the signified or the signifier, language has neither ideas nor sounds that existed before the linguistic system, but only conceptual and phonic differences that have issued from the system. The idea or phonic substance that an idea sign contains is less important than the other signs that surround it.'[40] Now while Saussure thus bracketed the question of reference, of the relation between word and object, he tended to accord equal importance to signifiers and signified, conceived as two parallel series composed respectively of words and concepts. The attempt to extend this structural conception of language to the more general study of the human world, particularly by Lévi-Strauss, involved according primacy to signifiers over signified, so that meaning became a matter of the interrelations of words.[41] Derrida and other poststructuralists took the further step of denying any systematicity to language. Rather than occurring within the kind of closed structure which Lévi-Strauss took from Saussure, the production of meaning was now conceived as consisting in the play of signifiers proliferating to infinity.

This move, while a legitimate response to contradictions internal to Saussurian theory, had the distinct attraction for Derrida of providing support for a philosophical critique of what he calls the metaphysics of presence, the doctrine that reality is directly given to the subject. For any attempt to halt the endless play of signifiers, above all by appealing to the concept of reference, must, he argues, involve postulating a 'transcendental signified' which is somehow present to consciousness without any discursive mediation. Rejection of a (radicalized) Saussurian theory of meaning thus depends on what Wilfred Sellars called 'the myth of the given', of a *parousia* in which reality is immediately given to the subject.

To appreciate the force of this argument we must consider the kind of philosophy of language presupposed by the metaphysics of presence. It is constituted, paradoxically, by a question-mark over language itself. Consciousness, according to the myth of the given, has direct access to reality and therefore has no need of a discursive intermediary. Signification is dispensable, at best a convenience, useful as an aid to memory or a means to economy of thought, at worst an impurity that clouds our vision. This epistemology renders plausible an atomistic conception of language, in which words signify individually by virtue of their reference to an object (or, in some versions, an idea which in turn stands for or is caused by an object). They are attached to their referents by a mind already acquainted with these objects or ideas. Such a theory of meaning is to be found in both the empiricisms and the rationalisms of the seventeenth century, in Locke's *Essay* as well as the Port Royal *Logic*. The revolutionary significance of Saussure's *Course* lay chiefly in its demolition of atomism. Words, as we have seen, no longer signify by virtue of their referring to objects, by rather through their relation to other words. The subject, consequently, is no longer directly constitutive of language, endowing words with meaning by dubbing objects to which it has independent access. Meaning is now autonomous, produced through the interrelations of signifiers.

This holist account of language has broader philosophical implications. It establishes that the subject cannot act, as Husserl believed, as the unmediated, 'self-present', starting-point for the constitution of the world: consciousness is necessarily mediated, imbricated with discourses which transcend the subject. But, as Dews observes, 'Derrida's response to this collapse of Husserl's philosophical project is *not*, like that of Adorno or Merleau-Ponty, to move "downstream" towards an account of subjectivity as emerging from and entwined with the natural and social world, but rather to move "upstream", in a quest for the ground of transcendental consciousness.'[42] The subject is subordinated to the endless play of difference, but his move takes us not into, but beyond, history. Difference is indeed an inadequate concept for characterizing the process of signification. Derrida offers various terms – for example, trace, archewriting and above all *différance* – to emphasize that it is impossible to escape from the metaphysics of presence. I have written elsewhere of *différance*:

> This neologism is what Lewis Carroll would call a 'portmanteau word'. It combines the meanings of the two words 'to differ' and 'to defer'. It affirms, first, the priority of play and difference over presence and absence, and secondly, the necessity within difference of a relation to presence, a presence always deferred (into the future or past) but nevertheless constantly invoked. Presence is as intrinsic to difference as absence.[43]

The play constitutive of signification thus necessarily involves both the disruption of presence, which is always part of a chain of substitutions which transcend it, and the reference to presence, but a presence which can never fully be achieved but is constantly deferred. *Différance* is thus 'the obliterated origin of absence and presence'.[44] *Différance* can only be conceptualized by means of a language which necessarily, by virtue of the nature of *différance* itself, involves the metaphysics of presence: *différance*, since it is ontologically prior to both presence and absence, is therefore unknowable. From this contradiction springs the practice of deconstruction which involves contesting the metaphysics of presence on its own terrain – a terrain from which there is any case no escape. 'The passage beyond philosophy does not consist in turning the page of philosophy (which usually amounts to philosophizing badly), but in continuing to read philosophers *in a certain way*.'[45]

Not surprisingly, various authors have detected in Derrida's argument strong filiations with the German idealist tradition. Dews argues that 'Derrida ... is offering us a philosophy of *différance* as the absolute' – an absolute which, like Schelling's, is unknowable by the procedures characteristic of modern scientific rationality.[46] Schelling, however, believed that the absolute could be grasped intuitively; Derrida, by contrast, relies on the endless play of signifiers to provide us with an intimation of *différance*, though no more than that, because of the necessarily metaphysical nature of language. This position has a more recent precursor. Ferry and Renaut sarcastically comment that while, for example, '*Foucault=Heidegger+Nietzsche*', '*Derrida = Heidegger + Derrida's style*', and argue that 'it seems that nothing intelligible or enouncable appeared in Derrida's work which was not (in respect of content) a pure and simple reprise of the Heideggerian problematic of the ontological difference.'[47] Similarly Habermas observes that 'Derrida's deconstructions faithfully follow the movement of Heidegger's thought.' The Heideggerian theme of the self-occultation of Being is repeated in the conception of *différance* as 'the obliterated origin of presence and absence': 'In the metaphor of the archewriting and its trace, we see again the Dionysian motif of the god making his promised presence all the more palpable to the sons and daughters of the West by its poignant absence.'[48]

The difficulty with Derridean textualism is not so much that, like traditional idealism, it involves the denial of the existence of objects independently of thought – or rather, in this case, discourse. In this sense Derrida's celebrated declaration that '*[t]here is no outside-text*' is misleading. In the light of his conception of *différance*, as Frank Lentricchia observes, '*[i]l n'y a pas de hors-texte* must mean, then, questioning not only the authority of presence but also "its simple and symmetrical contrary, absence or lack". *Il n'y a pas de hors-texte* must not be read as positing an ontological "nothing" outside the text.'[49] But if textualism does not deny the existence of extra-discursive objects, it does deny our ability to know these objects. For such knowledge would seem to require some reliable mode of access to that object. But for Derrida the notion of such access is an instance of the metaphysics of presence, involving the idea of some direct, unmediated contact with a reality outside the play of signifiers. One might compare this position with that of Kant, who believed that we could not know things in themselves, but only sense-impressions organized by the categories of the understanding inherent in the structure of transcendental subjectivity underlying experience. The difference is that Derrida sets *différance* in the place of the unknowable *Ding-an-sich* and, resolving the subject into the play of presence and absence, sets the categories themselves in motion.

Whether one finds this a tenable position depends partly on one's broader theoretical objectives. Lentricchia in his devastating critical survey of Derrida's American followers has shown how the notion of deconstruction can legitimize a genuine idealism narcissistically preoccupied with an endlessly self-generating textuality.[50] But this is not the only available version of textualism. Thus Norris offers a reading of deconstruction as, not 'a species of Nietzschean irrationalism', but as, in the hands of Derrida and de Man at least, a form of *Ideologiekritik* whose 'point of departure is to argue with the utmost *logical* rigour to conclusions which may yet be counter-intuitive or at odds with common-sense (consensual) wisdom'.[51] One might indeed regard this interpretation of textualism as an example of such a procedure, since Norris tends to present deconstruction as a form of close reading bearing a strong resemblance to the methods of analytical philosophy – a conclusion which certainly accords ill with the natural response particularly to Derrida's more extravagantly literary texts.

Nevertheless Derrida himself is concerned to establish the politically oppositional character of his philosophy. Thus, reflecting in 1980 on his intellectual trajectory, he declared: 'I have been increasingly preoccupied with the necessity of making a fresh start on questions said to be classically institutional.' More specifically,

> how is it that philosophy finds itself, rather than inscribing itself, within a space which it seeks but is unable to control . . . ? How is one to name the structure of this space? I do not *know*; nor do I know whether there can ever be what may be called *knowledge* of such a space. To call it socio-political is a triviality which does not satisfy, and even the most indisputable of what are said to be socio-analyses have often enough very little to say on the matter, remain blind to their own inscription, to the law of their own production performances, to the stage of their own inheritance and of their self-authorization, in short to what I call their writing.[52]

This passage is interesting because of the characteristic oscillation it involves between alluding to the social conditions of discourse ('questions said to be classically institutional') and cutting the ground from under any analysis of these conditions because of its blindness to *différance*, of which 'writing' is merely one of the avatars. ('The archewriting', says Habermas, 'takes on the role of a subjectless generator of structures.')[53] We may gesture towards, but never know the *hors-texte*. That this oscillation is a fundamental feature of Derridean textualism may be confirmed by considering another example. Derrida contributed a piece to the catalogue of an exhibition of anti-apartheid art which opened in Paris in November 1983. Largely composed of windy banalities ('Hasn't *apartheid* always been the archival record of the unnameable?'), this text, 'Racism's last word', was criticized for its lack of historical specificity by two American literary theorists, to which Derrida responded in a rather bad-tempered, and abusive article. The main philosophical point at issue was whether or not Derrida's denial of the existence of the *hors-texte* was responsible for his failure to attend to the evolution of racial domination in South Africa. Perhaps more interesting is the contrast he draws between apartheid, which he describes as a 'concentration of world history' – or more specifically of 'a European "discourse" of the concept of race bound up with the operation of the Western multinationals and nation-states', and the opposition to it, which depends on 'the future of another law and another force lying beyond the totality of this present'. But it is impossible now to anticipate the nature of this 'law' and 'force'. Commenting on the paintings, Derrida says: 'their silence is just. A discourse would compel us to reckon with the present state of force and law. It would draw up contracts, dialecticize itself, let itself be reappropriated.'[54]

So the resistance to apartheid must remain inarticulate, must not seek to formulate a political programme and strategy: any attempt to do so would simply involve reincorporation into 'the present state of law and force' and perhaps even into the 'European discourse of racism'. If this argument is valid, then the resistance was lost long ago: far from being silent, it is indeed positively garrulous, resorting to define itself to a variety of different discourses – social democracy, Stalinism, black exclusivism, syndicalism, revolutionary socialism, even Islamic fundamentalism.[55] But the contention of these discourses – the stuff of any real liberation struggle – for Derrida presumably amounts merely to variations on the theme of the 'present state of law and force'. No wonder that Ferry and Renaut talk about Derrida's *'negative ontology'*:[56] we can only allude to, but not (at risk of 'reappropriation') seek to know anything lying beyond 'the totality of the present'. Habermas suggests that 'Derrida, all denials notwithstanding, remains close to Jewish mysticism',[57] one of whose main characteristics, as Gershom Scholem observes in his classic study, is that it transforms the personal God of the Scriptures into 'the *deus absconditus*, the God who is hidden in his own self, [and] can only be named in a metaphorical sense and with the help of words which, mystically speaking, are not real names at all.'[58] Apartheid is 'the archival record of the unnameable' because it represents the culmination and therefore the truth of the European civilization which, not only produced the 'discourse' of race but which, reproduced now on a world scale, is the source of the categories in terms of which we are all compelled to think. It is therefore the *alternative* to apartheid which is unnameable, because it lies beyond these categories.

Whatever Derrida's personal political commitments (which do not seem in any case to rise much above a fairly commonplace left liberalism), he is unable rationally to ground them because he denies himself the means either to analyse those existing social arrangements which he rejects or to justify this rejection by outlining some more desirable state of affairs. This position finds its roots in – Heidegger aside – a philosophy of language which moves from the rejection of the atomistic theories of meaning typical of seventeenth-century epistemology to the denial of any relation of discourse to reality. But this move is unnecessary.

Contemporary analytical philosophy of language contains theories of meaning as vigorously anti-atomistic as anything in the Saussurian tradition. In the writings of Quine, for example, language is conceived holistically, as 'a fabric of sentences'.[59] Yet the concepts of reference, and still more of truth are central to the single most ambitious attempt to develop a holistic theory of meaning, that of Donald Davidson. The meaning of sentences is given by their truth-conditions, Davidson argues, and truth in turn is to be defined, following Tarski, by means of the concept of satisfaction, the relationship between predicates and the objects of which they are true. 'The study of sense thus comes down to the study of reference.' Davidson tends to treat the concept of reference not as an epistemological grounding for meaning, but rather as an explanatory concept which allows the truth-theorist to give a structural account of the way in which words derive their meaning from their ability to occur in an indefinite number of different sentences. Nevertheless, he insists that 'language is an instrument of communication because of its semantic dimension, the potentiality for truth or falsehood of its utterances and inscriptions,'[60]

The concept of reference indeed became in the 1970s one of the main preoccupations of English-speaking philosophers, largely as a result of the work of Saul Kripke, Hilary Putnam and Keith Donnellan. What is striking about these discussions is their refusal to base their accounts of reference on any notion of the subject with direct access even to the contents of its consciousness. Thus the moral of

Putnam's work on natural-kind terms ('gold', 'tiger', etc.) is that 'meanings ain't in the head': the sense of these words is fixed by their reference, which in turn depends partly on the inner structure of their referent, partly on the 'linguistic division of labour' through which the community as a whole, not individual speakers, acquires knowledge of that structure.[61] This account of reference has been taken further by Tyler Burge, who argues that an individual's mental states cannot be identified independently of her social context and physical environment.[62] The late Gareth Evans's remarkable study of reference is similarly 'firmly anti-Cartesian' in its rejection of any self-present subject of thought.[63]

There is, of course, little agreement about the epistemological drift of recent work in analytical philosophy of language, as the debates between 'realists' and 'anti-realists' should make clear.[64] Indeed, Richard Rorty has made wicked use of Quine and Davidson to arrive at conclusions highly congenial to textualism. I consider some of the arguments involved in the following chapter. Nevertheless, what the work alluded to above shows is that the rejection of atomism does not, on the face of it, require the abandonment of the concept of reference: indeed, Davidson's theory of meaning *combines* holism and realism. There is more than one way out of the myth of the given.

## 3.4 APORIA 2: RESISTANCE

These difficulties encountered by textualism are one instance of a more general dilemma highlighted by Habermas. He argues that the radicalization of the Enlightenment involves *Ideologiekritik*, which seeks to demonstrate how theoretical discourses secrete, and are shaped by socio-political interests:

> with this kind of critique enlightenment becomes reflective for the first time; it is performed with respect to its own products – theories. Yet the drama of enlightenment first arrives at its climax when ideology critique *itself* comes under suspicion of not producing (any more) truths – and the enlightenment attains second-order reflectiveness. Then doubt reaches out to include reason, whose standards ideology critique had found already given in bourgeois ideals and has simply taken at their word. *Dialectic of Enlightenment* takes this step – it renders critique independent even in relation to its own foundations.[65]

Horkheimer and Adorno were consequently confronted with what Habermas calls a 'performative contradiction': 'If they do not want to renounce the effect of a final unmasking and still want to *continue with critique*, they will have to leave at least one rational criterion intact for their explanation of the corruption of *all* rational criteria. In the face of this paradox, self-referential critique loses its orientation.' Derrida, Habermas argues, faces the same dilemma: 'subject-centred reason can be convicted of being authoritarian in nature only by having recourse to its own tools.'[66] This contradiction can be traced back to Nietzsche, as Habermas observes. The paradoxical nature of Nietzsche's attempt to demonstrate by means of rational argumentation the perspectival and indeed instrumental nature of knowledge has led to various salvage attempts: ascribing to him, for example, a multi-dimensional epistemology which finds some place for the classical conception of truth as correspondence between sentences and states of affairs or, at the opposite extreme, insisting on the fundamentally aesthetic nature of his philosophy, which thereby renders epistemic considerations of, at best, secondary importance.[67]

The paradox arises in Derrida's case thanks to a radically anti-realist philosophy of language which denies us the possibility of knowing a reality independent of discourse. This anti-realism compels him, as we have seen, to question the possibility of giving an account of the relationship between forms of discourse and social practices, whether the latter sustain or challenge existing relations of domination. By contrast, the 'worldly' poststructuralism of Foucault and Deleuze attaches central importance to this relationship. Far from operating on the inside of discourse, they seek thoroughly to contextualize it. Thus Foucault declared: 'I believe one's point of reference should not be the great model of language and signs, but that of war and battle. The history which bears and determines us has the form of a war rather than a language: relations of power, not relations of meaning.'[68] Deleuze and Guattari polemicized against 'the imperialism of the signifier' and drew on Hjemslev and Bakhtin in order to develop a pragmatic theory of language starting from the irreducibly social character of the utterance.[69] The nature of this pragmatics was captured by Foucault's notion of 'power-knowledge': 'There is no power-relation without the correlative constitution of a field of knowledge, nor at the same time any knowledge that does not presuppose and constitute at the same time power-relations.'[70] The will to truth is but one form of the will to power; the appropriate analysis of theoretical discourses belongs, as Nietzsche argued, to the genealogy of forms of domination, not to an epistemological history of the growth of knowledge. The result is an anti-realism as radical as Derrida's in its rejection of any account of theories in terms of their ability more or less accurately to characterize independently existing states of affairs, but one imbricated in a pragmatics of discourse and power rather than implying, as do the textualists, that it is impossible to escape the bonds of discourse.

This very different kind of poststructuralism permitted an orientation on history entirely absent from Derridean textualism. Probably the most lasting contribution of French Nietzscheanism will turn out to be the series of great historical texts in which Foucault explored the constitution of modernity – the *Histoire de la folie* (1961), *Surveillir et punir* (1975), and the *Histoire de la sexualité* (1976, 1984), towards the end of his life by way of a detour through antiquity. The appearance of continuity is, however, misleading. Foucault himself argued that, while always concerned with 'a history of truth', 'an analysis of "truth games (*jeux de vérité*)"', of the games of true and false across which being constitutes itself historically as experience, that is to say as what can and must be thought', his thought had undergone a 'theoretical displacement' from works such of the 1960s such as *Les Mots et les choses* concerned with 'truth-games in relation to each other' to the genealogical study of 'truth-games in relation to relations of power', in *Surveillir et punir* and the first volume of the *Histoire de la sexualité*.[71]

This 'displacement' was, however, motivated by more than theoretical considerations. It involved a particular interpretation of May 1968, one which rejected any attempt to see it as a vindication of the classical revolutionary socialist project. Rather, Foucault contended, 'what has happened since 1968, and arguably what made 1968 possible, is profoundly anti-Marxist.'[72] 1968 involved the decentralized contestation of power rather than an attempt to replace one set of social relations with another. Any such attempt could only succeed in establishing a new apparatus of power-knowledge in place of the old, as the experience of post-revolutionary Russia showed. Foucault sought to give this argument – in itself hardly original, indeed a commonplace of liberal thought since Tocqueville and Mill – a new inflection by offering a distinctive account of power. Rather than being unitary power is a multiplicity of relations infiltrating the whole of the social body. Consequently no causal priority can be assigned as it is by Marxism, to the economic base. Moreover, power is productive: it does not operate by repressing individuals, circumscribing their activity, but rather by *constituting* them – Foucault's main example is the 'disciplinary' institutions such as the prison which emerged in the early nineteenth century. Finally, power necessarily evokes resistance, albeit as fragmentary and decentralized as the power-relations it contests.[73]

This conception of power immediately raises the problem inherent in the Nietzschean critique of the Enlightenment, which uses the latter's own tools. Foucault declares: 'It seems to me that power is "always already there", that one is never "outside" it, that there are no "margins" for those who break with the system to gambol in.' But if this is so, if power is omnipresent, how is it possible, as Foucault did, to write the genealogy of modern disciplinary society? Foucault's answer, in the 1970s at least, seems to involve relating genealogy to the forms of resistance which he argues are intrinsic to power-relations. Thus he talks of 'a reactivation of local knowledges – of minor knowledges as Deleuze might call them – in opposition to the scientific hierarchization of knowledges and the effects intrinsic to their power'.[74] But are these 'local knowledges' any more than the oppositional other of the prevailing apparatus of power-knowledge? This is related to the general problem of resistance in Foucault's work, to which a number of commentators have drawn attention. As Hubert Dreyfus and Paul Rabinow observe, 'resistance is both an element of the functioning of power and a source of its perpetual disorder.'[75] But where does resistance derive its capacity to be the latter, given the omnipresence of power? Foucault tentatively points towards the body as both the locus of power's operations, and the source of resistance to these operations, but hesitates between conceiving the body as power's malleable raw material, and as a fixed natural essence.[76] This equivocation is symptomatic of what Dreyfus and Rabinow describe as 'a series of dilemmas' in Foucault's work about truth, resistance and power: 'In each set there is a seeming contradiction between a return to the traditional philosophic view that description and interpretation must ultimately correspond to the way things reallly are, and a nihilist view that physical reality, the body, and history are whatever we take them to be.'[77]

One way out of these dilemmas is to adopt a far more thorough-going naturalism, one which treats power as a secondary phenomenon. This is the course taken by Deleuze and Guattari in their *magnum opus*, *Capitalisme et schizophrénie*. In the first volume, *L'Anti-Oedipe* (1972), their argument centres on the concept of 'desiring production', reflecting their efforts in the wake of 1968 to marry Marx and Freud. Desire, they claim, is positive, productive, heterogeneous, multiple; social formations differ according to the manner in which they 'code' and 'territorialize' the flux of desire. Presumably as a result of the influence of Foucault (who emphatically rejected 'the Deleuzian concept of desire'),[78] the concept of desiring production does not appear in the second volume, *Mille plateaux* (1980). There it is replaced by a concept bearing a strong family resemblance to the Foucauldian concept of the apparatus (*dispositif*) uniting 'the said and the unsaid', that of the assemblage (*agencement*), which is used by Deleuze and Guattari to denote the multiplicities of heterogeneous elements ramifying to infinity and spilling over into each other, forming the plateaux whose very form the book seeks to mirror.

Deleuze and Guattari continue, however, to insist on the primacy of desire over power: 'Our only differences with Foucault bear on the following points: 1) assemblages do not seem to us first of all power but desire, desire being always assembled, and power a stratified dimension of the assemblage; 2) the diagram [or formal structure of an assemblage] . . . has lines of flight which are primary, and are not phenomena of resistance or reaction in an assemblage, but points of creation and of deterritorialization.' In other words, the flux of desire, assembling the organic and the inorganic, the human and the natural, the discursive and the social, into contingent and changing unities, constantly breaking down the boundaries which these unities constitute, is primary. The tendency to resist the dominant forms of power is not generated by these forms themselves, but arises from desire's natural tendency to overreach itself, to 'deterritorialize'. The difficulties of these position are twofold. First, it seems to involve erecting what looks suspiciously like a version of *Lebensphilosophie*, in which the desire which overturns and outflanks power is identified with life itself, but with a life which opposes itself to the organic unities of bodies, states, societies. Deleuze and Guattari indeed espouse a 'material vitalism'. Second, this naturalistic metaphysic explains resistance, but at the price of making power itself a mystery. It is true that *Mille plateaux* contains elaborate accounts of the impulse towards 'territorialization' and 'stratification', of desire's tendency to confine itself within power-relations. But unless one buys the *Lebensphilosophie*, there is no reason to accept these accounts. Whatever the undeniable splendours of many passages in Deleuze's writings, as a corpus they suggest mainly that the only escape from Foucault's dilemmas lies in adopting a modernized variant of Nietzsche's ontology of the will to power.[79]

It would be better to say that this is the only escape so long as one accepts the central Foucauldian thesis of the omnipresence of power. Of the various devices used to insulate this thesis from criticism, perhaps the most important is an appeal to theoretical pluralism. Thus Paul Patton dismisses an attempt of mine at a global comparison between classical Marxism and Foucauldian genealogy as displaying 'a monoperspectivism that turns all theoretical difference' symptomatic of a 'will to totalize', that is, 'a refusal to accept the possibility of difference and discontinuity at the heart of human history, and a corresponding refusal to allow that there can be irreducibly different perspectives, each in its own way critical of existing social reality', a perspective reflecting the will 'to *govern* a multiplicity of interests' characteristic of 'state philosophy'.[80] This argument rules out by fiat the possibility that Marxian and Foucauldian social theory might be fundamentally incompatible with one another. The substance of Foucault's and Deleuze's positions is effectively smuggled in under the guise of a methodological preference for pluralism. Marxism, as Patton acknowledges a theory of social totality, is reduced to merely one fragment of an inherently multiple theoretical field, and thereby rendered into material appropriate for incorporation into a Nietzschean perspective which treats the class struggle as one instance of the struggle for domination traversing human history. The rhetoric of difference Patton espouses serves to conceal that the Foucauldian conception of an apparatus of power-knowledge is as much a theory of totality as Marx's. As Dews observes, 'power – often spoken of in the singular – becomes a constitutive subject on the Kantian or Husserlian sense, with the social as its constituted subject.'[81] It is perhaps fortunate, therefore, that the claim that *any* totalization serves some will to power is quite unsupported by argument or evidence, unless one counts Foucault's embarrassing enthusiasm for André Glucksmann's worthless *Les Maîtres penseurs*.[82]

Patton's defence of Foucault and Deleuze does, however, highlight the political sources of their ideas – the post-1968 rejection by many left intellectuals of any perspective of global social transformation, a reaction to dashed revolutionary hopes and to the rise of the 'new social movements' (feminists, gays, ecologists, black nationalists, etc.). Patton argues that the experience of these movements shows that 'change in existing social relation does not have to be mediated by the totality. The conditions that sustain oppression can be altered piecemeal.'[83] This political judgement sums up the evolution of many of the generation of 1968 in the course of the 1970s – from revolutionary *groupuscule* to single-issue campaigns and then to social democracy, a process which took an especially concentrated form in France because of the sudden and traumatic collapse of the French Communist Party under the impact of François Mitterrand's revived Socialist Party. The denunciation of Marxism as the philosophy of the Gulag by the ex-Maoist *nouveaux philosophes* in 1976–7 was an event of no intellectual significance but of some political moment, since it marked the transition of the French intelligentsia – *marxisant* for a generation – into the ranks of social democracy and neo-liberalism (see section 5.6 below.)[84]

Although Foucault's Nietzschean theory of power-knowledge was an important influence on those abandoning Marxism, the concept of resistance retains in his writings a definite political content, providing a rationale for various oppressed groups resisting their oppression. One sign of the degeneration of French poststructuralism in the 1980s – no doubt a consequence of the climate that has made Paris today, in Anderson's words, 'the capital of European intellectual reaction'[85] – is the evacuation of any political content from the concept of resistance. Thus Lyotard, the author after 1968 of a philosophy of desire analogous to Deleuze's and Guattari's, has come to distrust any form of political action, regarding with suspicion even the eminently moderate student demonstrations in Paris in December 1986.[86] The task has become, not to seek any revolutionary change, or even to articulate the political aspirations of a particular oppressed group, but to 'wage a war on totality; let us be witnesses to the unpresentable; let us activate the differences and save the honour of the name.'[87] Despite his stated opposition to 'the complete aestheticization of the political', Lyotard seems to conceive resistance in essentially aesthetic terms. He favours, over the defence of 'natural rights', 'resistance in and through writing as . . . inscription which attends to the uninscribable'.[88] Since, as we saw in section 1.3 above, Lyotard characterizes Postmodern art as involving an attitude to the sublime that no longer (unlike Modernism) regrets the unpresentability of the whole, it is clear that the burden of resistance must now fall on art.

Perhaps the limit-point of this degeneration is provided by the work of Jean Baudrillard. To the Foucauldian concept of power as well as the Marxist notion of production he counterposes the idea of seduction – unlike them cyclical, reversible, purposeless. The Nietzschean antecedents of this concept are clear enough, as are those of the related concept of challenge, whose 'only term is the immediacy of a response or of death. Everything linear, including history, has an end; challenge alone is without end since it is indefinitely reversible.'[89] The social is the product of the imposition of a linear order upon the cyclical, a process subverted in the consumer society of late capitalism, which is characterized above all by 'hyperreality', the collapse of any distinction between true and false, real and imaginary. The only appropriate form of resistance in these circumstances is the refusal of any political action, which could only succeed in restoring in a perhaps more repressive form the imploding social, but the inert, apathetic absorption of the 'silent majority' in the images showered on them by the mass media: 'withdrawing into the private could well be *a direct defiance of the political*, a form of actively resisting political manipulation.' I discuss Baudrillard's views on contemporary 'hyperreality' in chapter 5 below. It is, however, difficult to see his attack on any form of collective action – with the exception of the terrorism of groups such as the Red Army Fraction, whose 'blind, non-representative, senseless' acts correspond to 'the blind senseless and unrepresentational behaviour of the masses' – as anything more than a facile attempt to trump the Foucauldian concept of resistance with one even further removed from the conventional political strategies of the left.[90] Baudrillard's posturings do not allow him to escape from the same problem confronting Foucault and Deleuze: 'This . . . remains a mystery: why does one respond to a challenge? For what reason does one attempt to play better, and feel passionately to answer such an arbitrary injunction?'[91] Why indeed? Unless one is prepared to locate the sources of the urge to dominate in the very structure of reality – as in different ways Nietzsche's ontology of the will to power and Deleuze's *Lebensphilosophie* do – then omnipresent power and resistance and the cycles of challenge and seduction float free, equally unsupported by any cogent argument.[92]

## 3.5    APORIA 3: THE SUBJECT

In his last works Foucault began to explore a path which might allow him to escape from the dilemmas discussed in the previous section. This involved reopening the question of subjectivity. As we saw in section 3.1 above, central to the poststructuralist *démarche* was the demotion of the subject from constitutive to constituted status. Foucault was perhaps the most eloquent and extreme advocate of this move. Thus he declared in 1976: 'The individual is not a pregiven entity which is seized on by the exercise of power. The individual, with his identity and characteristics, is the product of a relation of power exercised over bodies, multiplicities, movements, desires, forces.'[93] But subsequently he seemed to shift ground, perhaps in response to the difficulty with grounding resistance given the omnipresence of resistance. Foucault wrote in a fascinating late essay: 'Power is exercised only over free subjects, and only insofar as they are free. By this we mean individual or collective subjects who are faced with a field of possibilities in which several ways of behaving, several reactions, and diverse comportments may be realized.'[94] If power acts on pregiven subjects, then resistance can easily be explained as arising from the clash between the subjects' independently formed desires and the imperatives of power, but we seem in doing so to have taken a big step back into the 'philosophy of the subject' previously rejected by Foucault.

The question of the subject came to occupy the focus of the second and third volumes of the *Histoire de la sexualité*, published days before Foucault's death in June 1984. Characteristically, just as he had in the mid-1970s denied that he had ever been concerned with language, Foucault now played down the question of power: 'I am very far from being a theoretician of power. At the limit, I would say that power, as an autonomous question, does not interest me.'[95] He announced a new 'theoretical displacement', away from power-knowledge towards 'truth-games in the relation of self to self and the constitution of oneself as a subject, by taking as domain of reference and field of investigation what one could call the "history of the man of desire"'. More specifically, he was concerned to trace the origins of the distinctively Western and modern notion that the truth of the subject is to be found in sexuality, a belief of which psychoanalysis is merely the latest version. To understand its formulation at the beginning of the Christian era Foucault had to go further back, and explore conceptions of sexuality in classical antiquity. He also had to construct new theoretical tools, in particular that of an 'aesthetic of existence' or 'technology of the self', 'those reflective and voluntary practices by which men not only set for themselves rules of conduct, but seek to transform themselves, to modify themselves in their singular being, and to make of their life a work which bears certain aesthetic values and responds to certain stylistic criteria'. The main example Foucault gives of such 'arts of existence' is the *chrésis aphrodisión*, government of pleasures, practised by the citizens of classical Athens, by which they sought to master themselves, to shape themselves into the kind of moral subject capable both of managing their households of women and slaves, and of participating in the government of their city.[96]

These 'modifications' (as Foucault called them) appear to mark a major shift away from the idea that '[t]he individual is ... not the *vis-à-vis* of power' but 'one of its prime effects'.[97] To adapt a famous remark of Edward Thompson's, the subject now seems to be present at its own making. The classical 'technology of the self' analysed by Foucault in the second and third volumes of the *Histoire de la sexualité* seems to involve practices of *self*-constitution and *self*-government. The claim that this involves a return on his part to the 'philosophy of the subject' has been contested.[98] Ferry and Renaut argue that Foucault equivocates between two conceptions of the subject – on the one hand, 'the atemporal, anhistoric structure of the human being as a being which characterizes itself by relation to itself', on the other, the historically specific 'modern' form of subjectivity, 'which it is necessary to criticize while reconstituting its genesis'.[99] The point, then, of studying the Greek *chrésis aphrodisión* is to discover the existence of other forms of subjectivity which demonstrate that the present form is not ineluctably imposed on us by our very nature. 'Among the cultural inventions of mankind there is a treasury of devices, techniques, ideas, procedures, and so on, that cannot exactly be reactivated, but at least constitute, or help to constitute, a certain point of view which can be very useful as a tool for analysing what's going on now – and to change it.' The kind of change Foucault had in mind is indicated by his question: 'Couldn't everyone's life become a work of art? Why should the lamp or the house be a work of art, but not our life?'[100]

As Foucault readily acknowledged in the interview from which this last quotation is taken, the idea of making one's life a work of art comes straight from Nietzsche: 'To "give style" to one's character – a great and rare art! It is practised by those who survey all the strength and weaknesses of their nature and then fit them into an artistic plan until every one of them appears as part and reason and even weaknesses delight the eye.'[101] Indeed, Nietzsche anticipated Foucault's analysis of the Athenian ruling class, describing them as a 'leisure class' characterized by 'the will to give form to oneself' (see section 3.1 above). But how does one 'give form to oneself' if, as Nietzsche and Foucault both seem to believe, there is no antecedently existing self? This problem is explored in most depth by Nehemas in his discussion of Nietzsche's injunction 'to become what one is': 'if there is no such thing as the self, there seems to be nothing that one can in any way become.' Nehemas argues that we must see 'becoming what one is' as a process, 'a matter of incorporating more and more characteristics under a constantly expanding and evolving rubric.' This process of incorporation involves above all assuming responsibility for one's properties and actions. 'The creation of the self therefore appears to be the creation, or imposition, of a higher-order accord among our lower-level thoughts, desires, and actions. It is the development of the ability, or the willingness, to accept responsibility for everything that we have done and to admit what is in any case true: that everything we have done actually constitutes who each one of us is.'[102] As we have seen (section 3.1 above), Nehemas's prime example of such self-creation is Nietzsche himself, who declared in *Ecce Homo*: 'I do not want in the least that anything should be different than it is; I myself do not want to become different.'[103]

The importance of the process which Nehemas describes seems to me unquestionable, but I doubt whether it can properly be called 'self-*creation*'. For one thing, some principle of individuation is required in order to allocate the right characteristics to the right persons. Nietzsche, for example, would not have liked to 'accept responsibility' for Wagner's life. Nehemas effectively concedes the point: 'Because it is organized coherently, the body provides the common ground that allows conflicting thoughts, desires, and actions to be grouped together as features of a single subject.'[104] This criterion of physical identity (and continuity?) offers a means of distinguishing correct and incorrect ascriptions of properties and actions to different individuals.[105] By thus acknowledging the irreducible distinctness of persons, however, we have gone a long way towards setting limits to the process of self-creation. My particular characteristics circumscribe my likely achievements. If I am tone-deaf or blind then I cannot appreciate, let alone produce music or painting respectively. My past actions – a act of personal or political betrayal, for example – may give a shape to the rest of my life which is, quite simply, inescapable. My bad temper may bedevil my personal life, helping to undermine my most important relationships with others. Of course, as the last example indicates, unalterable characteristics shade off into those which can be modified. Nevertheless, the process of making sense of one's life, described by Nehemas as 'self-creation' is constrained by the facts of one's character and history. Nietzsche, when talking in the passage cited above about giving style to one's character, seems to have in mind a sort of balancing process in which strengths and weaknesses are integrated into an overall conception of oneself – but these strengths and weaknesses are surely at least in part given independently of this conception.

There are other constraints, shared by all or many individuals. For one thing, the abilities particular to human beings as a species – which the anti-humanism of '68 thought' allowed it to ignore – set limits to the scope of 'self-creation'. Even with all the aid of technology, I cannot expect to include the kind of experiences had by a dolphin among my own. For another, there is the matter of the brute inequalities in resources which find expression above all in class divisions. Nietzsche argues that '[i]t will be the strong and domineering natures that enjoy their finest gaiety' in the self-discipline involved in accepting 'the constraint of a single taste', while 'it is the weak characters without power over themselves that *hate* the constraint of style.'[106] As Nehemas points out, 'Nietzsche does not consider that every agent has a self.'[107] Foucault, more democratic, asks why 'everyone's life couldn't become a work of art?' The answer, of course, is that most people's lives are still (contrary to the theories of 'post-capitalism' discussed in chapter 5) shaped by their lack of access to productive resources and their consequent need to sell their labour-power in order to live. To invite a hospital porter in Birmingham, a car-worker in Sao Paolo, a social security clerk in Chicago, or a street child in Bombay to make a work of art of their lives would be an insult — unless linked to precisely the kind of strategy for global social change which, as we saw in the previous section, poststructuralism rejects.

This discussion of the later Foucault shows that his apparent rediscovery of the subject does not represent an escape from the dilemmas involved in the notion of power-knowledge without the adoption of a much stronger theory of human nature and agency than is found anywhere in the Nietzschean tradition.[108] It also takes us full circle, since we have seen how perhaps the most important poststructuralist thinker remained wedded to the end of his life to the Aestheticism central to Nietzsche's own thought. To understand why such ideas should have been so readily received in the 1980s we must examine the social and political context of their reception. This I do in chapter 5. But let us first consider the thought of poststructuralism's greatest critic.

# 4
# THE LIMITS OF
# COMMUNICATIVE REASON

On the wings of synthesis one can fly to such a height that the blood turns to ice and the human body freezes, to a height which no flyer has ever attained, but whither with a cigar between their teeth thousands of scholars have soared.

*Valerian Maikov*

## 4.1  IN DEFENCE OF THE ENLIGHTENMENT

Jürgen Habermas is without any doubt the major philosopher of the contemporary Western left. This description can be defended on three grounds – first, quite simply the scale, range and quality of his writings; second, Habermas's attempt to reconstruct historical materialism as a theory of social evolution, and in particular to provide a defensible account of the contradictionary process of capitalist modernization; third, his taking up the cudgels in defence of the Enlightenment project of 'the rational organization of everyday social life'.[1] All these three aspects of Habermas's work are present in *The Philosophical Discourse of Modernity* (1985), where he draws both on his vast and penetrating knowledge of intellectual history and on the theory of communicative action basic to his analysis of modernity in order to develop a devastating and uncharacteristically vivid critique of the tradition stemming from Nietzsche and Heidegger and currently represented by the two strands of poststructuralist thought discussed in the last chapter.

It is important, I think, to stress the political character of Habermas's philosophical intervention against poststructuralism. His work since the late 1970s has been preoccupied with the revival throughout Western capitalism of various strands of conservative thought involving the partial or complete rejection of modernity. This re-emergence of what to Habermas seemed to be the irrationalism of the prewar

European right had, quite obviously, particularly threatening overtones in the Federal Republic: the fear of reactionary challenges to
liberal democracy informs Habermas's vigorous involvement, for
example, in the *Historikerstreit*, the debate about German history
provoked by Ernst Nolte's claim that the Nazi Holocaust was merely
a reaction to, and copy of the totalitarian dynamic inherent in
socialism.[2] Habermas's critique of poststructuralism has to be seen in
this context. Thus he distinguishes between the 'old conservatives',
who 'recommend a withdrawal *anterior* to modernity', the 'neocon-
servatives' who accept 'technical progress, capitalist growth and
rational administration' – what Habermas calls 'societal modernization' – but 'recommend a politics of defusing the explosive content of
cultural modernity', and the 'young conservatives', who

> recapitulate the basic experience of aesthetic modernity. They claim
> as their own the revelations of a decentred subjectivity, emanci-
> pated from the imperatives of work and usefulness, and with this
> experience they step outside the modern world. On the basis of
> modernistic attitudes they justify an irreconcilable antimodernism.
> They remove into the sphere of the far-away and the archaic the
> spontaneous powers of imagination, self-experience and emotion.
> To reason they juxtapose in Manichean fashion a principle only
> accessible through evocation, be it the will to power or sovereigni-
> ty, Being or the Dionysiac force of the poetical.[3]

The idea that poststructuralism should be seen as akin to conservative nostalgia for an idealized precapitalist organic order has encountered much resistance in the English-speaking world, where the
reception of Foucault, Deleuze and (to a lesser extent) Derrida has
been mainly by the left intelligentsia. Thus Frederic Jameson dismisses
Habermas's defence of modernity as specific to 'the national situation in which Habermas thinks and writes' and therefore
'ungeneralizable'.[4] This response is, however, too hasty. The case for
connecting poststructuralism's critique of discursive reason and the
traditional right's rejection of modernity is well put by Christopher
Norris. He takes as his starting-point Lyotard's discussion of narrative, the distinctive form of knowledge in premodern societies.
Popular narratives – folktales – are, according to Lyotard, characterized by the fact that they are self-legitimizing, they do not require
justification in terms of some 'metanarrative', whether that be some
abstract theory of rationality or one of the 'grand narratives' of
Enlightenment thought, in which individual stories are integrated into
an unfolding totality – Reason, Spirit, the Protetariat. Postmodernity
is precisely the condition in which such metanarratives turn out to

have the properties of popular narratives, to be the source of their own legitimacy, a cluster of language-games merging into the heterogeneity of ordinary discourse.[5]

Norris observes:

> As the idea gains ground that *all* theory is a species of sublimated narrative, so doubts emerge about the very possibility of *knowledge* as distinct from the various forms of narrative gratification. Theory presupposes critical distance between its own categories and those of a naturalized mythology or commonsense system of assumptions. Simply to collapse that distance – as Lyotard does – is to argue away the very grounds of rational critique.

The very notion of theoretical enquiry – of *theória* – since its first formulation in Greek thought is that of a discourse which is *not* identical with, say, popular narrative. By collapsing the distinction between the two levels of discourse, Norris argues, Lyotard makes political critique of the status quo impossible:

> The 'postmodern condition' – as Lyotard interprets it – thus seems to share the essential characteristics of all conservative ideology, from Burke to the current New Right. It rests, that is to say, on the idea that *prejudice* is so deeply built into our traditions of thought that no amount of rational criticism can hope to dislodge it. Any serious thinking about culture and society will have to acknowledge the fact that such enquiries have meaning only within the context of a certain informing tradition.[6]

Although Norris's criticisms are directed at Lyotard, they are of more general application. Poststructuralism denies that theory can detach itself from the immediate context of meanings and purposes in which it is formulated. Consequently any critique of existing conditions cannot base itself on any general principles, but must proceed allusively, as Derrida does when he appeals to the 'unnameable'. Similarly, the hermeneutics of Heidegger and Gadamer claims that understanding depends on a preunderstanding determined by social practices whose nature cannot be fully grasped since they are presupposed by and implicit within the act of understanding itself; tradition, far from being dissolved by the rational criticism of enlightenment, is the essential prerequisite of, and therefore sets limits to, any such critique.[7] Habermas's philosophy of language is intended in part as a response to the hermeneutic tradition (see section 4.2 below); for the present, however, it is sufficient to note that Foucault and Derrida, like Heidegger, seek to question theory's claim critically to reflect on the existing network of social practices which supposedly determine the limits of our understanding.

*The Theory of Communicative Action* (1981) elaborates Habermas's philosophy of language as the basis of his theory of modernity. It also provides the conceptual framework on which he relies in his critique of poststructuralism. The *Theory*, indeed, is itself a political intervention. Habermas has explained why he came to write the book, whose central focus is the modernization as a process of rationalization, in late 1977: 'The tense German political situation, which was becoming more and more like a pogrom following Schleyer's kidnapping, drove me out of the theoretical ivory tower to take a stand.' Liberal democracy seemed to be under threat both from extreme left – the terrorists of the Red Army Fraction – and extreme right, whose demands for greater repression gained respectability thanks in part to the revival of conservative thought. At the same time, the rise of new social movements such as the Greens seemed to offer a challenge to modern industrial civilization itself:

> my real motive in beginning the book in 1977 was to understand how the critique of reification, the critique of rationalization, could be reformulated in such a way that would offer a theoretical explanation of the crumbling of the welfare-state compromise and of the potential for a critique of growth in new movements, without surrendering the project of modernity or descending into post- or anti-modernism, 'tough' new conservatism or 'wild' young conservatism.[8]

Habermas is therefore concerned to undertake a critical defence of modernity, one that emphasizes its incompleteness, its failure to realize its potential. In this respect his work can be seen as a continuation of the Marxist tradition, and more particularly of the early Frankfurt school. Habermas says of Adorno: 'he remains true to the idea that there is no cure for the wounds of Enlightenment other than the radicalized Enlightenment itself.'[9] There is no doubt that this is also his own stance. There are, nevertheless serious weaknesses in Habermas's attempt to elaborate this position which make his critique of poststructuralism – and more generally of 'post- or anti-modernism' – vulnerable. More specifically, as I try to show in the rest of this chapter, his theory of communicative action leads him to fall into almost as one-sided a defence of modernity as its critique by Nietzsche and his successors.

## 4.2  FROM WEBER TO HABERMAS

Habermas follows Weber in conceiving 'the modernization of European society as a result of a universal-historical process of rationalization'. In starting from Weber's account of modernization as the differentiation of autonomous subsystems – above all the market and the state – regulated by instrumental rationality, Habermas takes the same course as Lukács and the early Frankfurt school. In *History and Class Consciousness*, Lukács interpreted rationalization as reification, as the consequence of the penetration of all the spheres of social life by commodity fetishism, the reduction, produced by capitalist economic mechanisms, of all relationships between people to relations between things regulated by the market. The obverse to this process of reification was, Lukács believed, the proletariat, conceived in highly Hegelian terms as the 'identical subject-object of history' whose inevitable assumption of revolutionary consciousness would shatter the reified structures of capitalist society. Horkheimer and Adorno took over, and indeed considerably enriched Lukács's analysis of reification but gave up any expectations of proletarian revolution. At the same time, as Habermas argues, they 'detach the concept [of reification] from the special historical context of the rise of the capitalist system' and 'anchor the mechanism that produces the reification of consciousness in the anthropological foundations of the history of the species, in the form of the existence of a species that has to reproduce itself through nature.' The triumph of instrumental reason therefore ceased to be, as Lukács argued, the consequence of a historically specific and transitory constellation of circumstances and became instead the inevitable outcome of humanity's need to reproduce itself, involving a transhistoric tendency to dominate persons and nature alike which finds its culmination in late capitalism. Hence the 'performative contradiction' which Habermas discovers in *Dialectic of Enlightenment* as well as in the Nietzschean critique of modernity (see section 3.4 above): how can Horkheimer and Adorno continue to practise a critical theory of society when reason itself is identified with the urge to dominate? Adorno sought to continue rational critique by means of negative dialectics which sought both to expose existing contradictions and allusively to evoke an emancipated society reconciled with nature, in particular by articulating the hints of such a society implicit in the abstract and distorted structures of Modern art. As Habermas observes:

> In the shadow of a philosophy that has outlived itself, philosophy

intentionally retrogresses to gesticulation. As opposed as the intentions behind their respective philosophies of history are, Adorno is in the end very similar to Heidegger as regards his position on the theoretical claims of objectivating thought and of reflection: The mindfulness [*Eingedenken*] of nature comes shocking close to the recollection [*Andenken*] of being.[1]

Habermas identifies with the variant of the discourse of modernity founded by Marx, which 'conceive[s] of rational practice as reason concretized in history, society, body, and language'.[11] But the 'performative contradiction' inherent in the thought of the early Frankfurt school is, he believes, unavoidable as long as we remain within the framework of 'the philosophy of consciousness', central to which is 'the relation of a solitary subject to something in the objective world that can be represented and manipulated'. The monologic conception of subjectivity central to Western thought since Descartes necessarily involves an instrumental conception of rationality: the world is presented to the subject thus conceived as a means to its own ends, and therefore reason is constituted within the framework of a means-ends relationship shaped by the subject's urge to dominate an environment that is essentially alien and external to it. Within this paradigm one is caught in a dilemma between the neo-conservative acceptance of a modernity dominated by instrumental reason or the radical critique of this modernity which, by its identification of instrumental rationality with reason *tout court*, denies itself any criteria by means of which to justify this critique or specify a more desirable state of affairs. This dilemma can be escaped 'only if we give up the paradigm of the philosophy of consciousness – namely a subject that represents objects and toils with them – in favour of the paradigm of linguistic philosophy – namely, that of intersubjective understanding or communication – and put the cognitive-instrumental aspect of reason in its proper place as part of a more encompassing *communicative rationality*.'[12]

Habermas thus proposes that we replace a monologic with a dialogic conception of subjectivity and rationality. Hence the importance of *The Theory of Communicative Action*, fundamental to which is the distinction between two kinds of action – first, 'action oriented to success', instrumental and strategic action, in which the individual subject pursues its goals in relation to an environment which, whether physical or social, is conceived as an alien object; second, communicative action, where 'the actions of the agents involved are co-ordinated not through egocentric calculations of success but through acts of reaching understanding.' Reaching understanding, 'the inherent telos of human speech', consists in 'a process of reaching agreement [*Einigung*] among seeking and acting subjects'. On the basis of an analysis which draws on the speech-act philosophy of language developed by Austin, Grice and Searle, Habermas argues that understanding necessarily involves the listener's acceptance of a 'redeemable validity-claim' made by the speaker: 'a speaker can *rationally motivate* a hearer to accept his speech-act offer because . . . he can assume the *warranty* [*Gewähr*] for providing, if necessary, convincing reasons that would stand up to a hearer's validity claim.' Only in this way can uncoerced agreement between subjects be obtained: 'only those speech acts with which a speaker connects a criticizable validity claim can move a hearer to accept an offer independently of external force.'[13]

This theory of communicative action serves Habermas in various ways. In the first place, by embedding quite a strong conception of rationality in everyday discourse he is able to rule out any form of relativism or scepticism as incoherent: 'For a human being that maintains itself in the structures of ordinary-language communication, the validity-basis of speech has the binding force of universal and unavoidable – in this sense transcendental – presuppositions . . . If we are not free then to reject or accept validity-claims bound up with the cognitive potential of the human species, it is senseless to "decide" for or against reason, for or against the expansion of the potential of reasoned action.'[14] Secondly, as the last phrase quoted suggests, this conception of communicative rationality has political consequences. Implicit in the aspiration of uncoerced agreement that is the goal of every speech act is the conception of a society based on such agreement: 'The Utopian perspective of reconciliation and freedom is ingrained in the conditions for the communicative sociation of individuals; it is built into the linguistic mechanism of the reproduction of the species.'[15]

Thirdly, this complex and differentiated conception of rationality, in which instrumental reason is merely 'a subordinated moment', allows Habermas to avoid the one-sided conception of rationalization shared by both Weber and the early Frankfurt school. 'The communicative potential of reason has been simultaneously developed and distorted in the course of capitalist modernization', he argues.[16]

The development of Western capitalism involved 'a selective pattern of rationalization, a jagged profile of modernization.'[17] Only certain aspects of rationality, understood broadly and in terms of communicative action, have been embodied in modernity. Hence the latter's incompleteness; contrary to the diagnosis offered by Nietzsche and his followers, it suffers not from 'an excess' but from 'a deficit of rationality'.[18]

To capture the 'jagged' character of modernization, Habermas draws the distinction between systems and lifeworld that is fundamental to the second volume of *The Theory of Communicative Action*. It is, in a sense, his version of the distinction between social structure and human action. The concept of system refers to the functional consequences of actions for the reproduction of a given society, that of lifeworld (*Lebenswelt*) to those mechanisms through which social actors arrive at a shared understanding of the world; the latter concept therefore is concerned with agents' intentions, the former with processes that, in Hegel's phrase, go on behind their backs. The distinction is an analytical one, referring to aspects of any social order which only take distinct institutional form as a result of modernization: indeed, the differentiation of system and lifeworld is constitutive of modernity. The more fundamental of the two is the lifeworld: Habermas uses the term (which derives from the phenomenological hermeneutics of Husserl) to refer to the implicit shared understandings presupposed by any speech act. These understandings, embodied in tradition, form 'the horizon within which communicative action is "always already" moving'. It is 'prior to any possible disagreement and cannot become controversial in the way that intersubjectively shared knowledge can be; at most it can fall apart'.[19]

But if Habermas's discussion of the lifeworld incorporates some of the central insights of hermeneutics, he denies that the traditional knowledge implicit in every speech act is immune from rational criticism. Against Gadamer he insists that 'the reflected appropriation of tradition breaks up the nature-like substance of tradition and alters the position of the subject in it.'[20] One feature of modernization is precisely that 'the need for understanding' is less 'covered *in advance* by an interpreted lifeworld immune from critique' and more 'met by the interpretive accomplishments of the participants themselves, that is, by way of risky (because rationally motivated) agreement'.[21] This shift in the relative weight in taken in speech by the lifeworld and the pursuit of rationally motivated agreement is bound up with the general process of rationalization. Habermas follows Weber and Parsons in seeing this as involving essentially differentiation – specifically, in two respects, of the lifeworld itself.

First, there is the differentiation of 'independent cultural spheres'. Science, law and morality and art constitute themselves as distinct cultural practices, each regulated by its own specific principles. This process of autonomization involves what Habermas calls the 'rationalization of world-views'. On the one hand, the confusion of nature and culture characteristic of myth is ended: the world is disenchanted, a sharp distinction drawn between the physical world governed by causal laws and the human world imbued with meanings and purposes. In consequence, a distinctively modern, 'decentred' understanding of the world develops in which nature is no longer a projection of human preoccupations. On the other hand, this process of rationalization involves the formalization of reason itself. Rationality no longer consists in certain substantive views, but in the *procedures* by means of which we come to hold our views. These procedures are those implicit in every speech act: 'The unity of rationality in the multiplicity of value spheres rationalized according to their inner logics is secured precisely at the formal level of their argumentative redemption of validity-claims.'[22]

Habermas's insistence on the procedural character of modern reason forms the basis of his critique of Weber, on whom he draws heavily for his own account of rationalization. For Weber, 'the real reason for the dialectic of rationalization is not an unbalanced institutional embodiment of available cognitive potentials: he locates the seeds of destruction of the rationalization in the very differentiation of independent cultural spheres that released that potential and made that rationalization possible.' Weber sees this differentiation as the emergence of an epistemic pluralism which confronts with each other different perspectives the reasons for choosing between which are irredeemably subjective. But, Habermas argues, 'Weber did not distinguish between the particular value *contents* of different traditions and those universal *standards* of value under which the cognitive, normative and expressive components of culture become autonomous value-spheres and developed complexes of rationality with their own logics.'[23] The differentiation of science, morality and art involves the explicit articulation of the tacit presuppositions of communication which require every speaker to undertake rationally to justify the 'validity-claim' involved in her utterance. Reason, therefore, does not disintegrate as a result of modernization, but rather assumes a more complex, self-conscious and formal shape.

Modernization involves, however, a second form of differentiation, between system and the lifeworld itself. It is a necessary condition of capitalist development that system integration should detach itself from social integration. The reproduction of society, previously effected through the transmission of tradition comes increasingly to depend on the emergence of 'systemic mechanisms that stabilize non-intended consequences of action by way of functionally intermeshing action *consequences*'. Two self-regulating subsystems separate themselves off from the lifeworld – the market and the state. The co-ordination of action comes to depend less and less on agents'

implicit shared understandings, and more and more on the impersonal operations of the economic and political subsystems. Market and
state function in isolation from the fabric of everyday life, using
'[d]elinguistified media of communication such as money and power'
to 'connect up interactions in space and time into more and more
complex networks that no one has to comprehend or be responsible
for'. Consequently, 'the conversion of communicative action over to
media-steered interaction . . . "technicize[s]" the lifeworld in the sense
that the expenditure and risk of consensus-forming processes are
obviated while the prospects for purposive-rational action are
enhanced.'[24] The prevalence of instrumental rationality which Weber
and the early Frankfurt school regarded as characteristic of modernity
is therefore a result of what Habermas calls 'the uncoupling of system
and lifeworld'.

Habermas's account of this process draws heavily on Parsons – for
example, in the conceptualization of money and power as 'steering
media'.[25] Like Parsons, he sees this differentiation of system and
lifeworld as, in certain respects at least, to be welcomed. Herein lies
one of Habermas's main disagreements with Marx. As Albrecht
Wellmer puts it:

> Marx lumped together two different kinds of phenomena which at
> least *we* ought to keep separate: exploitation, pauperization and
> degradation of the working class, the dehumanization of work and
> the lack of democratic control of the economy, on the one hand,
> and the emergence of formal law based on universalist principles of
> human right together with the functional and systemic differentia-
> tion of modern societies, on the other. Because in his critique of
> alienation, Marx lumped together these two different types of
> phenomena, he could believe that the abolition of capitalist proper-
> ty was sufficient to clear the road not only for an abolition of the
> inhuman features of modern industrial societies, but also for an
> abolition of all the functional differentiations and the systemic
> complexities which had come with it – and therefore for the
> recovery of an immediate unity and solidarity among human beings
> in a communist society.[26]

Habermas, by contrast, believes that such an 'abolition of all the
functional differentiations and the systemic complexities' of modernity is both impossible and undesirable. Marx, he argues,

> fails to recognize the *intrinsic* evolutionary *value* that media-steered
> subsystems possess. He does not see that the differentiation of the
> state apparatus and the economy *also* represents a higher level of

system differentiation, which simultaneously opens up new steering possibilities and forces a reorganization of the old, feudal class relationships. The significance of this level of integration goes beyond the institutionalization of a new class relationship.[27]

Underlying the positive judgement that Habermas passes on 'system-differentiation' is a theory of social evolution in which the development of the productive forces is subordinated to 'learning processes . . . in the dimension of moral insight, practical knowledge, communicative action, and the consensual regulation of action-conflicts – learning processes that are deposited in more mature forms of social integration, in new *production relations* and these in turn first make possible the introduction of new production forces.' The differentiation of 'independent cultural spheres' and in particular of law and morality is not simply a symptom of capitalist reification, but rather makes possible the 'consensual regulation of action-conflicts (accomplished under the renunciation of force)' which 'provides for the continuation of communication by other means'. The evolution of 'normative structures' such as law and morality is no mere reflex of the economic base, but has 'an *internal history*' which is 'the pacemaker of social evolution'.[28] Modernization is therefore to be welcomed not simply because its functional differentiation widens the scope for instrumental action and therefore enhances society's ability to meet its needs, above all economically; it also evolves forms of social integration which develop and formalize the pursuit of un-coerced agreement characteristic of everyday speech.

Modernization has, however, a dark side summarized by what Habermas tends to call the paradox of rationalization: 'The rationalization of the lifeworld had to reach a certain maturity before the media of money and power could be legally institutionalized in it.' The autonomization of the market and the state thus presupposes the differentiation of the lifeworld into independent cultural spheres, and more especially the development of a formalized legal system. 'The internal dynamic of these two functionally intermeshed systems, however, also reacts back upon the rationalized life-forms of modern society that made them possible, to the extent that processes of monetarization and bureaucratization penetrate the core domains of cultural production, social integration, and socialization.'[29] The result is 'the colonization of the lifeworld': 'cognitive-instrumental rationality surges beyond the bounds of the economy and the state into other, communicatively structured areas of life and achieves dominance there at the expense of moral-political and aesthetic-practical rationality.'[30] It is this process which is responsible for the social pathologies of late capitalism, where economic contradictions are displaced, thanks to the Keynesian welfare-state compromise between labour and capital, on to the cultural sphere, producing, through the resulting politicization of the market, an increased demand for legitimation which the progressive monetarization and bureaucratization of everyday life prevent from being met.[31]

These pathologies give rise to their specific forms of conflict, which 'are not ignited by distribution problems but by questions having to with the grammar of forms of life'. Class conflict is institutionalized thanks to the welfare-state compromise, and therefore the workers' movement no longer represents a fundamental challenge to the status quo. Instead:

> A line of conflict forms between, on the one hand, a centre composed of strata *directly* involved in the production process and interested in maintaining capitalist growth on the basis of the welfare-state compromise, and, on the other hand, a periphery composed of a variegated array of groups that are lumped together. Among the latter are those groups that are further removed from the 'productivist core of performance' in late capitalist societies, that have been more strongly sensitized to the self-destructive consequences of the growth in complexity or have been more strongly affected by them.

Habermas has in mind, of course, the 'new social movements' – feminists, ecologists, campaigners against nuclear power and for peace – which emerged in the 1970s, and which in many cases directly involve 'resistance to tendencies toward a colonization of the lifeworld'.[32]

Habermas's response to these movements is ambivalent. On the one hand, he firmly welcomes the challenge they represent to the destructive extension of instrumental rationality to contexts appropriately regulated by the discursive regulation of validity-claims. On the other hand, he fears that the movements' rejection of instrumental rationality could be generalized into the renunciation of reason *tout court*. Hence the danger represented by poststructuralism, whose more 'worldly' wing (Foucault and Deleuze) does identify resistance with the decentralized contestation of power by the movements. Habermas insists that '[m]odern lifeworlds are differentiated and should remain so in order that the reflexivity of traditions, the individuation of the social subject, and the universalistic foundations of justice and morality do not all go to hell.'[33] Rather than seek the 'de-differentiation' of modernity, those concerned to resist the colonization of the lifeworld should concentrate on 'building up restraining barriers between system and lifeworld and . . . building in sensors for the exchanges between system and lifeworld'.[34] In particular, the greater democratic regulation of state and market, which must of necessity be allowed a degree of autonomy, would render the instrumental rationality of these subsystems more accountable to the communicative rationality embedded in the lifeworld. Habermas's argument is thus intended to show that the feasible goals of the movements can be attained, not through the destruction of moderni- ty, but through the preservation of its positive achievements – the rationalization of the lifeworld – and the realization of the further potential implicit in the structures of communicative reason itself.

## 4.3   THE SPECTRE OF KANT: LANGUAGE, SOCIETY AND REALITY

Something of the scale and quality of Habermas's project should be clear from the foregoing summary. We are plainly confronted here with a figure of considerable stature, certainly dwarfing the *epigoni* of poststructuralism – Lyotard, Baudrillard and *tutti quanti*, and offer- ing a formidable challenge to the critique of modernity developed above all by Foucault. Plainly central to this challenge is Habermas's theory of rationality. Since I criticize this theory below, let me first underline the considerable virtues of Habermas's *démarche*. It in- volves the espousal of certain poststructuralist themes. Thus Haber- mas rejects the traditional aspiration to First Philosophy, to provide an *a priori* foundation of knowledge in either the ontological structure of Being or the transcendental presuppositions of experience.[35] Furthermore, like the poststructuralists, he recognizes the exhaustion of 'the philosophy of consciousness' – of the attempt to assign a constitutive role to the subject. What, however, disting- uishes Habermas from Foucault and Derrida is his insistence that it is still possible to construct a theory of rationality, despite the failure of all efforts to base such a theory on the philosophy of consciousness. The nature of rationality is instead to be elicited from the structure of *inter*subjectivity – more specifically, from the presuppositions of every speech act, the aspiration that everyday discourse involves towards rationality motivated agreement.

This strategy seems to me to be basically correct. In other words, Habermas is right, I think, to believe that a conception of what it is to be rational is involved in the orientations that language-users take up towards each other. It is his manner of implementing this strategy which is, in my view, disastrous.[36] There is, to begin with, the strange idea that communication involves the speaker 'offering' and the hearer 'accepting' the speech act, a transaction dependent on the former undertaking rationally to justify her utterance. Understanding is thereby disjoined from the addressee simply hearing an utterance in a language she knows, and comes to depend upon her recognizing undertakings made by the addressor but distinct from the content of the speech act itself. Not only does this involve an appeal to a highly problematic notion of tacit knowledge – understanding involves the hearer implicitly knowing that the speaker intends that she should recognize *her* (the speaker's) intention to perform a speech act that is normatively appropriate, true and sincerely expressed[37] – but seems to a case of the model of understanding as a kind of mental shadow of utterances which Wittgenstein dismantled in the *Investigations*.[38]

Then there is the idea that understanding consists in agreement. The hearer understands the speech act because she recognizes the speaker's undertaking to give reasons for whatever the utterance claims is (or will or should be) the case. But why should understanding so depend on an orientation towards rationally motivated agreement? We all hear a myriad of utterances with which we are unlikely ever to agree. Does our understanding of these utterances depend upon our recognition (via the speakers' 'offers' discursively to redeem their validity-claims) of the possibility of agreeing with them? Surely not. If you say to me 'Hitler was right', I can understand you perfectly well even though there is not the slightest chance of my agreeing with you however long we argue about it. Perhaps this is a bad example since it involves a disagreement which might move all too quickly from the exchange of words to that of blows. But we can think of other cases where this danger is at least less pressing, of the atheist to whom the words 'God exists' is addressed: she understands, but rejects what she hears. Perhaps these counter-examples are too simple-minded. Habermas says that 'not every linguistically mediated interaction is an example of action oriented to reaching understanding', but 'the use of language with an orientation to reaching understanding is the *original mode* of language use.'[39] We might think of cases where understanding seems to go along with the refusal to contemplate agreement as parasitic upon this 'original mode'. This is, however, a dangerous move to make, since it begins to undermine the conceptual link that Habermas wishes to establish between rationality and the presuppositions of everyday speech. Once the 'ideal speech situation' oriented to rationally motivated agreement ceases to be implicit in every speech act, the connection between understanding and rationality has been broken. There is also the problem of how one would then distinguish between 'normal' and 'deviant' utterances.

Involved in Habermas's identification of speech with action oriented to achieving rationally motivated agreement is the contrast suggested by the following remark: 'only those speech acts with which a speaker connects a criticizable validity-claim can move a hearer to accept an offer independently of external force.'[40] The alternative to uncoerced agreement is imposed consensus. We would be right to hear Kantian overtones in this passage and others like it. Language is the sphere where we treat others as ends in themselves, whose agreement must be voluntarily elicited, rather than as means which we can compel to serve our purposes: 'Our first sentence expresses unequivocally the intention of universal and unconstrained consensus ... Perhaps that is why the language of German idealism ... is not quite obsolete.'[41] As Anderson comments, 'where, we might say, structuralism and poststructuralism developed a kind of diabolism of language, Habermas has unruffledly produced an angelism.'[42] The trouble is that Habermas's philosophy of language cracks under the weight of the metaphysical burden which he loads on to it. For the contrast between voluntary and coerced agreement depends upon the idea that understanding involves the hearer *accepting* the speaker's 'offer'. But why should any such transaction be involved? Challenging this kind of theory, which makes understanding depend upon the assumptions participants in discourse make about each other's intentions, Michael Dummett argues:

> In the normal case, the speaker simply says what he means. By this, I do not mean that he first has the thought and then puts it into words, but that, knowing the language, he simply speaks. In the normal case, likewise, the hearer simply understands. That is, knowing the language, he hears and thereby understands; given that he knows the language, there is nothing that his understanding the words consists in save his hearing them.[43]

On this view of understanding, the speaker's and hearer's orientation on reaching agreement is simply irrelevant; it is their participation in a shared social practice – that of using the same language – that allows one to understand the other. This may seem to beg the question – Habermas might argue that using the same language presupposes the intention to achieve rationally founded consensus. Further consideration is required of the role of agreement in language, which is, I think, fundamental, but quite different from that assigned it by Habermas. Take the following remark of Wittgenstein's:

If language is to be a means of communication there must be agreement not only in definitions but also (queer as this may sound) in judgements. This seems to abolish logic but does not do so. – It is one thing to describe methods of measurement, and another to obtain and state results of measurement. But what we call 'measuring' is partly determined by a certain constancy in results of measurement.[44]

Agreement, then, is not the telos of speech but its prerequisite. What can Wittgenstein be saying here? It might seem that he is merely arguing that each language involves a set of social conventions to regulate correct usage. This interpretation has been undermined, however, by discussion of those passages in the *Investigations* where Wittgenstein challenges the idea that a rule can guide practice.[45] In any case, the concluding sentence of the remark says that more than agreement in 'methods of measurement' is required: in addition there must be 'constancy in results of measurement'. On what will such constancy depend? In the first place, surely, on the constitution of the world. We 'agree in judgements' because many of the beliefs our assertoric sentences state accurately represent the nature of the world we share. 'Agreement in judgements' is contingent upon the objective properties of the natural and social environment with which we must cope. It is also contingent, surely, upon our own constitution. It is *we* who must cope with this environment – human beings with a common nature which guarantees a considerable overlap in perspective even among members of very different societies. It is this which Wittgenstein seems to have in mind in the preceding remark (where, incidentally, he also rejects a consensus theory of truth): '"So you are saying that human agreement decides what is true and what is false?" – It is what human beings *say* that is true and false; and they agree in the *language* they use. That is not agreement in opinions but in form of life.' Agreement in judgements is not simply a matter of shared beliefs but of shared nature. What Wittgenstein meant by 'form of life' is complex and controversial, but it is reasonably clear, I think, that the expression refers not so much (as is often thought) to the practices specific to a particular society, but to conduct flowing from our human constitution itself. Thus, considering the case of an explorer faced with an alien language, Wittgenstein says: 'The common behaviour of mankind is the system of reference by means of which we interpret an unknown language.'[46] As Colin McGinn observes: 'His view is that what underlies (if that is the word) our practices and customs with signs is our human nature in interaction with our training: this is what explains our unreflectively going on as we do.'[47]

This naturalistic conception of language is akin to one of the most important developments in postwar analytical philosophy. Quine in particular has challenged the idea – originating ultimately in Kant's distinction between analytical and synthetic judgements – that language has a formal structure, consisting in conventions distilled in the meanings of words, and separate from the content of our utterances, which involve, crucially, assertions about the state of the world. Quine's attack on the analytic–synthetic distinction implied a quite different conception of language, expressed in this celebrated metaphor: 'The lore of our fathers is a fabric of sentences . . . It is a pale grey lore, black with fact, white with conventions. But I have found no substantial reason for concluding that there are any quite black threads in it, or any white ones.'[48] On this view, there is no sharp distinction between matters of meaning and those of fact, between the form and the content of language. Quine's argument has been taken much further by Davidson, for whom interpreting another's speech consists in ascribing to her broadly the same beliefs as one holds to be true oneself, on the grounds that to entertain the possibility that the speaker's beliefs are systematically false is to deny her rationality. Even when this Principle of Charity is weakened to a Principle of Humanity which simply requires that the speaker's beliefs be ones that it is intelligible for someone in her situation to hold rather than beliefs that the hearer herself holds to be true, the underlying thrust of the theory remains the same: interpretation involves assuming that the speaker is rational in a sense that involves setting her in the context of the world which she shares, along with their common human nature, with the hearer.[49] Davidson has in recent years tended to highlight the way in which this theory of interpretation undermines any attempt to distinguish between the form and content of language, arguing, for example, that 'language is a condition for having conventions' rather constituted by them.[50]

The differences between the naturalism which is such a striking feature of contemporary analytical philosophy of language and Habermas's theory of communicative action shed light on the nature of his epistemology itself. Wellmer aptly characterizes Habermas's conception of communicative rationality as '(a) a *procedural* conception of rationality, i.e., a *specific* way of coming to grips with incoherences, contradictions and dissension, and (b) a formal standard of rationality which operates on a "meta-level" *vis-à-vis* all those "substantive" standards of rationality'.[51] Thus we saw in the previous section that, for Habermas, the differentiation of the 'independent cultural spheres' – science, law and morality and art – involves the elaboration of formal standards of rationality shared by all three. Once again, we are confronted with a strikingly Kantian perspective. Habermas's very classification – science, morality and art – reproduces the structure of Kant's three *Critiques*, concerned as they are with, respectively, pure theoretical reason, pure practical reason, and aesthetic and teleological judgements. Kant's differentiation of reason also focuses on form: thus knowledge consists in the application of the categories of the understanding to sense-impressions, while it is their universal character which gives the key to the nature of moral judgements. The difference is that Kant roots rationality in features inherent in the transcendental subject while for Habermas it arises from the nature of linguistic *inter*subjectivity.

Habermas's insistence on the procedural nature of rationality leads him in some strange directions. Thus he argues that moral philosophy should concern itself solely with the establishment of ethical cognitivism, that is, the doctrine that ethical assertions are amenable to rational adjudication rather than being merely commands or expressions of desire or taste:

> According to my conception, the philosopher ought to explain the moral point of view, and – as far as possible – justify the claim to the universality of this explanation, showing why it does not merely reflect the moral intuitions of the average, male, middle-class member of a modern Western society. Anything further than that is a matter for moral discourse among participants. Insofar as the philosopher would like to justify specific principles of a normative theory of morality and politics, he should consider this as a proposal for the discourse between citizens. In other words: the moral philosopher must leave the substantive questions which go beyond a fundamental critique of value-scepticism and value-relativism to the participants in moral discourse, or tailor the cognitive claims of normative theory from the outset to the role of a participant.[52]

Elsewhere Habermas says: 'Cognitive ethics separates off the good life and concentrates on strictly deontological, universalizable aspects, so that what remains from the Good is only the Just.'[53] But it's not clear that we even have that, since Habermas denies that Rawls's *Theory of Justice* is a 'philosophical work'. In elaborating two principles of justice Rawls 'is speaking as a citizen of the United States with a certain background, and it is easy to make – as has been done – an ideological critique of the concrete institutions and principles which he wants to defend.'[54] And Rawls's failure to detach his principles from his own socio-political context is no mere contingent failure, Habermas seems to suggest: *any* theory of justice will founder on the same rock. This does seem fairly perverse. How can the formulation and rational justification of ethical principles avoid discussion of concrete social worlds, both actual and possible? How can they eschew giving some account of the person? And how can consideration of human beings and their social relationships eschew empirical enquiry? One of the great merits of Rawls's book – and indeed of its neo-liberal pendant, Nozick's *Anarchy, State, and Utopia* – is their rehabilitation of substantive political theory, which seeks to ground principles of justice in quasi-empirical conceptions of human nature and of society. Habermas's formalist metaethics flies in the face also of the most interesting direction taken by analytical moral philosophy, which is concerned with the relationship between ethical realism – according to which moral judgements must be taken at face value, as assertions bearing a truth-value like any other assertion – and the varying social contexts in which human beings find themselves.[55] It also leaves Habermas vulnerable to Rorty's riposte, which is to concede to Habermas his procedural conception of philosophy's role but then to 'swerve off' and 'privatize philosophy' by giving up the attempt to provide a theoretical justification for political projects. Politics, Rorty argues, should be left to 'superficial dreamers – people like Edward Bellamy, Henry George, H. G. Wells, Michael Harrington, Martin Luther King', who propose 'concrete ways in which things might get better . . . They supply local hope, not universal knowledge.'[56] Rorty in his characteristically narcissistic way poses the issue in terms of the role of philosophy, but it is really that of whether theoretical enquiry can play any part in guiding political practice. The conclusion – that it cannot – is highly congenial to Rorty's liberalism, 'the attempt to fulfil the hopes of the North Atlantic bourgeoisie', as he calls it, but it is surely a highly damaging one for Habermas's attempt to rehabilitate the 'radicalized Enlightenment'.[57]

This scission between formalist metaethics and substantive political philosophy indicates, in my view, that any defensible theory of rationality cannot be purely procedural but must incorporate a factual account of human beings and their place in the world. This claim is, indeed, a corollary of the rejection of the analytic–synthetic distinction. If the clarification of meanings cannot be divorced from empirical enquiry into the structure of the world, then philosophy must be seen as continuous with rather than an *a priori* foundation of the sciences. Habermas in principle eschews 'First Philosophy', but by conceiving rationality as essentially procedural, threatens to rehabilitate a founding role for philosophy, albeit a rather ethereal version of philosophy. The difficulty with the naturalistic epistemology which I have counterposed to Habermas's is, of course, that by setting rationality in the context of human beings in their natural and social environment it seems to threaten to dissolve it into that context, a danger which I shall try to illustrate – and dissolve – by considering the question of truth.

The most important contemporary epistemological naturalism is perhaps Davidson's philosophy of language. This is, as we saw in section 3.3 above, both holist – following Quine he conceives language as a 'fabric' of interconnected sentences – and realist – the sense of an individual sentence is given by its truth-conditions, truth is understood in accordance with the classical definition, so that a sentence is true or false in virtue of the state of the world. Now Rorty has tried to claim this philosophy of language for pragmatism, understood as 'the doctrine that there are no constraints on inquiry save conversational ones – no wholesale restraints derived from the nature of the objects, or of the mind, or of language, but only those retail constraints provided by the remarks of our fellow-inquirers'.[58] He argues that '"true" has no explanatory use'; it may be of some technical value in allowing us, for example, to distinguish between using and mentioning sentences, as is done by Tarskian truth-sentences of the form '"p" is true if and only if p', which Davidson uses to give the sense ( = truth-conditions) of sentences, but this does not amount to the grounding of knowledge in a relation between sentences and the world.[59] (For what it is worth, Davidson firmly rejects this interpretation of his work.)[60]

Habermas also espouses a pragmatist theory of truth. Following Dewey he identifies truth with warranted assertibility: to say that a sentence is true is to say that it is justified. This does not, however, amount to reducing truth to whatever the participants in a conversation choose to accept (Rorty's position), since a sentence is justified if the participants to the discussion freely accept it on the basis of rational argumentation.[61] This definition of truth in terms of ideal consensus is a lineal descendant of Peirce's, where a sentence is true if it is what would be accepted were enquiry continued indefinitely. The flaw in all such theories is that a sentence may be warrantedly assertible, not merely in terms of the current state of knowledge, but also in terms of whatever consensus arises from discussion in an ideal speech situation uncontaminated by inequalities of power, and still be false. It is quite possible for not simply our best contemporary theories, but also for those accepted by the kind of ideal consensus which Habermas projects as the telos of speech, to be wrong. One of the great merits of the classical theory, where truth is a matter of the state of the world, not of whatever we might agree, even in the best circumstances, is that it allows for this possibility.

Now both Habermas and Rorty would respond that the classical theory of truth, precisely because it is so strong – even our best theories may turn out to be false, is a metaphysical fifth wheel, of no use when it comes to actually making sense of the world. And both of them would be wrong. For one thing, the liability according to the classical theory of even the most 'justified' theory to falsehood implies a fallibilist conception of knowledge, in which theories are understood as hypotheses subject to revision. For another, the objectivity of truth – independently of even the most ideal consensus, the truth-value of a sentence depends on whether the world is the way it says it is – suggests that we impose some constraints upon the revision of our theories, that there may, from the point of view of attaining the truth, be better or worse of revising them. *Pace* Rorty, there are more than 'conversational' constraints on enquiry. The most interesting attempt to give an account of these constraints, by Lakatos, involves a fascinating fusion of his two teachers, Lukács and Popper, in which acceptable revisions must both cohere with a theoretically articulated scientific research programme and predict 'novel facts', sometimes successfully.[62] The latter requirement, of empirical corroboration, demands that acceptable theories offer an independent test of the accuracy of their representations of the world. Truth, conceived in classical terms, acts as, in Popper's words, a 'regulative ideal', requiring the acceptance of constraints on the revision of our beliefs.[63]

If the line of thinking sketched out in the previous paragraph is correct, then the kind of philosophical naturalism which I have argued provides a better account of rationality than Habermas's is consistent with epistemological realism. It may indeed require it, since the Davidsonian strategy involves the idea that we understand others only if we regard them as rational, which means ascribing to them beliefs which, if not true, are ones whose acceptance is intelligible in the circumstances of those who hold them. It is hard to see how any reflective justification of these ascriptions can avoid distinguishing between true and false beliefs, which in turn takes us towards the issues of truth and knowledge touched on above. In any case, Habermas's procedural conception of rationality does not seem tenable. Defining truth in terms of ideal consensus does not provide an account of the *grounds* on which a particular sentence is warrantedly assertible. Habermas indeed concedes that 'the "evidential dimension" of the [i.e., his] concept of truth is badly in need of further clarification.'[64] The danger is that Rorty, a poststructuralist in pragmatist garb, will drive a coach and horses through so etiolated a theory of rationality. A purely formal conception of reason cannot defeat the foes of Enlightenment.

## 4.4   THE SPECTRE OF MARX: ECONOMY, POLITY AND CONFLICT

If Habermas's theory of communicative rationality is too thin to be able to resist the poststructuralist critique of reason, it is at the same time too strong an account of social modernity, tending to exaggerate the extent to which the Enlightenment project has been realized in contemporary society. In both cases the source of the difficulty lies in a conception of sociality as action oriented on agreement. We can see this if we consider Habermas's social theory at three levels of increasing concreteness.

First of all, there is Habermas's critique of Marxism. The fundamental weakness of Marx's 'praxis philosophy', according to Habermas, is that it remains within the problematic of 'the philosophy of consciousness': 'praxis philosophy, which accords privileged status to the relationship between the acting subject and manipulable wordly objects, conceives the self-formative process of the species (on the model of self-externalization) as a process of self-creation. For it, not self-consciousness but labour counts as the principle of modernity.' Humanity is conceived as a macro-subject acting on and transforming its environment in order to meet its needs. The form of action involved is therefore instrumental, governed by a purposive rationality which is oriented on the most efficient attainment of pregiven ends. This 'production paradigm' suffers as a theory of society from certain inherent defects, Habermas argues: first, it cannot explain how 'the paradigmatic activity-type of labour is related to all the other cultural forms of expression'; secondly, it is equally unable to tell us 'whether any normative activity at all can still be derived from the metabolic interaction between society and nature'; thirdly, identifying practice with production limits the explanatory reach of Marxist social theory given 'the historically foreseeable end of a society based upon labour'. The theory of communicative action incorporates those aspects of Marxism that are of lasting value – in particular, a conception of history as an evolutionary learning process, and an insight into the selective nature of capitalist rationalization – into a philosophical framework whose conception of social action is dialogic rather than monologic.[65]

This argument derives its plausibility from a contrast between production conceived as instrumental action and normatively regulated social interaction. Thus Habermas says that 'practice in the sense of norm-governed interaction cannot be analysed on the model of the productive expenditure of labour-power and the consumption of use-values.'[66] This opposition between labour and interaction long predates Habermas's elaboration of the theory of communicative action – it is central to his writings of the 1960s. But does it accurately represent Marx's own theory? There are strong reasons for doubting this. In the first place, Marx's philosophical anthropology, developed in the *Economic and Philosophic Manuscripts of 1844* and *The German Ideology*, does not simply treat labour as a monologic relationship between society and nature. Central to the theory of alienated labour elaborated in the *Manuscripts* is the distortion of social relationships involved, while Marx, in criticizing the subjective idealism of the Young Hegelians, argues for the social character of language and thought – an idea taken much further by Mikhail Bakhtin and his co-thinkers in the 1920s in their attempt to formulate a systematic philosophy of language based on the dialogic nature of speech.[67] This is not to say that Marx's anthropology is unproblematic: criticism has recently been directed at his model of self-realization as the full use of the person's essential powers, and the place of ethics in historical materialism has also been the subject of much controversy.[68] Nevertheless, it is hard to see how Habermas can offer satisfactory answers to the questions raised by these discussions, since his ethereal conception of rationality abstracts from the bodily character of human existence – which any anthropology oriented on achieving an emancipated society must confront – and issues in a neo-Kantian metaethics which privileges norms and duties at the expense of other, arguably more important forms of ethical life such as the virtues.[69]

Secondly, is the opposition between instrumental labour and norm-governed interaction an exhaustive or adequate one from the point of view of explanatory social theory? It is plain that Marx thought not. He distinguished between the forces and relations of production, between the technically determined labour-process through which use-values are produced and the relations of effective control over the means of production and labour-power on the basis of which exploitation and class struggle develop (see section 2.1 above). The relations of production are reducible *neither* to the instrumental action which we can more or less plausibly see as occurring in the labour-process, *nor* to norm-governed social interaction whose implicit telos is consensus; rather they constitute a sphere of assymetrical power-relations, unequal distribution of wealth and income, antagonistic class interests, and irreconcilable social struggle.[70] Habermas's 'reconstruction' of historical materialism effectively writes the relations of production out of the picture. They are subordinated to the consensual structures of social integration: 'The institutional core around which the relations of production crystallize lays down a specific form of social integration. By *social integration* I understand, with Durkheim, securing the unity of a social lifeworld through systems and norms.'[71] The distinction between system and lifeworld takes over from that between the forces and relations of production, with the latter now equated with the autonomous normative structures of law and morality.

But since the differentiation of system and lifeworld is a *product* of capitalist modernization, and in particular of the rationalization of the lifeworld, how are we to explain this historical process? Habermas does at times toy with classical Marxism, telling us that the 'impulses toward a differentiation of the social system emanate from the domain of material reproduction.'[72] Elaborating on this argument would, however, require according the relations of production a specificity and explanatory autonomy that are largely missing from Habermas's social theory. In the absence of a materialist account of the mechanisms of social change, he slides towards a strange kind of idealism in which the stages of development of the individual person are assimilated to those of humanity. Habermas speaks of 'the homologous structures of consciousness in the histories of the individual and the species': both involve 'learning processes' in which the individual or collective subject gradually evolves more advanced forms of moral consciousness culminating in 'a universal ethics of speech' where norms are justified argumentatively.[73] It is not surprising, therefore, to find Habermas, despite his criticisms of 'praxis philosophy', coming dangerously close to reinstating a kind of social macro-subject when he argues that 'even modern, largely decentred societies maintain in their everyday communicative action a virtual centre of self-understanding' and 'a diffuse common consciousness'.[74] History becomes, in the absence of any account of the antagonisms which give rise to exploitation and class struggle, the process through which the aspiration towards rationally founded consensus implicit in every speech act becomes ever more explicitly articulated in normative structures and moral consciousness.

At a second and more concrete level, Habermas's consensual conception of the social leads him to exaggerate the extent to which late capitalism has overcome the kind of economic contradictions analysed by Marx in *Capital*. He argues that 'Marxian orthodoxy has a hard time explaining government interventionism, mass democracy, and the welfare state.' The three are connected:

> Welfare-state mass democracy is an arrangement that renders the
> class antagonism built into the system innocuous, under the
> condition, however, that the capitalist dynamics of growth, pro-
> tected by measures of state intervention, do not grow weak. Only
> then is a mass of compensation available that can be distributed
> according to implicitly agreed upon criteria, in ritualized confronta-
> tions, and channelled into the roles of consumer and client in such a
> way that the structures of alienated labour and alienated political
> participation develop no explosive power.[75]

Under late, 'organized' capitalism political control of the economy
secures, thanks to Keynesian techniques of demand management,
class peace, albeit at the price of displacing these contradictions onto
other spheres.

I shall have much more to say about contemporary capitalism in
chapter 5. Suffice it to say here that Habermas's analysis suffers from
two fundamental weaknesses. The first is that it leaves out of account
the return since the late 1960s of the classic cycle of boom and slump,
involving two major global recessions, in 1974–5 and 1979–82.
Moreover, while it is open to argument how far capitalism has over
the last couple of decades returned to a condition of 'disorganization',
it is clear that the ability of the nation-state to manage economic
activity within its borders has been very significantly reduced. These
developments makes it very hard to sustain the idea that of 'repoliti-
cization' of the relations of production has bought a large measure of
economic stability at the expense of the cultural reproduction of the
system. However precisely we characterize them, the internal contradictions of the capitalist mode of production still have an effectivity
which no measure of control by individual states has been able to
overcome. Secondly, Habermas's account of the 'legitimation crisis'
which he claims has supplanted the classical form of capitalist crisis
focuses on the destabilizing effects of changes which have, he believes,
undermined the masses' normative integration into the existing order.
But it is at least arguable that social stability depends not on the
subordinate classes' belief in the legitimacy of the status quo but on a
fragmentation of social consciousness which prevents them from
developing a comprehensive perspective on society as a whole.[76]

These specific criticisms aside, what is interesting is the direction of
Habermas's argument: the explanatory weight is taken by the development of normative structures – which make possible the political control of the economy – or their internal dysfunctions – which
produce legitimation crises. The same emphasis is to be found when
we consider, at a still more concrete level, Habermas's views on
democracy. The institutions of parliamentary democracy represent

for him a mechanism for the consensual regulation of social life. 'The normative meaning of democracy can be rendered in social-theoretical terms by the formula that the fulfilment of the functional necessities of *systematically* integrated domains of action shall find its limits in the integrity of the lifeworld, that is to say, in the require-ments of domains of action dependent on *social* integration.'[77] Democratic forms are therefore necessarily in conflict with capitalism, which is governed by the imperative of system-integration regulated by the market.

Given this conception of liberal democracy (Habermas is careful to distance himself from calls for 'so-called direct democracy'),[78] it is not surprising that Habermas should set himself in opposition to its critics from both left and right. Indeed, he sees a close kinship between the two, denouncing 'those left-wingers in the Federal Republic, and today above all in Italy, who drive out the Devil with Beelzebub, by filling the gap left by the non-existent Marxist theory of democracy with [Carl] Schmitt's fascist critique of democracy'.[79] The polemic against Schmitt from which this passage is drawn is a bravura piece of writing, in which Habermas's passions seem directly engaged. And it is easy enough to see why this might be so. Schmitt belongs, as Habermas observes, to the *galère* of conservative thinkers – others were Heidegger, Gottfried Benn, Ernst Jünger – who explicitly lashed the swastika to the mast of the Counter-Enlightenment, welcoming the Hitler regime as the realization of their critique of modernity.[80] But more than that – Schmitt's system of ideas does make him a kind of diabolic other, a Mephistophelean mirror-image of Habermas. Counterposed to Habermas's universalism and rationalism, is Schmitt's decisionism: 'Sovereign is he who decides the exception' – the locus of political power lies with the agency which responds to a moment of extreme peril to the state with a creative intervention springing *ex nihilo*, irreducible to any general principle.[81] Corres-ponding to this theory of sovereignty is a conception of the political as 'the most intense and extreme antagonism', founded in the relationship of friend and enemy which reflects the permanent possibility of war inherent in social life and which finds its highest expression in the world system of rival nation-states – a view quite antithetical to Habermas's consensual conception of the social.[82] Finally, Schmitt treats discussion, for Habermas a necessary feature of rationality, as distinctive to the liberal bourgeoisie, which 'shares the class characteristic of wanting to evade the decision. A class that shifts all political activity onto the play of conversation in the press and in the parliament is no match for social conflict.'[83]

Schmitt indeed sees discussion – 'an exchange of opinion that is governed by the purpose of persuading one's opponent through argument of the truth or justice of something or allowing oneself to be persuaded of something as true and just' – as the essence of parliamentary government. But this form of political rule emerged in the period of liberal constitutionalism prior to the progressive introduction of universal suffrage in the second half of the nineteenth century. It was only in these circumstances, where parliamentary discussion occurs within a restricted bourgeois elite, that 'laws arise out of a conflict of opinions (not out of a struggle of interests).' However,

> [t]he situation of modern parliamentarism is critical today because the development of modern mass democracy has made argumentative public discussion a formality. Many norms of contemporary parliamentary law, above all provisions concerning the independence of representatives and the openness of sessions, function as a result like a superfluous decoration, useless and even embarrassing, as if someone had painted the radiator of a modern central heating system with red flames in order to give the appearance of a blazing fire. The parties ... do not face each other today discussing opinions, but as social and economic power-groups calculating their mutual interests and opportunities for power, and they actually agree compromises and coalitions on this basis. The masses are won over through a propaganda apparatus whose maximum effect relies on an appeal to immediate interests and passions. Argument in the real sense that is characteristic for genuine discussion ceases.[84]

These lines, published in 1926, describe the Weimar republic, but who can deny their applicability to contemporary liberal democracy? I certainly will not, writing under Mrs Thatcher's third term of government, and shortly after the farce of the 1988 presidential election in the United States, governed as it was by the thirty-second sound-bite and smart knocking copy. Habermas is able easily to dismiss Schmitt's solution to the crisis of liberal democracy, which consists in ditching parliamentary institutions and civil liberties and putting in their place 'a Caesarist and racially homogeneous *Führerdemokratie*', and he rightly argues that '[t]he medium of discussion that is public and guided by argument . . . is in fact essential to for any democratic justification of political authority.'[85] But can he deny the accuracy of Schmitt's diagnosis of the condition of contemporary liberal democracy? Indeed, he says that 'the tendency to disintegration of a public sphere of the liberal type – a formation of opinion in discursive style mediated by reading, reasoning, information – have intensified since the late fifties. The mode of functioning of electronic media testifies to this, above all the centralization of organizations which privilege vertical and one-way flows of second- and third-hand information, privately consumed.' Having first identified this tendency in *Strukturwandel der Öffentlichkeit* (1962), Habermas now speaks of the 'really existing surrealism' of life under late capitalism.[86]

Of course, to recognize the evacuation of liberal democratic institutions of much of their political content is not to advocate their abolition by the extreme right. Despite Habermas's sarcastic reference to the 'nonexistent Marxist theory of democracy', the classical revolutionary socialist tradition – Marx and Engels, Lenin and Trotsky, Luxemburg and Gramsci – always rejected the idea that Marxists should be indifferent to reactionary attacks on the rights and institutions of liberal democracy. (The infantile leftist stance of refusing to defend bourgeois democracy against the right has, however, strong roots in Germany – in the council communism of Pannekoek and Görter, in third-period Stalinism, and in the romantic Maoism which flourished after 1968 – which may help to explain why Habermas tends to 'bend the stick' in the opposite direction.) But the classical Marxists also insisted on tracing the class roots of liberal democracy, which set limits to the possibilities of mass participation, and on setting the goal of a higher form of democracy in which representation would be based on collective organization at work and in the community rather than on an atomized and passive electorate. The danger with Habermas's defence of liberal democracy against the neo-conservatives is that it can lead him close to an apologetic position: thus in his intervention in the *Historikerstreit* over the uniqueness of the Nazi Holocaust he tends so strongly to stress the democratic virtues of the *Bundesrepublik* as to play down such infringements of civil liberties as the *Berufsverbot* and the constitutional ban on 'extremist' parties, and to treat its integration into the Western political order as a necessary break with the authoritarian past.[87]

Habermas's view on democracy illustrate his more general tendency to autonomize normative structures, to treat society as 'a *moral reality*'.[88] There is obviously considerable scope for serious and illuminating disagreement about the extent to which a more advanced form of democracy than that presently existing is feasible. But such discussion would require probing and historically informed enquiry into the social conditions of specific modes of political rule.[89] Enquiry of this sort is likely to proceed more fruitfully within the framework of classical historical materialism than on the basis of Habermas's 'reconstruction', where the development of forms of social integration rather than the interaction of technological development and class struggle becomes 'the pacemaker of social evolution'. As Anthony Giddens – himself hardly an uncritical admirer of Marxism – complained of *The Theory of Communicative Action*: 'Too much Weber! Too little Marx!'[90] The point can be made more generally about Habermas's diagnosis of modernity. To put it in the terms Marx used when discussing the conflict between the bourgeois defenders and Romantic opponents of capitalism (see section 2.1 above): Habermas in rightly rejecting the critique of Enlightenment developed by Nietzsche and his successors, which opens the door to the imposed return of a fictive 'original fullness' – the project of Heidegger, Schmitt et al. in their Nazi period, tends to fall into an equally one-sided exaggeration of the extent to which modernity has already realized the Enlightenment project. Marx celebrated capitalism both because it immeasurably developed human powers and because it created the class which would achieve 'its blessed end'. Along that path – I argue in the following and final chapter – lies the true radicalization of the Enlightenment.[91]

# 5
# SO WHAT ELSE IS NEW?

The 19th Century is not yet over.
*Richard Sennett*

## 5.1 THE MYTHS OF POSTINDUSTRIALISM

The idea of postindustrial society is, of course, nonsense. As formulated by Daniel Bell, for example, the concept denotes the latest stage in a progression: from traditional to industrial and now to postindustrial society. Each stage is differentiated by what might be thought of as a (rather crude) version of what Marx called the productive forces: traditional society is based on agriculture, and industrial, surprisingly enough, on modern manufacturing industry involving the scientific control of nature and the use of artificial energy sources. Postindustrial society is characterized by the shift from goods production to a service economy, and by the central role played by theoretical knowledge as the source of both technical innovation and policy formulation. Changes in social structure are then read off these technological changes. Postindustrial society is a 'knowledge society', dominated increasingly by a university-trained professional and technical elite. The big corporations are shifting from an 'economizing mode' of activity, 'in which all aspects of organization are single-mindedly reduced to becoming means to the goals of production and profit' to a 'socializing mode', one 'in which all workers are guaranteed lifetime jobs, and the satisfaction of the workforce becomes the primary levy on resources'. Consequently, Bell argues, 'today, we in America are moving away from a society based on a private enterprise market system toward one in which the most important economic decisions will be made at the political level, in terms of consciously defined "goals" and "practices"'.[1]

It is easy enough to pour scorn on such announcements of the death of capitalism, which reflect the circumstances of their initial formulation, during the long economic boom of the 1950s and 1960s.[2] It is indeed hard to take seriously the alleged shift from 'economizing' to 'sociologizing' modes in the wake of the holocaust of manufacturing jobs at the end of the 1970s and the great bull market of the mid-1980s, in the era of concessions and leveraged buyouts, of privatization and greenmail, of Ivan Boesky and Gordon Gecko. Bell's argument was very much a development of the orthodoxy among English-speaking social scientists in the immediate postwar period, whose main themes were the separation of ownership from control, the consequent rise of a managerial technocracy, the fragmentation of social classes into clusters of overlapping interest groups, and – another of Bell's bright ideas – the 'end of ideology', of polarized politics whose stake was the global transformation of society. The formulation of the concept of postindustrial society can perhaps be best seen as an attempt – undergirded by a technological determinism which would make the most vulgar Marxist blench – both to give some coherence to these themes and to provide them with an economic rationale.

Commentators were quick to point out the misinterpretation of economic trends committed by theorists of postindustrial society.[3] The rise in the proportion of output and employment taken by services which is indeed one of the major secular changes in twentieth-century capitalism has taken place primarily at the expense of agriculture rather than manufacturing industry. Employment in manufacturing has in any case never accounted for a majority of the workforce: the all-time peak was achieved briefly by Britain in 1955, when industry accounted for 48 per cent of employment.[4] The period since the early 1970s has seen a more pronounced shift away from manufacturing and towards services in the Western economies, but this trend requires far more careful analysis than it has been given by those left intellectuals who eagerly seized on them to announce the disappearance of the industrial proletariat, a response summed up by André Gorz's book *Farewell to the Working Class*.[5]

In the first place, this process of 'deindustrialization' typically involved in a fall in the share of employment and output accounted for by manufacturing. In other words, it was primarily a *relative* change – typically industry's share of the workforce fell rather than the absolute number of industrial employees. The sectoral shift from manufacturing to services may in large part be accounted for by rapid rises in the productivity of labour in manufacturing industry, which meant that a smaller proportion of the workforce can produce a considerably larger quantity of goods; productivity growth in services is by comparison notoriously sluggish – in the United States between 1970 and 1984 it rose by only 0.8 per cent per annum in commercial banking, and actually fell at an annual rate of 0.4 per cent in eating and drinking places.[6] It is perhaps significant that manufacturing's share of output has generally fallen less sharply than its share of employment: thus in the United States manufacturing declined from 25.8 per cent of employment in 1964 to 19.6 per cent in 1982; its share of GDP volume, however, experienced a much less pronounced fall, from 24.8 per cent in 1964 to 22.8 per cent. Taken together, these figures suggest a considerable rise in manufacturing productivity. Even the sectoral shift from manufacturing to services is not universal. Japan, the most successful postwar economy, experienced between 1964 and 1982 a *fall* in services' share of GDP volume, from 51.7 to 48.8 per cent, and a *rise* in manufacturing's share, from 24.1 to 39.9 per cent. The Japanese case indeed refutes the commonly held theory that the decline of manufacturing relative to services is a consequence of economic 'maturity' and rising per capita income. Japanese per capita income is considerably higher than British, but services take up a larger share (55.6 per cent in 1982) and service manufacturing a much smaller share (24.9 per cent) of GDP volume in the United Kingdom.[7]

There are in any case good reasons for doubting that there is any necessary tendency for services to supplant manufacturing. The rise of white-goods industries, for example, involved the substitution of goods for services – of domestic appliances such as vacuum cleaners and washing machines, produced by factory labour and distributed through the market, for services provided within households either by unpaid female labour or by domestic servants. Similarly, the general trend away from public transport to the private motor car means that personal transportation is secured by the purchase of a good rather than a service. Finally, the transformation of mass entertainment in the twentieth century has involved the progressive replacement of services provided by cinemas, music halls and the like, with consumer durables – gramophones, television sets, video-recorders etc. Michael Prowse argues that slow productivity growth in services means that 'the relative price of directly supplied services rises relative to that of goods, encouraging the purchase of manufactured goods' and thereby providing 'a continual incentive for entrepreneurs to manufacture goods which can substitute for previously purchased services'. He suggests that 'the principal reason why the share of services may have risen is that the manufacturing industries in some Western countries have grown moribund and are no longer performing their long-run function of producing tangible goods to substitute for directly purchased services.'[8] It is the uncompetitiveness of their manufacturing industries which, Prowse believes, explains the relatively rapid deindustrialization of Britain and the US. The complacency with which the Thatcher and Reagan administrations greeted the decline of manufacturing as part of what they depicted as the historically inevitable transition to a services economy attracted sharp criticism from more thoughtful commentators such as Prowse concerned about the future prospects of British and American capitalism.[9]

The social consequences of the (usually only relative) decline of manufacturing employment have not been those anticipated by Bell. The increasing proportion of the workforce classified as white-collar employees is often confused with, but is of course not equivalent to the expansion of service industries – the latter employ hospital cleaners and waiters as well as bank clerks and stockbrokers, while draughtspeople and typists, as well as machine-minders and labourers, work in factories. In any case, white-collar employment embraces at least three distinct class positions – 'managerial capitalists' who are, in effect, salaried members of the bourgeoisie, the 'new middle class' of upper-echelon professional, managerial and administrative employees, and routine white-collar workers whose insecurity, relatively low earnings, and lack of job control place them in the same fundamental position as manual workers.[10] Employment in the service industries proper hardly matches the profile of the 'knowledge-society' elite portrayed by Bell. Average gross weekly earnings in US manufacturing were $396 in 1986, in services $275. The Reagan administration made much of the fact that the 20 fastest growing occupations in the 1980s were almost all involved in 'the handling of information' – a motley crew of computer programmers, analysts and operators, data-processing-machine operators and mechanics, travel agents, astronautical engineers, psychiatric aides, and paralegal aides. Altogether, however, this group was smaller than the growth in fast-food workers. 22 per cent of the 17.1 million nongovernment service jobs created in the US between 1972 and 1984 was accounted for restaurants and retail trade, a sector where hourly earnings were 38 per cent below those in manufacturing.[11]

'Deindustrialization' has been a painful process, with socially regressive results. Nowhere is this better illustrated than in California, the paradigmatic 'postindustrial society', strategically located on the Eastern edge of the dynamic Pacific economy, with 70 per cent of its workforce employed in services in 1985, ideally suited, thanks to Hollywood and Silicon Valley, to supply the world market with entertainments and information.[12] The 1979–82 recession virtually wiped out the state's car, steel, tyre and other basic industries. High unemployment combined with an influx of (often illegal) immigrants to push down wages. Labour-intensive low-wage industries consequently expanded, in manufacturing as well as services. Employment in textiles, where California can now compete with Hong Kong and Taiwan, grew. As Mike Davis commented, 'LA industry has been turned back from "Fordism" to "Bloody Taylorism" of an almost East Asian standard.'[13] A similar pattern can be observed in service industries, whose wages are on average 40 to 50 per cent lower than in basic manufacturing. Consequently, despite California's fabled wealth and dynamic growth rates, the state's per capita income fell from 123 per cent of the US average in 1960 to 116 per cent in 1980 and 113 per cent in 1984. In Philip Stephens's words, '[t]he benefits of growth have been enjoyed most by the entrepreneurs in Silicon Valley and by the small proportion of the population with large property and financial assets.'[14]

The revival of nineteenth-century sweated trades in the richest cities on earth is part of a broader set of changes one of whose most important features – usually ignored by the parochial theorists of 'postindustrial society' – is the rise of the newly industrializing countries in the Third World.[15] One major consequence of the emergence of new centres of capital accumulation – and manufacturing production – has been the considerable *growth* of the industrial working class on a global scale. Paul Kellogg writes:

> Employment in manufacturing grew by 65 per cent in Turkey between 1960 and 1982, 179 per cent in Egypt between 1958 and 1981, 623 per cent in Tanzania between 1953 and 1981, 57 per cent in Zimbabwe ... 1970–80, 212 per cent in Brazil 1970–82, 34 per cent in Peru 1971-1981 and an astonishing 2,500 per cent in South Korea between 1956 and 1982! On a world scale, this has meant in the 11 years between 1971 and 1982, a 14.1 per cent rise in industrial employment. It is true that in this period 'developed market economies' (North America and Western Europe in particular) experienced an industrial employment decline of 6½ per cent. But 'developing market economies' shot up by 58 per cent, and 'centrally planned economies' by 16 per cent to more than make up the difference ... On a world scale there are more industrial workers than at any time in history ... The industrial working class in the 36 leading industrial countries ... , between 1977 and 1982, increased its numbers from 173 to 183 million. This understates the picture considerably because 1982 was the worst year of the worst recession in the post-war era, a recession that saw *millions* of industrial layoffs in the West.[16]

I discuss how best to interpret these changes in section 5.3 below. What is certain is that detecting in them the rise of postindustrial society is the wrong way. Nevertheless, contemporary theorists – Habermas as well as his postmodernist foes – have been all too eager to announce the 'obsolescence of the production paradigm', by which they mean Marxism. It is hard to take seriously much of what is written on this subject. Craig Owens probably wins first prize for the silliest argument. He says that 'Marxism privileges the characteristically masculine activity of production as the *definitively human* activity ... women, historically consigned to the spheres of non-productive or reproductive labour, are thereby situated outside the society of male producers, in a state of nature.'[17] The adverb 'historically' is especially delightful, since, of course, women's labour played a central productive role in the peasant households that were typically the basic economic unit of precapitalist agricultural societies.[18] The transformation of the household from a unit of production to a unit primarily of consumption where female domestic labour is devoted chiefly to the reproduction of labour-power is a historical novelty peculiar to industrial capitalism. It naturally does not follow that women are confined under capitalism to this reproductive role: one of the most important contemporary employment trends in the advanced economies is the progressive incorporation of women into wage-labour.[19]

Baudrillard is less ignorant than Owens, but he makes a similar kind of criticism of Marxism, accusing it of ethnocentrism and indeed 'theoretical racism' for projecting the categories specific to industrial capitalism on to 'primitive' societies, where production 'is continually negated and volatilized by reciprocal exchange which consumed itself in an endless operation'.[20] But historical materialism is not (as Baudrillard seems to believe) committed to claiming that each social formation has as its overriding motive production for production's sake; Marx indeed saw this as a peculiar feature of capitalism. All historical materialism asserts is that even preclass societies which engage in redistributive practices such as generalized reciprocity which are not in any but the most formal sense governed by the desire to maximize utilities must find some way of securing their material reproduction, and that the combination of productive forces and relations will shape each society in ways that the actors do not recognize. When confronted by Baudrillard's apparent denial that 'primitive' societies are subject to material constraints one is tempted to agree with Perry Anderson that 'classical Marxism' is 'a kind of common sense'.[21]

Habermas is, of course, in a different league from postmodernist *littérateurs* like Owens and Baudrillard. But he too sees the 'production paradigm' as increasingly inapplicable to contemporary society.

For example, he speaks of 'the historically forseeable end of a society based on labour'.[22] He seems to have in mind here what he regards as the declining importance of manual goods-producing labour. But, as we have seen, the contraction of manufacturing employment in the advanced economies has been exaggerated, and is counterbalanced by the expansion of the industrial working class on a global scale. It does seem in any case rather narrow to identify work with industrial labour. Despite the long dole queues of the 1970s and 1980s, usually some nine tenths of the population of working age in the Western economies are in some kind of employment, in most cases as wage-earners. The fact that manual industrial workers no longer form the majority of wage-labourers does not of itself imply the beginning of the end of the 'work-based society'. Wage-labour has if anything become a more pervasive feature of social experience in the past half century, with the decline of peasant agriculture and the growing involvement of women in the labour-market. The fact that much of this labour now involves interacting with other people rather than producing goods does not change the social relations involved: one striking feature of contemporary industrial relations is the spread of trade unionism to the 'caring professions' (health, teaching, social work, etc.) – 1988 saw major industrial disputes involving nurses in both Britain and France. The fact that fewer people are employed in material production does not in any case alter the fact that no one can survive without the industrial goods manufactured by these people. Not only do human beings continue to have the same mundane needs for food, clothing, shelter and the like, but rising living standards and the associated expansion of mass consumption entail a *proliferation* of material goods, particularly given the tendency noted above for services to be replaced with consumer durables. The enormous expansion of human productive powers which has taken place under capitalism makes possible a drastic reduction in the working day, and in that sense an abolition of the 'work-based society'. But that possibility could only become a reality as a result of the overthrow of capitalist social relations, which still depend on the exploitation of wage-labour. And even the socialist society which emerged from such a transformation would still rest on what Marx called 'the kingdom of necessity', upon the material production of the physical use-values without which human existence would cease. It is a measure of current intellectual disarray that as cogent a thinker as Habermas should lose sight of such fundamental realities.

## 5.2   THE SPECTRE OF HEGEL: JAMESON ON POSTMODERNISM

Belief in the existence of a postmodern era does not necessarily depend upon the bankrupt idea of postindustrial society. A number of Marxist – or at least *marxisant* – writers have related what they see as the emergence of postmodern culture to changes within the capitalist mode of production. The most important defender of this view is Frederic Jameson, who argues that 'to grant some historical original-ity to a postmodernist culture is also implicitly to affirm some radical structural difference between what is sometimes called consumer society and earlier moments of the capitalism from which it emerged.'[23] Jameson had already begun to develop such an analysis in his brilliant discussion of Surrealism in *Marxism and Form*, first published in 1971. The Surrealists' 'profane illuminations', their discovery of unconscious psychic investments almost magically pre-sent in everyday objects, reflected, he argued, 'a not yet fully industrialized and systematized economy' where 'the human origins of the products of this period – their relationship to the work from which they issued – have not yet been fully concealed; in their production they still show traces of an artisanal organization of labour while their distribution is still predominantly assured by a network of small shopkeepers.' Today, by contrast,

> in what we may call postindustrial capitalism, the products with which we are furnished are utterly without depth: their plastic content is totally incapable of serving as a conductor of psychic energy . . . All libidinal investment in such objects is precluded from the outset, and we may ask ourselves, if it is true that our object universe is henceforth unable to yield any 'symbol apt at stirring human sensibility' [Breton], whether we are not here at the presence of a cultural transformation of signal proportions, a historical break of an unexpectedly absolute kind.[24]

This passage contains *in nuce* Jameson's more recent analysis of the 'cultural logic of late capitalism'. Postmodernism has become, he argues, a 'cultural dominant'. Art produced under its reign is char-acterized by a peculiar depthlessness, a draining away of any emo-tional content; instead, it celebrates the disintegration of the subject and offers mere pastiches of a historical past nostalgically reduced either to a lost world of political commitment or to a source of glossy retro-style images; the strange exhilaration Postmodern art induces is an instance of the 'hysterical sublime', of the excitement and terror with which we respond to the realization that the workings of the global economic system can no longer be represented or imagined. In all these respects, however, Postmodernism mirrors the nature of that system. '[T]here have been three fundamental moments of capitalism . . . market capitalism, the monopoly stage or the stage of imperialism, and our own – wrongly called postindustrial, but what might be better called multinational.' To each stage corresponds a particular technology – steam (market), electricity and automobiles (monopoly), computers and nuclear power (multinational) – and also a 'cultural dominant' – Realism in the case of market capitalism, Modernism in the case of imperialism. 'Postmodernism corresponds to the third phase, 'late or multinational or consumer capitalism, . . . the purest form of capitalism yet to have emerged, a prodigious expansion of capital into hitherto uncommodified areas . . . one is tempted to speak in this connection of a new and historically original penetration and colonization of Nature and the Unconscious: that is, the destruction of precapitalist third world agriculture by the Green Revolution, and the rise of the media and the advertising industry.'[25]

Jameson's attempt thus historically to contextualize Postmodernism is brilliantly and imaginatively executed. He displays the mark of the genuine cultural critic in moving with breathtaking facility from theoretical generalities to specific cases, above all in his celebrated use of the baroque interior of the Bonaventure Hotel in Los Angeles to illustrate the way in which 'postmodern hyperspace . . . has finally succeeded in transcending the capacities of the individual human body to locate itself, to organize its immediate surroundings perceptually, and cognitively to map its position in a mappable external world.' But Jameson's skilful interweaving of universal and particular has a definite political point. He wishes to avoid passing moral judgement – whether positive or negative – on Postmodernism. Readily dismissing 'the complacent (yet delirious) camp-following celebration of this aesthetic new world (including its social and economic dimension, greeted with equal enthusiasm under the slogan of "post-industrial society")', Jameson nevertheless insists that 'if postmodernism is a historical phenomenon, then the attempt to conceptualize it in terms of moral or moralizing judgements must finally be identified as a category-mistake.' Postmodern art cannot be simply dismissed as mystificatory but must also 'be read as peculiar new forms of realism (or at least of the mimesis of reality)'. This response is the only one consistent with Marx's approach to capitalism in the *Communist Manifesto*, 'a type of thinking . . . capable of grasping the demonstrably baleful features of capitalism along with its extraordinary and liberating dynamism simultaneously, within a single thought, and without attenuating the force of either judgement. We are, somehow, to lift our minds to a point at which it is possible to understand that capitalism is at one and the same time the best thing that has ever happened to the human race, and the worst.'[26]

Jamesons's general stance is plainly in line with Marx's perspective on capitalism (see section 2.1 above), and therefore with the argument developed throughout this book. It is also easy enough to sympathize with his desire to avoid the kind of elitist denunciation of new cultural forms which so disfigures Lukács's writings on Modernism. Jameson's attitude to Postmodernism recalls rather the 'Brechtian maxim' quoted by Benjamin: 'Don't start with the good old things but the bad new ones.'[27] Instead of nostalgically hanging on the exhausted forms of Modernism, Jameson suggests, we should be exploring the critical potential inherent in Postmodernism. He is, in fact, rather parsimonious about illustrating the subversive possibilities of new forms, but this is not where the main difficulty lies. It is, rather, methodological.

Jameson is the most distinguished contemporary practitioner of Hegelian Marxism. For him Marxism is distinguished above all by 'an imperative to totalize', to conceptualize the various fragments of social life as aspects of a comprehensive and integrated set of relationships. The difference between Jameson and Lukács, whose *History and Class Consciousness* is the most important attempt to identify the Marxist method with the concept of totality, is twofold. First, Jameson conceives the social totality not as an entity that can in any sense be directly experienced but as 'an absent cause, ... inaccessible to us except in textual form'. History, 'conceived in its vastest sense of the sequence of modes of production and the succession and destiny of the various human social formations', acts as the 'final horizon' of all textual analysis, but its theoretical function is primarily that of providing the basis for criticism of the partial and limited character of narratives which do not take it into account. 'This negative and methodological status of the concept of "totality"' means that 'Marxism subsumes other interpretive modes of systems', making use of poststructuralism, for example, as Jameson himself does in his study of Wyndham Lewis (see section 1.3 above), but at the same time pressing them beyond their limits, incorporating them within a broader totalization. Second, whereas *History and Class Consciousness* conceptualizes mediations between different social practices in terms of the homologies they display, Jameson follows Althusser, Lukács's most important Marxist critic, whose structural conception of the social totality 'insists on the interrelatedness of all elements in a social formation, only it relates them by way of their structural *difference* and distance from one another, rather than by their ultimate identity ... Difference is then here understood as a relational concept, rather than as the mere inert inventory of unrelated diversity.' Thus, '[t]he current poststructuralist celebration of discontinuity and heterogeneity is ... only an initial moment in the Althusserian exegesis, which then requires the fragments, the incommensurable levels, the heterogeneous impulses of the text to be once again related, but in the mode of structural difference and determinate contradiction.'[28] Jameson's conception of totality is thus rather like the *deus absconditus* of the scholastics and mystics, present only in its absence. This *démarche* involves pressing into the service of the Lukácian tradition Althusser's critique of the Hegelian 'expressive totality, i.e., a totality of all whose parts are so many *"total parts"*, each expressing the others, and each expressing the social totality which contains them, because each in itself contains in the immediate form of its expression the essence of the totality itself.'[29] If successful it would be a remarkable feat, since Althusser regarded Lukács's analysis of reification in *History and Class Consciousness* as a prime example of such a totality, which reduced different social practices to expressions of some essence whose structure they share.[30] But it is not clear whether Jamesons's synthesis of Lukács and Althusser works, at least with respect to Postmodernism. One has the impression, rather, that Jameson's attempt to relate a distinctively Postmodern art to a new 'multinational' phase in capitalist development is precisely an example of the kind of mistake Althusser sought to diagnose in his critique of expressive totality.[31] Thus, Jameson tells us that the 'mode of contemporary entertainment literature' which he calls '"high tech paranoia"', in which the circuits and networks of some putative global computer hook-up are narratively mobilized by labyrinthine conspiracies of autonomous but deadly interlocking and competing information agencies in a complexity often beyond the capacity of the normal mind', is 'a degraded attempt to think the impossible totality of the contemporary world system', 'the whole new decentred global network of the third stage of capital'.[32] This looks a lot more like a relationship of homology than one of structural difference. More generally, Jameson's discussion of Postmodern art, despite its many felicities, does tend to involve forcing into a single mould a diversity of cultural phenomena which do not obviously belong together: his treatment of 'nostalgia film' is a case in point.[33]

The upshot of this criticism is not that Jameson is wrong to insist on the necessity of totalization. He points out that poststructuralist celebrations of fragmentation and difference 'must be accompanied by some initial appearance of continuity, some ideology of unification already in place, which it is their mission to rebuke and to shatter'.[34] One could indeed argue, as I do in section 3.4 above, that when, for example, Foucault develops his account of the 'disciplinary society' constituted by the 'apparatus' of 'power-knowledge', he is implicitly totalizing. Jameson is also right to highlight the bankruptcy of any political strategy which does not involve recognition of the *systemic* character of capitalism.[35] The trouble is that Jameson's tendency to reduce the diversity of social life to exemplars of a single essence runs the risk of giving totalization – or rather Marxist totalization, which, unlike poststructuralism, is explicit in its attempt to relate different practices as parts of the same whole – a bad name. Matters are not helped by his attempt to go beyond good and evil in his attitude towards postmodern capitalism. There is in fact no inconsistency between the scientific analysis and the ethical appraisal of a social phenomenon, and by suggesting otherwise Jameson is likely to merely to encourage the ascription to him of a Hegelian teleology in which progress is woven into the texture of history.[36] The importance in this context of Althusser's argument remains: evolutionism can be avoided by Marxism only on the basis of a complex conception of totality, one recognizes the 'differential temporality' of the various levels of the social formation, each having 'a *peculiar time*, relatively autonomous and hence relatively independent, even in its dependence, of the "times" of the other levels' so that the totality must be seen as the '*intertwining of the different times* ... , i.e., the type of "dislocation" (*décalage*) and torsion of the different temporalities produced by the different levels of structure, the complex combination of which constitutes the peculiar time of the process's development.'[37] Such a totality will be necessarily 'unrepresentable', knowable only by means of a complex articulation of theoretical concepts, rather than these being, as Jameson believes, features only of 'multinational capitalism'.[38]

## 5.3   A BREAK IN CAPITALISM?

Jameson's substantive thesis, that capitalism has undergone a fundamental change, does not of course founder simply because of the reductive way in which he conceptualizes the cultural consequences of this supposed change. In fact, however, his attempts to make out this thesis are not very well elaborated. In *Marxism and Form* it is 'postindustrial monopoly capitalism', dominant since the 1940s, and characterized in terms drawn from Paul Baran's and Paul Sweezy's

*Monopoly Capital*, which is responsible for the depthless, affectless
nature of cultural products.[39] By 1984, however, Jameson had come
to repudiate the notion of 'postindustrial society', to locate the
moment of change around 'the end of the 1950s or the early 1960s',
and to cite as his economic authority Ernest Mandel's *Late Capitalism*, which 'anatomize[s] the historical originality of this new society',
now described as 'multinational' capital, a stage beyond the monopoly era.[40] As Mike Davis points out, this new periodization conflicts
with that used by Mandel whose 'central purpose [in *Late Capitalism*]
is to understand "the long *postwar* wave of rapid growth"', and who
'regards the real break, the definite ending of the long wave, to be the
"second slump" of 1974–75 ... The difference between Jameson's
and Mandel's schemes is crucial: was Late Capitalism born *circa*
1945 or 1960? Are the Sixties the beginning of a new epoch, or
merely the superheated summit of the postwar boom? Where does the
slump fit into an accounting of contemporary cultural trends?'[41]

Jameson does not say enough about the nature of 'multinational
capitalism' to sustain much serious discussion of these questions. The
slippages in his analysis (from the late 1940s to the early 1960s, from
monopoly to multinational capital), and rather casual uses of economic sources suggest that his belief in 'a cultural transformation of
signal proportions, a historical break of an unexpectedly absolute
kind' is more an intuition informing his criticism than an inference
from the empirical investigation of the contemporary world economy.
There are, however, more sustained attempts to show that capitalism
has moved into a new phase whose cultural correlate is Postmodernism. Let us consider two of them.

Scott Lash and John Urry argue that Western societies are currently
undergoing a transition from 'organized' to 'disorganized' capitalism.
Organized capitalism (the expression was coined by Hilferding), as
consolidated at the beginning of the twentieth century, involved in
particular: the concentration and centralization of industrial, commercial and banking capital; the separation of ownership and control; the growth of the professional, managerial and administrative
'service class'; the corporatist regulation of the national economy by
the state, big capital and organized labour; the sectoral dominance of
manufacturing and extractive industry; the spatial concentration of
large-scale industry in urban centres acting as the focus of coherent
regional economies; a cultural life bisected by technological rationality and its opposites, notably Modernism and nationalism. The rise of
disorganized capitalism consists in the disintegration of the state-
regulated national economic spaces characteristic of the earlier phase.
The expansion of a world market dominated by multinational

corporations undermines the economic power of the nation state; the growth of industrial investment in the Third World contributes to the decline of manufacturing industry in the West; the effect, combined with the further growth of the 'service class', is to undermine the coherence and strength of the labour movement, contributing to the erosion of corporatist bargaining and the decline of class-based politics; a series of spatial changes, such as the ruralization of industry, promote the decline of the great metropolitan centres and the disintegration of regional economies; cultural life becomes more fragmented and pluralistic, a change reflected in the rise of Postmodernism.[42]

While Lash and Urry adopt an implicitly multicausal explanation of the changes they describe, others, while covering the same ground, have preferred to concentrate on the relationship between production and consumption. Writers associated with the British journal *Marxism Today* argue that contemporary capitalism is experiencing the rise of 'post-Fordism'. The master-concept here is that of 'Fordism', most fully developed by the French Marxist 'regulation school' (Michel Aglietta, Alain Lipietz, Michel de Vrooy et al.), although these theorists cannot be held responsible for the use to which their ideas have been put.[43] Fordism is to be understood in the first instance as a system of mass production involving the standardization of products; the large-scale use of dedicated machinery suitable only for a particular model; the Taylorist 'scientific management' of labour; and flowline assembly of products. The high fixed costs involved required guaranteed mass markets. Consequently Fordism is characterized, secondly, by the articulation of mass production and mass consumption: the use of advertising etc. to encourage consumers to purchase standardized products; the formation of protected national markets; and the intervention of the state, employing techniques such as Keynesian demand management and transfer payments, to prevent catastrophic falls in demand. The crisis of the late 1960s and the 1970s represented the collapse of Fordism. In its place a new variant of capitalism, called (originally enough) post-Fordism, is taking shape. Just as Fordism was created by producers such as its eponymous founder post-Fordism is consumption-led. Computer-based distribution systems allow retailers to avoid the overstocking that was one of the main problems of Fordism; it also makes it possible the targeting of products on specific groups of consumers. Post-Fordism has seen the disaggregation of the mass market into segmented niches, where design has become a major selling-point – commodities are no longer bought simply for the use-value they have put also for the lifestyle connoted by their design. These changes correspond to, within the sphere of production, the development of 'flexible specialization'. New technology – such as flexible manufacturing systems – no longer needs be dedicated to a particular model and can be adapted to a variety of different purposes. The growing use of computers to co-ordinate production also makes possible just-in-time stock-keeping, significantly reducing overheads. Plant size falls, and the role of labour changes. The new methods of production no longer require the mass of semi-skilled machine-minders of Fordism, but a smaller multi-skilled core workforce capable, through quality circles and the like, of participating actively in the labour-process; below this (white, male, highly paid) group lies the 'peripheral' workforce, low-paid, temporary, often part-time, drawn from oppressed groups (women, blacks, etc.), shading off into the underclass sustained by a pared-down welfare state. Post-Fordism therefore means an increase in income and freedom for some, a decrease for others.[44]

The authors of these analyses of contemporary capitalism are typically guilty of a reductionism as ferocious as Jameson's but lack his ability to provide nuanced, precise and eloquent explorations of specific cultural phenomena. To read the accounts of 'New Times' in *Marxism Today* is to be confronted with an almost caricatured version of the kind of expressive totality criticized by Althusser, down to contrasted lists of the characteristics of 'Modern Times' and 'New Times'. Often the arguments seeking to establish connections between different phenomena are slovenly in the extreme. Stuart Hall, for example, whose decline into a master of obfuscatory rhetoric blurring essential conceptual distinctions is one of the minor intellectual tragedies of the 1980s, concedes that 'the debate still rages as to whether "post-Fordism" exists', but then blithely proceeds to assert that 'whichever explanation we finally settle for, the really startling fact is that *these* "new times" clearly belong to a time-zone marked by the march of capital simultaneously across the globe and through the Maginot Lines of our subjectivities'.[45] The mind-numbing reductionism displayed here comes strangely from so persistent a critic of classical Marxism's supposed tendency to collapse the ideologico-political superstructure into the economic base. Nevertheless, analyses of 'disorganized capitalism' and 'post-Fordism' do at least have the merit of seeking to show how systematic changes in the capitalist economy justify us in speaking of a distinctively postmodern era; furthermore, these accounts are supported empirically, at least to the extent that they refer to transformations which have actually occurred. The difficulty is that they grossly exaggerate the extent of the changes involved, and fail to theorize them properly.

These faults are most obvious in the case of the contrast drawn between Fordism and 'post-Fordism', which has been subjected to rigorous and devastating theoretical and empirical criticism. The Fordist mass production model is, in the first place, misrepresented by theorists of 'post-Fordism' – thus, to take the classic instance of the car industry, much equipment is not dedicated and can be reused for different models, and in any case long-term reliance on a single largely unchanging product such as the Ford Model T or the Volkswagen Beetle is quite exceptional; moreover, the field of application of mass production techniques was always primarily limited to the production of complex consumer durables (cars, electrical and electronic goods) and did not embrace basic consumer industries such as clothing and furniture or capital-intensive process industries such as steel and chemicals. Secondly, the thesis that mass markets for standardized products are breaking up has no empirical support. There is considerable replacement demand for such 'mature' consumer durables as cars, washing machines and refrigerators, to which now are added such new mass produced durables as video-recorders, walkmen, compact disc players, microwave ovens, dishwashers and food processors. The internationalization of trade has led to the fragmentation of markets as previously dominant domestic producers are confronted by importers, but the typical result is that mass producers survive by offering a range of models and by combining a relatively large share of the home market with rising exports. Thirdly, the novelty of 'flexible specialization' is much overstated. New technology – for example, robots in car factories – is still largely dedicated to the production of a specific generation of models. More importantly, the introduction of flexible manufacturing systems is expensive, requiring high-volume production in order to cover the costs involved.[46] Finally, the trend towards a workforce divided between a privileged 'core' and oppressed 'periphery' is also greatly exaggerated, and rests on the assumption – implausible in a period of intense international competition – that employers can guarantee some of their workers secure and well-paid employment.[47]

These criticisms leave the essentials of Lash's and Urry's analysis of 'disorganized capitalism' largely untouched.[48] They claim that the decline of 'organized capitalism' is, in economic terms, a consequence of the globalization of capital: 'what has happened now is that both "industry" and "finance" have been internationalized but with separate and uncoordinated circuits. This has then massively weakened the individual nation-state which places its economy within one or other vicious circle and makes the state unable to regulate or orchestrate its national currency.'[49] This general thesis is by no means original to Lash and Urry. It has, in fact, been advanced with great force and brilliance by a much more orthodox Marxist, Nigel Harris, who argues that the internationalization of capital involves three main trends, all evident during the long boom of the 1950s and 1960s but which have subsequently accelerated: the growth not simply of international trade but of intra-industry trade, reflecting the emergence of a 'global manufacturing system' in which plants in individual countries participate in a continual production process organized on a world scale; the expansion of investment by multinational companies increasingly detached from any national economic base; and the formation of an international financial system whose operations are outside of national governments. The cumulative effect of these changes – which are dramatized by the rise of the newly industrializing countries (NICs) of Latin America and the Pacific Rim – is 'the end of capitalism in one country': the nation-state can no longer manage economic activities within its territory in an era when the key actors become capitals operating on a global stage.[50]

Here far more than in the case of 'post-Fordism' we are dealing with developments whose reality and importance are undeniable. The global integration of capital is qualitatively greater than it was a generation ago; perhaps the most important corroboration of this assertion is the fact that the world market did not, under the impact of the slumps of the mid-1970s and early 1980s, disintegrate into the kind of protectionist trade blocs that were so important a feature of the Great Depression of the 1930s. Nevertheless, it remains open to question whether or not the changes which have occurred amount to the dawning of a new era of 'multinational' or 'disorganized' capitalism. David M. Gordon has recently subjected the claimed globalization of production and emergence of a new international division of labour to careful empirical analysis and come up with some startling results. In 1984 the less developed countries' (LDCs) share of world industrial country was 13.9 per cent, marginally less than the 14.0 per cent they achieved in 1948 as a result of import-substitution during the Depression and Second World War but subsequently lost during the long boom. Even during the most recent and more unstable period of 1973–84, the NICs' share rose only from 7.1 to 8.5 per cent, hardly a very dramatic shift. Far from Western capital flooding to the Third World, the share of foreign direct investment going to the LDCs remained roughly constant between the late 1960s and the early 1980s. Moreover, such investment, instead of seeking low-wage havens, was governed primarily by broader considerations such as local market size and political and economic stability. Gordon concludes that 'we have been witnessing the decay of the postwar global economy rather than the construction of a

fundamentally new and enduring system of production and exchange.' In response to this crisis, characterized by declining profit-
rates, globally synchronized business cycles, volatile exchange-rates
and internationally mobile money capital seeking speculative investments, he argues,

> the role of the state has grown substantially since the early 1970s;
> state policies have become increasingly decisive on the international
> front, not more futile. Governments have become more and more
> involved in active management of monetary policy and interest
> rates in order to condition exchange-rate fluctuations and short-
> term capital flows. They have become actually and potentially
> decisive in bargaining over production and investment agreements.
> And, small consolation though it may be, in an era of increasing
> monetarist conservatism, everyone including transnational cor-
> porations has become increasingly dependent upon co-ordinated
> state intervention for restructuring and resolution of the underlying
> dynamics of crisis.[51]

Gordon's emphasis on the continued, and in some respects increased, economic importance of the nation-state seems to me
fundamentally correct.[52] Thus, while the 1970s and 1980s have not
seen the return of the great interwar trading blocs, bodies such as that
policing the General Agreement on Trade and Tariffs have frequently
noted the growing tendency for governments to use various forms of
import control as a bargaining tool in their efforts to secure access for
their firms to other national markets: the conflicts of the US with, on
the one hand, Japan over electronic goods and, on the other, with the
EEC over the Common Agricultural Policy are cases in point. But the
most dramatic recent instance of state intervention came after Black
Monday, 19 October 1987, when Wall Street suffered the sharpest
fall in share prices in its history.

Faced with a threatened meltdown of the world's stockmarkets
which could precipitate a collapse of the financial system, the state
stepped in. Alan Greenspan, chairman of the US Federal Reserve
Board, issued a celebrated one-sentence statement on 20 October:
'The Federal Reserve, consistent with its responsiblities as the nation's
central bank, affirmed today its readiness to serve as a source of
liquidity to support the economic and financial system.'[53] The Fed
and the other major Western central banks cut interest rates and
pumped money into the banking system in order to keep financial
markets afloat. This large-scale intervention by the state averted the
kind of chain reaction which led from the Wall Street crash of
October 1929 to widespread bank failures and closures in the early

1930s and thence to the most profound recession in the history of capitalism. The resulting stimulation of demand helped to ensure that 1988 was a year, not of slump, but of unexpectedly rapid economic growth.[54]

The ability of Western states acting in concert to turn a threatened recession into a moderate boom suggests that rumours of the death of the interventionist state have been exaggerated. Indeed, much writing on the globalization of capital suffers from a lack of historical perspective. Martin Woolf argues:

> Before 1914 the world economy was in many respects as integrated as it is today and in certain important respects more so. Indeed it is possible to view the history of the international economy of the last 70 years as consisting of two attempts to restore the two main features of the liberal international economy of the 1870 and 1914 period. The first attempt foundered during the Great Depression. The second attempt at reconstruction began in the period immediately after the Second World War and has continued, with growing difficulty, to this day. The ratio of trade in manufactures to world output passed the 1913 level only in the late 1970s. This is consistent with the experience of the seven principal market economies. Ratios of trade (exports plus imports) to GDP in the mid-1980s were a little above pre-First World War levels in France and the United Kingdom. They were actually a little below those levels for Japan and had risen significantly above the pre-1914 levels only in the cases of the United States, Italy and Canada. (Reliable comparisons for Germany are impossible, for obvious reasons.) ... the world economy [in 1914] was almost as open to trade and, arguably, more open to flows of capital than today.[55]

It is perhaps misleading to equate the importance of international trade and investment to the pre-1914 world economy with the prevalence of *laissez faire*, given the pronounced tendency towards the 'organization' of individual national economies – the rise of oligopolies, monopolies and cartels, the fusion of banks and industry in the shape of finance capital, and the growing regulation of national economic life by what Hilaire Belloc called the 'servile state'.[56] It is nevertheless clear that Arno Mayer's 'Thirty Years' War of the general crisis of the twentieth century' between 1914 and 1945 (see section 1.2 above) did see a fragmentation of the world market and the formation of what Bukharin called 'national state-capitalist trusts': the exigencies of world war and economic slump promoted, within the advanced economies, a fusion of the state and private capital. This tendency was in some respects clearest not in the war economies of 1914–18 and 1939–45 but during the Great Depression of the 1930s, when every major power assumed powers of control over private investment as part of a drive to create a self-sufficient economic bloc under its control; the interventionist policies of the National Government in Britain, Roosevelt's New Deal, the Nazi programmes of rearmament and public works, and the First Five Year Plan in Stalinist Russia should thus be seen as variations on a theme, with the last case an extreme example of a general trend and not an antithesis to the others.[57] The destabilizing consequences of these simultaneous state-capitalist attempts to carve up the global economy precipitated the Second World War and the final destruction of the old European order. The postwar era has seen a gradual retreat from the fragmentation into statized blocs characteristic of 1914–45, for a variety of reasons: the institutional arrangements devised at the end of the Second World War in order to promote an American dominated free-trade order (the Bretton Woods agreement, etc.); the emergence in the 1950s and 1960s of a very large, relatively open global market in which competition between the major economies (the US, the EEC and Japan), thanks in part to their politico-military integration in the Atlantic alliance, and in marked contrast with the first half of the century, did not pass over into strategic conflict; the cumulative and unintended consequences of a series of policy decisions, reflecting in particular the weakening competitive position of the US relative to Western Europe and Japan, which led to the development of unregulated international financial markets (e.g., the creation of the Eurodollar market in the 1960s); and – perhaps most fundamental of all for those of an orthodox Marxist cast of mind – the cost reductions and productivity increases realized through the organization of globally integrated manufacturing processes.[58]

The fact remains, that despite the trends towards the internationalization of capital, the nation-state retains considerable power to affect the rate and distribution of capital accumulation within its borders. Belief to the contrary often presupposes an exaggerated view of state power at some earlier stage. This tends to involve giving credence to the main theorem of Keynesian economics, that state intervention can offset crisis tendencies and secure full employment, as the explanation of the postwar boom. The palpable failure of Keynesian methods to prevent two world slumps, in the mid-1970s and the early 1980s, is then taken as evidence that state intervention can no longer produce crisis-free economic growth. It is important therefore to stress the limits of state power during the apogee of 'organized capitalism' after 1914 and in the immediate postwar era. No state was able to achieve complete economic autarky during the fragmentation of the world market in the 1930s, not even Stalinist Russia: one of the main functions of the forcible collectivization of agriculture in 1928–9 was to increase Soviet grain exports – which rose 56-fold in 1928–31 – in order to finance the import of the plant and equipment required for industrialization, at the expense of millions of peasants who starved to death or were deported to the labour camps.[59] Furthermore, neither the long boom of the 1950s and 1960s nor the slumps of the 1970s and early 1980s can be seen as a consequence of the success and subsequent failure of Keynesian demand management. Keynes himself argued that the 'Trade Cycle is best regarded ... as being occasioned by a cyclical change in the marginal efficiency of capital', a concept roughly equivalent to the classical and Marxian notion of the general rate of the profit.[60] The long boom reflected not so much successful state intervention as the effect of very high levels of peacetime arms expenditure in offsetting what Marx called the tendency of the rate of profit to fall; it was the decline of this 'permanent arms economy' in the late 1960s which produced the crisis of profitability underlying the shift to global economic stagnation in the 1970s.[61] The stage was neither omnipotent before 1970 nor impotent thereafter.

The point – that the nation-state retains considerable economic strength – is important to underline because the 1980s witnessed a major demonstration of this truth, one all the more striking because the use of state power concerned was carried out under the covering fire of vast amounts of *laissez faire* rhetoric. The American economy experienced a sharp recovery in 1983–4 from the recession at the beginning of the decade; this boom was followed by an extended period of less rapid and stable but nonetheless real growth. The Reagan administration explained this return to prosperity as a consequence of its policy of promoting private enterprise. In fact, the opposite was true: Anatole Kaletsky described the American boom as the 'triumph of John Maynard Reagan', the result of 'a standard Keynesian policy of demand reflation'.[62] Two forms of state intervention were decisive. First, the Federal Reserve, having helped to precipitate the 1979–82 recession by a monetary squeeze intended to prevent further dollar depreciation, began in the summer of 1982 to increase the money supply in an effort to avert banking failures after Mexico defaulted on its debt – a policy continued by such measures as the rescue of Continental Illinois in 1984 and the Fed's response to Black Monday. Second, Reaganomics, involving as it did a redistribution of income from poor to rich via tax and welfare cuts and a very sharp increase in defence spending financed primarily by government borrowing, amounted to a considerable boost of effective demand, which operated through the mechanism of the multiplier to stimulate the US economy. The Reagan boom represented, not the magic of the market-place, but a remarkable exercise in 'military Keynesianism'.[63]

One of the most important developments in Western political economy during the second half of the 1980s was a certain generalization of this model. The British economy enjoyed in 1987–8 its first real boom since the early 1970s. Once again, it was a consequence not of deregulation and *laissez faire* but of government measures whose effect was to stimulate the economy: in 1986 the Thatcher government formally abandoned its previous attempts to control the money supply and allowed the pound sterling to depreciate against other currencies; the abolition of all controls on credit made possible a rise in personal sector debt from slightly over £100 billion in 1983 to £250 billion in 1987; in addition, Mrs Thatcher's second and third terms saw a determined shift towards a Reaganite mix of sharp cuts in personal taxation and in social security payments.[64] Of far greater moment to the world economy, the Japanese government responded to the 1985–6 recession, induced by the rise of the yen against the dollar, by adopting in May 1987 a package of classic Keynesian measures, including a massive programme of public works, designed to make up for lost exports with increased domestic consumption – a policy which allowed Japan, like Britain, to enjoy rapid economic growth in 1987–8. The response of all major Western governments to the October 1987 stock market crash underlined the Keynesian direction of policy. It is something of a historical irony: the remedies advocated by Keynes, wrongly credited with the long boom of the 1950s and 1960s, had a pronounced economic impact in a decade when his thought had fallen into intellectual disrepute, and been displaced in the favours of both policy-makers and academics by the reactionary Utopias of Hayek and Friedman.

The drift back to Keynesian measures did not amount to a solution to the problems facing the world economy. Mike Davis – whose writings on American capitalism in the Reagan era were nothing short of brilliant – described US economic recovery in the 1980s as 'a pathological prosperity'. He noted, *inter alia*, 'the general shift that is occurring in the profit-distribution process towards interest incomes, with the resulting strengthening of a neo-rentier bloc reminiscent of the speculative capitalism of the 1920s' and 'the striking reorientation of mainline US industrial corporations away from consumer-durable mass markets and towards volatile high-profit sectors like military production and financial services'.[65] The Reagan boom did not signify a revival in the global fortunes of American industry. On the contrary, the strength of the dollar in the first half of the 1980s – a consequence of the high interest rates required to attract the foreign lenders on whom the sale of US government debt come to depend – promoted further import penetration from Japan, Western Europe and the East Asian NICs; by the middle of the decade the mammoth US balance of payments deficit and foreign debt represented a major dislocation of international economic relationships. The speculative character of the boom, characterized as it was by frenzied merger battles, greenmail, leveraged buyouts, and the general features of a classic bull market, reflected the depressed state of industrial profitability and the consequent displacement of investment into securities and real estate. A presidential commission reported in 1985: 'Over the past twenty years, real rates of return on manufacturing assets have declined. Pretax returns are well below alternative financial investments and make many investors question the wisdom of putting funds in America's vital manufacturing sector.'[66] A variety of factors helped to internationalize the stock market boom – the development of a global securities market, financial deregulation (for example, the City of London's Big Bang in October 1986), a general expansion of credit. The *Financial Times* (*FT*) complained in the spring of 1987 that '[f]inancial markets seem to have broken free from real-world constraints and . . . are enjoying a heavenly dance on their own creation.' The biggest share prices took place in Japan, industrial powerhouse of world trade; on the Tokyo stock exchange, 'even the hardened professionals are beginning to blanch', the *FT* reported.[67]

Black Monday, like its predecessor, Black Thursday, 24 October 1929, represented the forcible correction of a situation in which the financial sector had been allowed to overextend itself by comparison with the relatively depressed industrial base of Western capitalism. But state intervention, although it prevented a repetition of the move from financial crash to world slump in 1929–31, could not abolish the contradictions which had given rise to the crash in the first place. The *Financial Times* observed almost a year after Black Monday: 'Governments around the world solved the immediate confidence crisis after the crash by throwing money at it, but they have now added inflation to the problems of distorted payments balances and overstretched banks.'[68] The 1980s were remarkable both for the sustained character of the recovery from the slump at the beginning of the decade and for the fragile foundations of this growth. A third major recession was averted thanks to a combination of state intervention, growing indebtedness and sheer good luck (David Stockman's account of economic policy-making in the first Reagan administration, *The Triumph of Politics*, removes any illusion that the recovery had anything to do with the wisdom or prudence of those in command of the American state). The relative prosperity of the mid and late 1980s did not mark the beginning of a new period of capitalist expansion comparable to the boom of the 1950s and 1960s, but represented an episode of overheated and unhealthy growth – in what Gordon rightly calls 'the decay of the postwar global enconomy'. Capitalism in the 1980s certainly fulfilled Nietzsche's injunction 'to *live dangerously*! Build your cities on the slopes of Vesuvius!'[69] Who can say when Vesuvius will explode again?

## 5.4   THE MIRROR OF COMMODITY FETISHISM: BAUDRILLARD AND LATE CAPITALIST CULTURE

One reason why many have seen an epochal break occurring some time in the past two decades, whether the outcome is thought to be 'postindustrial society' or a new phase on capitalism, is a widespread sense of a profound sea-change undergone by Western culture in this period. The same thought has been expressed in a variety of political and intellectual idioms. On the left, Christopher Lasch has announced the formation of a new, narcissistic, self, 'the final product of bourgeois individualism': 'Acquisitive in the sense that his cravings have no limits, he does not accumulate goods and provisions against the future, in the manner of the acquisitive individualist of nineteenth-century political economy, but demands immediate gratification and lives in a state of restless, perpetually unsatisfied desire.'[70] Further to the right, Daniel Bell has explored the 'cultural contradictions of capitalism': the moral foundations of bourgeois society in the Protestant ethic have been subverted by late capitalism's promotion of a mass market geared to the instant fulfilment of its desires, while cultural Modernism has undermined the old confidence in scientific reason.[71] For the novelists Saul Bellow and Martin Amis contemporary America is a 'moronic inferno' (the phrase is actually Wyndham Lewis's), a sinister, centreless chaos, in which the autonomous individual and the cultural tradition are increasingly displaced by a violent, illiterate mass lobotomized by television, all coherent understanding lost as, their attention span dwindling, they hop from channel to channel – a vision of the present to which Bellow and Amis have sought to give actuality in such novels as *The Dean's December* and *Money*.[72] The 1960s are generally treated as the turning-point in this cultural shift: thus Gilles Lipovetsky argues that the main consequence of the events of May 1968 was, quite contrary to the intentions of the actors, to promote the narcissistic individualism which he, like other commentators, regards as the dominant feature of the 1970s and 1980s.[73]

The funeral rites conducted by contemporary *Kulturkritik* for the autonomous, rational individual of modernity verge often on the apocalyptic. It is appropriate, therefore, that the social theorist *à la mode* should be Baudrillard, for whom apocalyptic pronouncements are a matter of course. The cultural phenomena on which others concentrate are for Baudrillard mere symptoms of a more fundamental change, which deprives us of the ability to talk of a world independent of our representations of it, to distinguish between true and false, real and imaginary. Postmodernity is characterized by 'simulation'. Unlike the problematic of representation, which is concerned with the relationship (of reflection, distortion or whatever) between images and 'a basic reality', simulation 'bears no relation to any reality whatever: it is its own pure simulacrum'. The kinds of distinction drawn by theoretical enquiry since the Renaissance revival of Platonism – between essence and appearance, for example – no longer makes sense in the era of the 'hyperreal', of *'that which is always already reproduced'*. Instead a world more or less adequately represented in images, we have a world *of* images, of hallucinatory evocations of a nonexistent real. This nightmare world is a historical product, of the technical changes making possible the mass reproduction of cultural products – above all, television, but, more fundamentally, of capitalism: 'it was capital which was the first to feed throughout its history on the destruction of every referential, of every human goal, which shattered every ideal distinction between true and false, good and evil, in order to establish a radical law of equivalence and exchange, the iron law of its power.' The result is a utterly depthless world, a hyperreality of pure surface: 'No more subject, focal point, centre or periphery: but pure flexion or circular inflection. No more violence or surveillance: only "information", secret virulence, chain reaction, slow implosion and simulacra of spaces where the real-effect comes into play.' *Ideologiekritik* is no longer appropriate, since '[i]deology corresponds to a betrayal of reality by signs; simulation corresponds to a short-circuit of reality and its reduplication by signs.'[74] Any conventional left strategy, whether of reform or revolution, no longer makes sense; the only form of resistance left is that of the silence and apathy of the masses, their refusal to be incorporated, manipulated or represented, even (or especially) by socialist parties (see section 3.4 above).[75]

Baudrillard's analysis is fundamentally Nietzschean in its denial of any reality beneath immediate experience and its rejection therefore of any 'depth model' of interpretation which would devalue the surfaces of things in favour of this underlying essence. He approvingly quotes Nietzsche's cry: 'Down with all hypotheses that have allowed the belief in a true world.'[76] What is distinctive about Baudrillard's position is that he ascribes what Nietzsche regards as properties of the world – properties which are given central importance in Modernist art, such as superficiality, ambivalence, instability, to a particular stage of social development: 'the important question . . . is that of the symbolic destruction of all social relations not so much by the ownership of the means of production but by *the control of the code*. Here is a revolution of the capitalist system equal importance to the industrial revolution.'[77] Consequently, 'now it is on the level of reproduction (fashion, media, publicity, information and communication networks), on the level of what Marx negligently called the nonessential sectors of capital (we can hereby take stock of the irony of history), that is to say in the sphere of simulacra and the code, that the global process of capital is founded.' The hyperreal is an aestheticized world: 'Today, when the real and the imaginary are confused in the same operational totality, the aesthetic fascination is everywhere . . . reality itself, entirely impregnated by an aesthetic which inseparable from its own structure, has been confused with its own image.'[78]

The United States, Baudrillard announced in *Amérique* (1986), is at once '*the last contemporary primitive society*', and the original version of modernity', in which all the tendencies towards hyperreality and simulation he had earlier described are most fully realized. The distinctive character of 'the American mode of life' is summed up by the country's great deserts, for '[t]he desert is a sublime form distanced from all sociality, from all sociality, from all sexuality,' Land of glittering surfaces, of '*the irrepressible development of inequality, of banality and of indifference*', the US has realized the 'anti-Utopia' of French poststructuralism, 'that of unreason, of deterritoralization, of the indeterminacy of the subject and of language, of the neutralization of all values, of the death of culture.' Herein lies the difference between America and Europe: 'We only manage to dream and from time to time to cross over to action – pragmatic America draws the logical consequences of everything that it is possible to conceive.' Europe – or rather her intellectuals – are still marked by 'the Revolution of 1789', 'with the seal of History, of the State and Ideology', acting as 'the unhappy consciousness of this modernity' which America has unreflectingly realized. 'In this sense, she is naive and primitive, she doesn't know the irony of the concept, she doesn't know the irony of seduction, she doesn't ironize about the future or destiny, she operates, she materializes.' Baudrillard's account of America is a version of the Myth of the Noble Savage, in which a stereotyped European view of Americans as naive, ignorant, unreflective, brutal, is taken over, but the value-judgement normally associated with this view reversed, so that Europeans are stigmatized as ineffectual onlookers, still preoccupied with the problematic nature of modernity, still concerned to criticize actuality and to seek Utopian political goals, while America pragmatically lives out their dreams – and nightmares. The fundamental contrast Baudrillard draws between America and Europe, however, remains stunningly banal, the mainstay of innumerable superficial essays over the past century and a half. Moreover, his enthusiasm for American 'hyper-reality' sometimes leads Baudrillard into straightforward apologetics, as when he tells us that there are '[n]o cops in New York', a city whose police force has in recent years become notorious for its racism and brutality.[79]

The upshot of Baudrillard's analyses is to license a kind of intellectual dandyism. In a world that has taken on the properties of a Modernist artwork, the radical intellectual must abandon the traditional task of theoretical enquiry, of uncovering the underlying structure responsible for the way things seem. Critique is senseless where '[t]here is no longer any critical and speculative distance between the real and the rational.'[80] All that is left is *belles lettres*, where unsubstantiated theoretical propositions rub shoulders, as in *Amérique*, with banal *aperçus*. Baudrillard's recent writing is an extreme case of what Jacques Bouveresse calls 'a type of work which attempts, with a very relative degree of success, to compensate for the absence of properly philosophical argumentation by means of literary effects and for the absence of properly literary qualities by means of philosophical pretensions.'[81] This oscillation between philosophy and *belles lettres* conceals the problem, intrinsic to the Nietzschean tradition, of the status of Baudrillard's own discourse. Some of his formulations seem to treat simulation as something that has *happened to* reality – 'reality itself, entirely impregnated . . . , has been confused . . .'. This sounds rather as if an antecedently existing world has undergone changes in its structure – the confusion of image and reality etc.; we could then analyse these changes, and explore the possibility of their not being as great as Baudrillard claims, and being themselves liable to be overtaken by events – could hyperreality itself be abolished, and by what? Counterposed to this relatively weak thesis is the idea that, given the nature of the hyperreal, characterized as it by the replacement of the real by its images, we can no longer coherently talk of any reality independent of these images. But if this is so, how can Baudrillard – or anyone else trapped within simulation, as presumably we all are – describe its nature, and outline the transition from the real to the hyperreal? Baudrillard is caught on the horns of one of the characteristic dilemmas of Nietzschean thought – how can he substantiate his claim that we have moved beyond a world to which theoretical enquiry is appropriate without relying on the assumptions and procedures of such enquiry (see section 3.3 above)? One way of avoiding this 'performative contradiction' is, as Habermas observes, to collapse the distinction between philosophy and literature, since 'consistency requirements . . . lose their authority or are at least subordinated to other demands – of an aesthetic nature, for example – if logic loses its conventional primacy over rhetoric.' Baudrillard's Aestheticism, like Derrida's, is an attempt to evade the aporias of the Nietzschean critique of reason.[82]

Treated purely as an empirical thesis, Baudrillard's claim that it is 'in the sphere of simulacra and the code . . . that the global process of capital is founded' is vulnerable to the arguments developed in sections 5.1 and 5.3 above. The proliferation of phenomena of 'reproduction (fashion, media, publicity, information and com- munication networks)' requires a vast expansion of material produc- tion; the greater circulation of images depends upon a variety of physical products – television sets, video-recorders, satellite discs and the like. More fundamentally, people do not live by MTV alone, but continue to have mundane needs for food, clothing and shelter meeting which makes the organization and control of production still the major determinant of the nature of our societies. Jejeune though Baudrillard's arguments are, there remains, however, a case to answer. Has there been a qualitative cultural break in the past two decades, pitching us into a moronic inferno of narcissists cretinized by television? If we refuse Baudrillard's categories – hyperreality, simulation, etc. – as a means of conceptualizing the changes which have supposedly overtaken Western culture we still cannot ignore the question itself. It is obviously impossible adequately to address in a few pages the complex issues raised. Nevertheless a few observations are worth making.

One is that it is a mistake to exaggerate the novelty of the cultural tendencies detected by contemporary commentators. Thus Richard Sennett argues that the origins of the narcissistic self, which knows no boundaries between itself and the world and demands the immediate gratification of its desires, and its broader context, the 'intimate society' in which social relationships are treated as pretexts for the expression of personality, lies in the erosion of an impersonal public life in nineteenth-century Europe. Sennett regards three main trends as responsible for 'the fundamental change in the ideas of the public and private which followed the great revolutions at the end of the [eighteenth] century and the rise of a national industrial capitalism in more modern times': first, the effects of the development of industrial capitalism itself, for example, 'the pressures of privatization which capitalism aroused in 19th Century bourgeois society', which made the nuclear family 'a refuge from the terrors of society'; second, the emergence of 'a code of the immanent', according to which the 'immanent, the instant, the fact, was a reality in and of itself', not requiring interpretation in the light of 'a pre-existent scheme in order to be understood'; third, the transformation of public life into a sphere where 'one could escape the burdens of [idealized family life] ... by a special kind of experience, one passed among strangers, or more importantly among people determined to remain strangers to one another', in which a silent and passive mass of spectators observed the extravagant expression of personality by a few – the Baudelairian *flâneur*, the Romantic artist, the political leader. The contemporary intimate society amounts to the abolition even of this public sphere. Thus politics becomes the means through which the personality of a 'charismatic' leader is projected to a mass audience by electronic media which render them both utterly passive and largely isolated from one another. But this and related phenomena are consequences of the nineteenth-century transformation of public life into a means of the expression of personality. 'Personality in public was a contradiction in terms; it ultimately destroyed the public term ... Thus the end of a belief in public life is not a break with 19th Century bourgeois culture, but rather an escalation of its terms.'[83]

If it can, then, be plausibly argued that contemporary narcissistic individualism has deep historical roots, it is also worth noting the existence of a particular way of theorizing the cultural processes whose present forms are under discussion, one which starts from Marx's concept of commodity fetishism. Marx argued that in a system of generalized commodity production, where the social activity of production in particular enterprises is mediated by the circulation of the products of labour in the market, 'the definite social relation between men themselves ... assumes here, for them, the fantastic form of a relation between things.'[84] David Frisby has shown how the notion of commodity fetishism provided the leitmotif for some of the most important German cultural criticism of the early twentieth century, including not merely the Marxists Walter Benjamin and Siegfried Kracauer, but also Georg Simmel, parts of whose *Philosophy of Money*, according to one reviewer, 'read like a translation of Marx's economic discussions into the language of psychology'.[85] Simmel, Kracauer and Benjamin all concentrated on the new modes of perception which developed as a result of the emergence of a modern, urban capitalism. What is striking is how contemporary many of their insights are. Simmel's remarks on the role of style as a means of at once maintaining a distance and establishing the existence of shared attributes in an intensely individualistic and subjective culture, though written at the turn of the century, could have been composed with the 1980s in mind.[86] Benjamin called novelty, 'a quality which does not depend on the use-value of the commodity', 'the quintessence of false consciousness, of which fashion is the tireless agent. This illusion of novelty is reflected, like one mirror in another, in the illusion of infinite sameness.'[87] The exchange of commodities reduces difference to identity, as the passage of time demotes each 'innovation' to merely one item in an endless sequence by virtue of the fact that it is no longer the 'latest' – an observation which, though formulated with respect to nineteenth-century Paris, retains all its relevance to a culture dominated by what Harold Rosenberg called 'the tradition of the new'.

There have been two more recent attempts to use the concept of commodity fetishism to make sense of the culture of twentieth-century capitalism. One is, of course, Horkheimer's and Adorno's critique of the 'culture industry' in *Dialectic of Enlightenment*. The other is the analysis developed by Guy Debord and other members of the Situationist movement in the 1960s. Parodying the opening sentence of *Capital*, Debord announced: 'The entire life of societies in which modern conditions of production reign announces itself as an immense accumulation of *spectacles*.' The spectacle, 'in all its specific forms, as information or propaganda, advertisement or direct consumption of entertainments', must be seen as 'a social relation among people mediated by images'. As such, 'the society of the spectacle' is the 'absolute fulfilment' of 'the principle of commodity fetishism'.[88] Baudrillard, while acknowledging the Situationists' influence, now rejects their ideas: 'We are no longer in the society of the spectacle . . . , nor the specific types of alienation and repression which this implied.'[89] The reason is presumably that concepts such as alienation and repression presuppose the existence of something that is being alienated or repressed. Debord is emphatic that the society of the spectacle involves a distorted form of social relationship: he writes of 'the global social praxis that is split into reality and image' and says that '[w]ithin a world *really on its head*, the true is a movement of the false.'[90] All this is anathema to Baudrillard, for whom real and image, true and false have become endemically confused in the hyperreal world of simulation.

The tradition which has built on Marx's theory of commodity fetishism is one, therefore, which is committed to the idea of pursuing the critique of existing reality as part of the struggle for what he called 'human emancipation'. To see this is a worthwhile project to continue is not by any means to endorse uncritically all, or even many, of the theoretical formulations used by those working within it – Adorno and Horkheimer took to extremes a danger inherent in the notion of commodity fetishism, namely a tendency to see the operation of the market as automatically inducing acceptance of capitalism by the masses;[91] and it is certainly not to accept the political conclusions drawn, whether it be the early Frankfurt school's pessimistic quietism or the ultra-left council communism of the Situationists. Nevertheless, one merit of the attempt to relate changes in social consciousness to the relative penetration of market relationships into everyday life is that it subjects apocalyptic *Kulturkritik* to the discipline of an empirical exploration of socio-economic processes.

In this context, the concept of Fordism developed by the regulation school can be put to good use. The concept's explanatory power is limited, since it provides no satisfactory account of the means by which capitalism was able during the long boom to offset the tendency of the rate of profit to fall, and of the reasons why these means failed in the 1930s and the 1970s;[92] moreover, theorists of Fordism (and even more of post-Fordism) tend, as we saw in the last section, to exaggerate the extent to which its distinctive techniques of production were ever prevalent. It remains the case, however, that the articulation of mass production and mass consumption is a central feature of twentieth-century capitalist economies. Aglietta argues that one consequence of Fordism was the systematic commodification of everyday life; 'With Fordism . . . , the generalization of commodity relations extended to their domination of practices of consumption. This was a mode of consumption restructured by capitalism, because the time devoted to consumption witnessed an increasing density in individual use in commodities and a notable impoverishment of noncommodity interpersonal relations.' The 'consumption norm' created by Fordism, Aglietta argues, 'is governed by two commodities: the *standardized housing* that is the privileged site of consumption; and the *automobile* that as the means of transport compatible with the separation of home and workplace'. Both commodities – and especially, of course, the motor car – were amenable to the techniques of mass production; the purchase of both required 'a vast socialization of finance', in the form of new or greatly extended forms of credit (hire purchase, mortgages, etc.). Furthermore, 'the two basic commodities of the mass consumption process created complementarities which effected a gigantic expansion of commodities, supported by a systematic diversification of use-values.' Finally, Fordist mass consumption required 'the creation of a *functional aesthetic* ("design")', involving the adaptation of use-values to the norms of mass, standardized production, which

> duplicated the real relationship between individuals and objects with an imaginary relationship. Not content to create a space of objects of everyday life, as supports of a capitalist commodity universe, it provided an image of this space by advertising techniques. This image was presented as an objectification of consumption status which individuals could perceive outside themselves. The process of social recognition was externalized and fetishized. Individuals were not initially interpellated as subjects by one another, in accordance with their social position: they were interpellated by an external power, diffusing a robot portrait of the 'consumer'.[93]

Despite the functionalism which pervades Aglietta's argument, it is suggestive in relating the cultural phenomena on which Horkheimer, Adorno and the Situationists all concentrated to certain transformations in capitalism. One question which theorists of postmodernity must address is whether any further, qualitative changes have occurred in the past 20 years which justify talk of a new historical epoch. Even Bell warns against making exaggerated claims to this effect:

> In terms of *daily life* of individuals, more change was experienced between 1850 and 1940 – when railroads, steamships, telegraph, electricity, telephone, automobile, motion picture, radio, and airplanes were introduced – than the period since when the future is supposed to have accelerated. In fact, other than television, there has not been one major innovation which has affected the daily life of persons to the extent of the items I enumerated.[94]

Television, one might well say, is a big exception. But surely its widespread use has primarily intensified trends towards privatization – the isolation of the household which is the main focus of life outside work – and the permeation of social existence by images which were already operative, as the writings of Horkheimer and Adorno in the 1940s make amply clear. And is it not arguable that the direction of change varies according to the dimension selected, that television makes possible a more active, though more privatized, viewing than cinema-going? The image of a mass audience autistically absorbed in television-watching may say as much about the prejudices of intellectuals as it does about the social world itself.

Lipovetsky by contrast represents what at time seems like the opposite extreme to pessimistic *Kulturkritik*. While much of his description of postmodernity is similar (if not identical) to Baudrillard's, his interpretation is quite different. The postmodern epoch is characterized by a 'process of personalization', which 'continued by other means the work of democratic-individualistic modernity'. Following Tocqueville rather than Marx, Lipovetsky doesn't see the postmodern 'seduction' reducing agents to alienation and passivity. On the contrary,

> the individual is forced permanently to choose, to take initiatives, to inform himself, to test himself, to stay young, to deliberate over the simplest acts: what car to buy, what film to see, what book to read, what regime, what therapy to follow. Consumption compels the individual to take charge of himself, it makes him responsible, it is a system of ineluctable participation, contrary to vituperations against the society of the spectacle and of passivity.[95]

Lipovetsky seems to be offering here a more precise description of late-capitalist alienation rather than, as he claims, demonstrating its non-existence. On his own account, 'personalization' involves an intense investment of *private* life and the reduction of the public sphere to the merest shell. And the limits to the participation on offer are plain enough. The classical democratic tradition from Machiavelli to Rousseau and Marx had something more extensive in mind when they spoke of freedom rather than the ability – constrained, of course, by class position and income – to choose between the various items of consumption offered by competing multinational corporations. 'Alienation' seems as good a term as any to sum up this society of privatized activity and public apathy.

One may, then, plausibly argue that late capitalist culture represents a continuation of trends operative throughout this century. Hobsbawm observes that the combination of technology (using the same 'basic devices: ... the mechanical reproduction of sound and the moving photograph') and the mass market characteristic of the 'culture industry' first emerged during the *fin-de-siècle* Age of Empire.[96] The decisive moment in the commodification of everyday life arguably came with the emergence of Fordism in the interwar years – particularly in the United States, of course, but its uneven impact can be traced elsewhere – and then during its consolidation after 1945. It is in this context that we may consider the question of the fate of Modernism, which we left hanging at the end of chapter 2.

## 5.5   THE COMMODIFICATION OF MODERNISM

The end of the Second World War marked the end of the distinctive
historical conjuncture which had produced Modernism in the first
place – the uneven and combined development of industrial capitalism which both disrupted existing regimes and offered apocalyptic
intimations of a radically different future. The postwar stabilization
and expansion of Western capitalism left the avant gardes, who had
dreamt of transcending the separation of art and life, beached. As
Perry Anderson put it, '[w]hat marks the typical situation of the
contemporary artist in the West, it might be said, is . . . the closure of
horizons: without any appropriable past, or imaginable future, in an
interminably recurrent present.'[97] What effects did this situation have
on Modernism? Very summarily, one can point to a number of
changes. One was a renewed emphasis on the autonomous and
abstract work of art. Aesthetics registered this shift. Adorno, for
example, attacked Benjamin and Brecht for stressing montage, whose
reliance on 'the ready made material supplied from the outside . . .
reveals a certain tendency to conformist irrationalism', as opposed to
'construction', which 'postulates the dissolution of materials and
components of art and the similar imposition of unity'.[98] Genuinely
critical art would not seek to resolve itself back into social life, but in
its fractured structure express its distance from, and rejection of, an
alienated and oppressive reality. When in 1939 Clement Greenberg
originally drew his celebrated distinction between avant-garde art,
fleeing social involvement for the purification of abstract form, and
kitsch, banal, commercialized mass culture, he was a Trotskyist who
looked to socialism for 'the preservation of whatever living culture we
have right now'.[99] After 1945, all revolutionary hopes gone, the
distinction served to canonize a new form of *l'art pour l'art*, as, in a
climate defined by the Cold War and the New York art market's
insatiable demand for Modernist works, Greenberg and another
ex-Trotskyist critic, Harold Rosenberg, became the chief propagandists of Abstract Expressionism, whose products they interpreted as
articulating the painter's personal alienation from a world no longer
amenable to change.[100]

Such a flight into abstraction did not, in fact, protect Modern art
from incorporation and commodification. Adorno himself believed
that 'among the dangers threatening modern art, not least is that it is
becoming inoffensive.'[101] One form taken by this danger is what
Russell Berman calls 'the obsolescence of shock'.[102] The shock
produced by the designed incoherence of avant-garde works of art

was, Peter Bürger argues, intended to 'direct the reader's attention to the fact that the conduct of one's life is questionable and that it is necessary to change it.' But '[n]othing loses its effectiveness more quickly than shock; by its very nature, it is a unique experience. As a result of repetition, it changes fundamentally: there is such a thing as expected shock ... The shock is "consumed".' As Modernism came to represent the norm of high culture, so techniques used by the avant-garde movements to subvert the institution of art itself were recuperated. Bürger observes:

> if an artist sends a stove-pipe to an exhibit today, he will never attain the intensity of protest of Duchamp's ready-mades. On the contrary, whereas Duchamp's *Urinoir* is meant to destroy art as an institution (including its specific organizational forms such as museums and exhibits), the finder of the stove-pipe asks that his 'work' be accepted by the museum. But this means that the avantgardiste protest has turned into its opposite.[103]

Saved for high art, Modernist techniques could then be integrated directly into the market. There was, of course, nothing new in this: the transformation of the work of art into a commodity was a precondition of the emancipation of art from its subordination to religious purposes. But the scale of the commodification of painting in particular has reached new heights since the Second World War. The functioning of artworks as investments reached its apogee appropriately enough during the bull market of the mid-1980s, and even survived the stock market crash. Individual paintings achieved astonishing prices: in 1987 Van Gogh's 'Sunflowers' was sold for $39.9 million, his 'Irises' for $53.9 million. Inevitably, artists adjusted themselves to the new situation – none better than the ineffable Warhol, who declared: 'Being good in business is the most fascinating kind of art.'[104] For those not content to gamble on posthumous greatness (and auction prices) 'being good in business' seemed to come down to high turnover. One young Manhattan artist, Barry X. Ball, recently said: 'This system doesn't work with someone who produces a small amount of work. There's a constant pressure to produce and turn it out fast. I've found it changes the way I work. I'm not allowed to make mistakes any more. I can't have old work to look at. I don't deliberate as much.'[105]

But it was in architecture that the most important incorporation of Modernism took place. Discussing one of the greatest urban reconstructions of the nineteenth century, the creation on the site of Vienna's old city walls of the Ringstrasse by the liberal administrations of the 1870s and 1880s, Carl Schorske observes: 'In Austria as elsewhere, the triumphant middle class was assertive in its independence of the past in law and science. But whenever it strove to express its values in architecture, it retreated into history.' So the Rathaus was built in Gothic style, the Parliament building in Classical style, and the University in Renaissance style.[106] The International Style forged by Modernist architects provided the bourgoisie of the mid-twentieth-century with the distinctive aesthetic means to put its stamp on the built environment. The career of Mies van der Rohe symbolizes this process: last director of the Bauhaus in the dying days of the Weimar republic, Mies developed a style – Kenneth Frampton calls it 'symmetrical monumentality' – which 'culminated in the development of a highly rationalized building method that was widely adopted in the 1950s by the American building industry and its corporate clientele ... Mies's approach offered the publicity-conscious client an impeccable image of power and prestige', its finest example being perhaps the Seagram building in New York.[107] Modernism gave capital the architectural language it had hitherto lacked.

Thus in a complex movement the recuperation of avant-garde techniques for autonomous art have gone hand in hand with the integration of Modernism into the circuits of capital. These developments are in turn connected with a much broader process, which Berman among others call 'the false sublation of art and life'.[108] In certain respects the avant-garde goal of the reintegration of art and life has been realized but in a distorted form, since life – capitalist society – remains untransformed. Crucial here is not so much the interpenetration of 'high' and mass culture – say, the regular use of Brechtian alienation devices by the television series *Moonlighting* – since there is nothing particularly new about such spillovers – *film noir* would be unrecognizable without the use of techniques culled from German Expressionist cinema, as the permeation of everyday life by images and sounds. Of decisive importance here is, of course, the culture industry in its many facets. It is fascinating, for example, to see the way in which Modernist artworks are used in advertising – thus images drawn from Magritte's paintings have become mass media clichés, used, for example, to publicize a British building society's interest rates.

Bergman argues that '[a]rt becomes the extension of politics, as the system of domination mechanizes its control; not even the most argus-eyed cop-on-the-block could compete with the omnipresence of music, the most romantic of arts', which

> tends to obliterate communication and to break down individual resistance, constructing instead the beautiful illusion of a collective, singing along in dictatorial unanimity. Yet because it is a false

collective in which no one is ever at home, it constantly collapses in a sado-masochistic antinomy: on the one hand, the autistic pseudo-privacy of the walkman, on the other, the megalomaniacal self-assertion of the ghetto-blaster ... and each of these gestures stands in an inverse relationship to the social status of the groups associated with the respective technical devices: the poorest sound the loudest.[109]

These developments – the recuperation of the avant garde for art, the incorporation and commodification of Modernism, the false sublation of art and life – seem much more important than any of the changes associated with the supposed emergence of a distinctively Postmodern art. Bürger lists the following trends, all of which have been claimed as exemplars of the Postmodern: 'a positive stance towards the architecture of the *fin-de-siècle* and hence an essentially more critical judgement of modern architecture; the softening of the rigid dichotomy between higher and lower art, which Adorno still considered to be irreconcilably opposed; a revaluation of the figurative paintings of the 1920s ...; a return to the traditional novel even by representatives of the experimental novel.'[110]

The idea that these shifts in sensibility represent a qualitative break in Modernism does not stand up to critical examination. I shall try to illustrate this claim – already developed in my discussion of the general arguments for a Postmodern cultural turn in chapter 1 – by considering a couple of specific developments, though the following brief remarks are something of a caricature of a proper analysis. Take, for instance, the return of figuration in painting. Bürger argues that this can be seen as a break from Modernism only on a very narrow conception of the latter, for example, that developed by Adorno, which, as we saw above, identifies Modern art, with 'the principle ... of a complete pervasiveness of form'. Such a view blocks 'the insight that the later development of an artistic material can run into internal limits'. Bürger gives the example of Picasso's move during the First World War from Cubism to Neo-Classicism, marked by his 1917 painting 'Olga in the Reclining Chair'. 'The idea that the possibility of a consistent continuation of Cubist material could have been exhausted' would give this development 'a consequentiality which Adorno's aesthetics does not allow us to recognize'.[111] The point admits of more general application. Greenberg argued that, by comparison with Cubism's evacuation of content from painting and pursuit of absolute form, Surrealism was 'a reactionary tendency which it attempting to restore outside subject matter'.[112] But a certain Neo-Classical revival was characteristic not simply of Surrealism but of *Neue Sachlichkeit* painters such as Grosz and Dix, whose use of figuration must be seen as part of one of the most innovative avant-garde movements of the 1920s.[113] Adorno's and Greenberg's privileging of abstraction seems more like a defensive attempt to preserve fragments of high culture from the advance of the culture industry and kitsch than a rounded analysis of Modernism. The fact that painters have in the past 20 years retreated from the extremes of abstraction reached after the Second World War does not, of itself, mark an epoch-making change, particularly since some of those prized as representative Postmodernist artists (Carlo Maria Mariani, for example) display a characteristically Modernist preoccupation with the process of artistic creation itself. What Greenberg called 'the imitation of imitating' still looms very large in contemporary art.[114]

It is, however, in architecture where Postmodernism has achieved the highest profile. One of the most interesting cultural developments since the early 1970s has been the politicization of architectural debate, a process which has perhaps gone furthest in Britain thanks to the intervention of the Prince of Wales, who has carved out a distinctive role as a populist defender of traditional architecture against the depredations of Modernism.[115] These debates must be seen in the context of the transformations undergone by the spatial relationships of advanced capitalist societies in the past generation. A major postwar trend has been the shift of population and industry out of the main metropolitan centres, a process which has gone furthest in the US with the development of the suburbs and the movement of investment out of the Northeast and Midwest to the Sunbelt, but which has been of great significance elsewhere, in Britain, for example.[116] David Harvey argues that this trend must be seen as part of the emergence of what he calls 'demand-side urbanization', the rise of the 'Keynesian city', 'a consumption artefact' whose 'social, economic, and political life [was] organized around the theme of state-backed, debt-financed consumption'. Thus suburbanization 'meant the mobilization of effective demand through the total restructuring of space as to make the consumption of the products of auto, oil, rubber, and construction industries a necessity rather than a luxury'. The urban crisis of the 1960s in the US marked the rebellion of those layers of the city population who had benefited least from the long boom, but the real break came with the onset of recession in 1973, which produced 'a changing thrust of urban politics away from equity and social justice and toward efficiency, innovation, and rising real rates of exploitation'.[117]

The impact of economic crisis on the cities – dramatized by New York's bankruptcy in 1974–5 – enforced a change in the character of urbanization. Two of the strategies outlined by Harvey as responses to this crisis seem of particular importance. One was the attempt by cities 'individually to improve their competitive position with respect to the spatial division of consumption.' As '[m]ass consumption of the 1960s was transformed into the less mass-based but more discriminating consumption of the 1970s and the 1980s', '[t]he city has to appear as innovative, exciting, and creative in the realms of life-style, high culture, and fashion.' Secondly, '[u]rban areas can . . . compete for those key control and command functions in high finance and government that tend, by their very nature, to be highly centralized while embodying immense power over all manner of activities and spaces. Cities can compete to become centres of finance capital, of information gathering and control, of government decision-making.'[118]

These two strategies are by no means incompatible; on the contrary, a city in which are concentrated corporate headquarters, banks and securities firms is likely to include among its population large numbers of the well-paid white-collar workers who form the main locus of upper-income consumption. The development of this kind of 'post-Keynesian city' requires the large-scale transformation of the built environment – the creation, for example, in run-down inner-city areas of up-market shopping malls, the construction of new office buildings, the 'redevelopment' of depressed waterside areas as concentrations of expensive housing. Such changes are, of course, the story of every major Western city in the 1980s. Mike Davis argues that the 'urban renaissance' of downtown Los Angeles reflects the 'hypertrophic expansion of the financial service sector', in which 'the transformation of a decayed precinct of downtown LA into a major financial and corporate-control node of the Pacific Rim economy . . . has gone hand-in-hand with a precipitous deterioration of the general urban infrastructure and a new-wave immigration that has brought an estimated one million undocumented Asians, Mexicans and Central Americans into the Inner City.' The abandonment of urban reform is symbolized by the fortress-line character of the new buildings: John Portman's Bonaventure Hotel, treated by Jameson as the acme of Postmodernism (see section 5.2 above), rather marks, with its inclusion of 'pseudo-natural, pseudo-public spaces within the building itself', a 'systematic segregation from the great Hispanic-Asian city outside'.[119] Similar patterns are repeated elsewhere: thus London, a key and expanding international financial centre, had in 1985 the largest concentration of unemployed in the industrialized world, and greater extremes of wealth and poverty than any other part of Britain.[120]

It is hardly surprising that in these circumstances the nature of the built environment should itself become a political issue, although often this has involved a considerable degree of mystification: thus advocates of a Classical revival such as Prince Charles displace attention from the real, socio-economic causes of mass inner-city poverty to the undeniable disasters wreaked by postwar slum-clearances and the translation of working-class city dwellers into high-rise blocks. The wretched consequences of these attempts by urban planners and Modernist architects during the long boom to re-fashion the city have been used to justify pursuing the most reactionary themes – from the idea that certain styles are divinely ordained to the revaluation of Nazi architecture.[121] But whether Postmodern architectural styles represent a genuine cultural break is open to question. Indeed it is arguable that such buildings as Michael Graves's Portland Building, a *cause célèbre* largely because of its collage-like facade, represent the increasing irrelevance of aesthetic considerations to major construction projects. Thus, according to Diane Ghirardo:

> The hoopla surrounding stylistic Post-Modernism is compensatory. The architect finds himself a media darling just as his significance dwindles. For nearly every project, the architect in a sense arrives last on the scene. Contemporary practice shrinks the role of the architect from that of an active agent in the construction of community and its structures to that of an exterior designer or interiors specialist. Leasing agents, developers, commercial loan officers, planning and zoning commissions make the important decisions, leaving the emarginated architect the trivial task of selecting finishes and glosses inside and out.[122]

On this analysis, architectural Postmodernism marks not a new aesthetic but the packaging needed to differentiate one skyscraper from another in an era when a building's individuality has come to be an important factor in marketing office space.[123] As Frampton puts it:

> Today the division of labour and the imperatives of 'monopolized' economy are such as to reduce the practice of architecture to large-scale packaging ... At its most predetermined, Post-Modernism reduces architecture to a condition in which the 'package deal' arranged by the builder/developer determines the carcass and the essential substance of the work, while the architect is reduced to contributing a suitably seductive mask. This is the predominant condition in city-centre development in America

today, where high-rise towers are either reduced to the 'silence' of their totally glazed, reflective envelopes or alternatively dressed in devalued historical trappings of one kind or another.[124]

It is hard, then, to see what has occurred in architecture, any more than developments in painting, as representing the end of Modernism. The architectural changes in particular seem rather to constitute a further stage in the process of commodification involved in the postwar triumph of the International Style. To stress the incorporation of Modernism, let alone that of its 'Postmodern' variants, does not require that we see all this as a betrayal of some original radical meaning. As I argue in chapter 2 above, Modernism in its heyday was characterized by its *ambiguity*, its capacity to express a variety of different political positions, from Marinetti's fascism to Brecht's Marxism, as well as, more frequently, to constitute precisely a flight *from* politics. The years since 1945 have not seen the Modernist revolution betrayed. Nor does the argument set out in this section imply the dismissal of all recent works – including those described as 'Postmodern' – as worthless rubbish. Good art can be produced in an immense variety of different conditions. What is true is that the innovative fire has gone out of Modern art. Franco Moretti's claim that the early years of this century represented 'the last *literary season* of Western culture' (see section 5.3 above) has more general application to a wide range of cultural practices: I have often been struck by the tedium that often overcomes one while walking through a gallery of twentieth-century painting arranged in chronological order, as one moves from the excitement of the early part of the century to the desperate and all too frequently sterile iconoclasm of recent artists. Genuinely interesting developments have often come, as Anderson observes, in a Third World context which reproduces a similar constellation of circumstances to those which gave rise to Modernism in the first place.[125] Think, for example, of the novels of Salman Rushdie, their author moving with apparent ease between Western metropolitan culture and the experience of a subcontinent unevenly and agonizingly integrated in global capitalism – a situation whose contradictions have, alas, become all too tragically manifest.

These considerations should underline, once again, the necessity of setting stylistic changes in a broader historical context. This raises the question also of politics. Art often seeks unsuccessfully to escape politics; sometimes it becomes itself a site of struggle, as the controversies over Modern architecture and *The Satanic Verses* make very clear. This point is especially relevant, since the belief that in cultural as well as broader historical terms we are entering a postmodern epoch presupposes a certain political background. I now turn, in the next and final section, to outlining this background.

## 5.6   THE CHILDREN OF MARX AND COCA COLA

We began with Lyotard, so let us finish with him (in more senses than one). He writes: 'Eclecticism is the degree zero of contemporary general culture: one listens to reggae, watches a western, eats McDonald's food for lunch and local cuisine for dinner, wears Paris perfume in Tokyo and "retro" clothes in Hong Kong; knowledge is a matter for TV games.'[126] It all depends, of course, on who 'one' is. This is more than an *ad hominem* remark, though it is a bit rich that Lyotard should ignore the majority of the population even in the advanced economies to whom such delights as French scent and Far Eastern travel are denied. To whom then is this particular combination of experiences available? What political subject does the idea of a postmodern epoch help constitute?

There is an obvious answer to this question. One of the most important social developments in the advanced economies during the present century has been the growth of the 'new middle class' of upper-level white-collar workers. John Goldthorpe writes: 'While in the early twentieth century, professional, administrative and managerial employees accounted for only 5–10 per cent of the active population in even the most economically advanced nations, by the present time they quite generally account in Western societies for 20–25 per cent.'[127] The new middle class, conceived as wage-earners occupying what Erik Olin Wright called 'contradictory class locations' between labour and capital and performing primarily managerial and supervisory tasks, is in all likelihood a considerably smaller group than these figures reflect – perhaps 12 per cent of the British working population.[128] Nevertheless, both because of the social power its members exercise, and because of the cultural influence it exerts on other white-collar workers who aspire to promotion into its ranks, the new middle class is a force to be reckoned with in every major Western society.[129]

Raphael Samuel has painted an evocative portrait of this salaried middle class, which, unlike the traditional petty bourgeoisie of small capitalists and independent professionals,

> distinguishes itself more by its spending than its saving. The Sunday colour supplements give it both a fantasy life and a set of cultural cues. Much of its claim to culture rests on the conspicuous display

of good taste, whether in the form of kitchenware, 'continental' food, or weekend sailing and cottages. New forms of sociability, like parties and 'affairs' have broken down the sexual apartheid which kept men and men in rigidly separate spheres.

Class hardly enters into the new middle class conception of themselves. Many of them work in an institutional world of fine gradations but no clear lines of antagonism.

The new middle class have a different emotional economy than [sic] that of their pre-war predecessors. They go in for instant rather than deferred gratification, making a positive virtue of their expenditure, and treating the self-indulgent as an ostentatious display of good taste. Sensual pleasures, so far from being outlawed, are the very field on which social claims are established and sexual identities confirmed. Food, in particular, a postwar bourgeois passion, . . . has emerged as a crucial marker of class.[130]

It is not hard to think of the economic conditions of such practices – thus saving becomes much less important when social position comes to depend less on accumulated capital than on skill in negotiating a managerial hierarchy, and when credit is readily available to expand consumption. It is also tempting to see Postmodernism as somehow the cultural expression of the rise of the new middle class.[131] This would, I think, be a mistake. For one thing the new middle class is less a coherent collectivity than a heterogeneous collection of strata, occupying the same contradictory position within the relations of production, but disarticulated by varying power-bases; for example, one important source of differentiation within the new middle class is likely to be employed in the public or private sector – a university lecturer, for example, does not always experience an identity of interest with a City bond-dealer.[132] For another thing, inasmuch as the term 'Postmodernism' has any genuine cultural referents – I have in mind the developments discussed at the end of the last section – these date from the 1960s or later, whereas the new middle class has been around a lot longer. This suggests the need for an analysis which, like Anderson's geneaology of Modernism (see chapter 2), seeks to isolate the historical conjuncture in which all the talk about a postmodern era began.

Two developments seem to me decisive. The first is what Mike Davis describes as 'the emergence of a new, embryonic regime of accumulation that might be called *overconsumptionism*', by which he means 'an increasing political subsidization of a sub-bourgeois, *mass* layer of managers, professionals, new entrepreneurs and rentiers'. Davis argues that American capitalism experienced in the 1970s and 1980s both the crisis of the old Fordist regime of accumulation based on the articulation of semi-automatic mass production and working-class consumption and a redistribution of wealth and income in favour, not simply of capital, but of an increasingly assertive new middle class. The tax and welfare cuts pushed through by the first Reagan administration meant that low-income families lost at least $23 billion in income and federal benefits, while high-income families gained more than $35 billion. 'The old charmed circle of the poor getting richer as the rich get richer is being superseded by the trend of poorer poor and richer rich, as the proliferation of low-wage jobs simultaneously enlarges an affluent market of non-producers and bosses.' The result is a 'split-level economy', involving 'as *Business Week* notes, a more sharply bifurcated consumer market structure, . . . with the masses of the working poor huddled round their K-Marts and Taiwanese imports at one end, while at the other there is a (relatively) "vast market for luxury products and services, from travel and designer clothes, to posh restaurants, home computers and fancy sports cars".'[133]

Although Davis's argument is somewhat weakened by his reliance on the regulation school's inadequate crisis theory, there seems to me little doubt that he is referring here to a phenomenon of general significance. The Reagan-Thatcher era saw, not the abandonment of Keynesianism, but an important reorientation of fiscal policy, one of whose main features was a redistribution from poor to rich – the British government's social security 'reforms' and drastic cuts in the taxation of those in higher-income brackets, both implemented in the spring of 1988, followed the pattern set by Reaganomics. Other developments promoted the expansion of upper-income consumption – for example, the heady growth of the financial sector thanks first to the boom in Third World lending in the 1970s and then to the bull market of the mid-1980s. The 1980s were after all the decade when the term 'Yuppie' became part of common parlance. The Yuppie was more than a subject of social comedy and object of *ressentiment* (hence the widespread *Schadenfreude* with which Black Monday and subsequent redundancies on Wall Street and in the City of London were greeted); she was a symbol of the large portion of the new middle class who did very well out of the Reagan-Thatcher era.

The 'pathological prosperity' (in Davis's words) which characterized the Western economies' recovery from the 1974–5 and 1979–82 recessions thus involved a certain reorientation of consumption towards the new middle class, a social layer whose conditions of existence tend to encourage high expenditure. But there something else that needs to be taken into account to make sense of the peculiar mood of the 1980s – the political fallout from 1968. 1968 was the year when a combination of crises – the May–June events in France, the student and ghetto revolts in the US, and the Prague Spring in Czechoslovakia – seemed to augur the breakup of the prevailing order both East and West. In the ensuing radicalization a generation of young Western intellectuals were won to militant political activity, often in one of the far left organizations, usually Maoist or Trotskyist in allegiance, which mushroomed at the end of the 1960s. Ten years on, the millenial expectations of imminent revolution that has flourished in 1968 had been dashed. The status quo proved to be more solidly based than it had seemed. Where change took place, perhaps most notably with the collapse of the Southern European dictatorships, the beneficiary was, at best, social democracy rather than revolutionary socialism. The far left disintegrated throughout Europe at the end of the 1970s. In France, where hopes had been raised highest, the fall was most precipitous. The *nouveaux philo-sophes* helped to convert the Parisian intelligentsia – largely *marx-isant* since the Popular Front and the Resistance – to liberalism. The parliamentary left won office in 1981 for the first time since the Fourth Republic amid an intellectual scene characterized by the complete rout of Marxism. As former Maoists vied to sign statements supporting the Nicaraguan *Contras*, the Left Bank had apparently been made safe for Nietzsche and NATO.[134]

Twenty years after, in 1988, with Western capitalism seemingly restabilized under the leadership of the New Right, the retreat of the generation of 1968 from the revolutionary beliefs of their youth had gone ever further. As Chris Harman remarked '[i]f the fashion in 1968 was to drop out and to drop acid, now, apparently, it is to drop in and drop socialist politics.'[135] The observations of the twentieth anniversary of 1968 were remarkable chiefly for the disillusioned retrospects of former student leaders. *Marxism Today*, which had made a marketing strategy out of the progressive abandonment of anything resembling socialist principle, was especially strident in its renunciation of revolutionary hopes which it had never shared. In France, however, there was at least a serious attempt to account for this extraordinary reversal of fortunes, a generation's movement from the barricades to Yuppiedom.[136]

The most striking explanation came from Régis Debray, whose own evolution from theorist of guerilla warfare threatened with execution by the Bolivian military for his collaboration with Che Guevara to presidential adviser in François Mitterrand's Elysée summed up a more general process. Debray argued that May 1968 acted as an instrument of modernization, eliminating the institutional obstacles to French capitalism's integration into a multinational,

Americanized, consumer capitalism. Thus the *événements* amounted
to

> [t]he most reasonable of social movements; the sad victory of
> productivist reason over romantic unreason; the gloomiest demon-
> stration of the Marxist theory of the finally determining role of the
> economic (technology plus relations of production). Industrializa-
> tion had to be given a morality not because the poets were
> clamouring for a new one but because industrialization required it.
> The old France paid off its arrears to the new; the social, political
> and cultural backlog all at once. The cheque was a large one. The
> France of stone and rye, of the apéritif and the institute, of *oui
> papa, oui patron, oui cherie*, ordered out of the way so that the
> France of software and supermarkets, of news and planning, of
> know-how and brain storming could show off its viability to the
> full, home at last. This spring cleaning felt like a liberation and, *in
> effect*, it was.[137]

On this account, the disillusionment of the generation of 1968 was
both an inevitable consequence of the objective logic of the events –
which was to modernize, not to overthrow French capitalism – and a
form of adaptation to the consumer society perfected as a result of
that crisis. Debray's argument has been taken further and generalized
by Gilles Lipovetsky, who contends that the revolts of the late 1960s
helped establish the predominance of the narcissistic individualism
identified by Lasch, Sennett and Bell as one of the main cultural
trends of the past 20 years. 'End of modernism: the 1960s are the last
manifestation of the offensive launched against Puritan and utilitarian
values, the last movement of cultural revolt, this time a mass
movement. But also the beginning of a postmodern culture, without
innovation and real audacity, which contents itself with democratiz-
ing the logic of hedonism' – a hedonism that has become a 'condition'
of the 'functioning' and 'expansion' of capitalism.[138]
A principal defect of this kind of explanation is its almost extravagant functionalism. Debray cheerfully espoused a Hegelian philosophy of history in which, by virtue of the ruse of reason, events serve
purposes unknown to the actors. 'The sincerity of the actors of May
was accompanied, and overtaken, by a cunning of which they knew
nothing. The pinnacle of personal generosity met the pinnacle of the
system's anonymous cynicism. Just as Hegelian great men are what
they are because of the world spirit, the May revolutionaries were the
entrepreneurs of the spirit needed by the bourgeoisie.'[139] Debray's
and Lipovetsky's reduction of 1968 to an episode in capitalism's
modernization – or postmodernization – left out of account the

possibility of other outcomes, and the fact that such expansion as the system did enjoy in the 1970s and 1980s depended on the *defeat* of the political challenge mounted by the struggles at the end of the 1960s.[140] As Alain Krivine and Daniel Bensaid – among the few French student leaders not to have renounced Marxism – observe, Debray and Lipovetsky give to 'the *fait accompli* the virtues of historical necessity. In their vision of May, the ruse of capital conveniently replaces that of reason.'[141] Even Krivine's and Bensaid's sometime cothinker, Henri Weber, one of the most talented of the generation of 1968, who subsequently abandoned revolutionary socialism for social democracy, has argued that '*the individualism of May was Promethean and communitarian,*' 'bearer of a more or less grandiose project for the transformation of society', convinced that 'there is no real self-realization except in and by the collectivity', so that 'there is a rupture, and not continuity' between it and 'the narcissistic and apathetic individualism of the end of the 1970s' with which Lipovetsky identifies it.[142]

Fundamentally, attempts such as Debray's and Lipovetsky's to explain away 1968 run aground on the fact of its sheer scale. The May–June events in France, after all embraced not just student barricades in the Latin Quarter and the occupation of the Sorbonne, but the greatest general strike in European history. They were simply the most dramatic episode in what Harman in his magisterial history of the period calls a 'three-fold crisis – of American hegemony in Vietnam, of authoritarian forms of rule in the face of a massively enlarged working class, and of Stalinism in Czechoslovakia' – a crisis which produced a *generalized* upturn of class struggle throughout Western capitalism which continued into, and was initially exacerbated by the onset of world recession after the 1973 oil crisis.[143] This upturn – the greatest Western Europe had seen since the aftermath of the Russian Revolution – comprised, alongside May–June 1968 in France, the Italian 'May in slow motion' which began in the autumn of 1969; the wave of strikes against the 1970–4 Heath government in Britain, which culminated in Heath's overthrow by the miners; the Portuguese Revolution of 1974–5; and the bitter industrial conflicts which accompanied the death agonies of the Franco regime in Spain during 1975 and 1976. While industrial militancy never achieved anything like this pitch in the US, the interaction of the antiwar movement, the black ghetto risings, and the student revolt helped produce at the end of the 1960s the worst American domestic political crisis perhaps since the Civil War. And there were echoes elsewhere – the *cordobazo* in Argentina, an explosion of worker and student militancy in Australia, the Quebec general strike of 1972.

The failure of these struggles to make any long-term inroads into the power of capital was a contingent one, reflecting not the immanent logic of the system but the dominance of the Western working-class movement by organizations and ideologies which, whether stemming from the social democratic or the Stalinist traditions, were pledged to achieving partial reforms within a framework of class collaboration. The intervention of the French Communist Party to end the general strike of May–June 1968 was repeated on numerous occasions elsewhere, from the Social Contract struck by the British Trade Union Congress with the Labour government of 1974–9 to the 1977 Moncloa pact through which the Spanish Communist and Socialist Parties pledged their support to Franco's heirs. Class compromises of this kind allowed Western capital to weather the great recessions of the mid-1970s and early 1980s and indeed to use them to restructure and to rationalize. As the working class of the advanced countries moved from the offensive to the defensive, the far left found itself isolated, no longer swimming with the stream; in these less favourable circumstances, many organizations collapsed, their activities succumbing to a 'crisis of militancy' provoked by the fact that their labours had not been met with the easy success they had expected.

The political odyssey of the 1968 generation is, in my view, crucial to the widespread acceptance of the idea of a postmodern epoch in the 1980s. This was the decade when those radicalized in the 1960s and early 1970s began to enter middle age. Usually they did so with all hope of socialist revolution gone – indeed, often having ceased to be believe in the desirability of any such revolution. Most of them had by then come to occupy some sort of professional, managerial or administrative position, to have become members of the new middle class, at a time when the overconsumptionist dynamic of Western capitalism offered this class rising living standards (a benefit often denied the rest of the workforce: hourly real wages in the US fell by 8.7 per cent between 1973 and 1986).[144] This conjuncture – the prosperity of the Western new middle class combined with the political disillusionment of many of its most articulate members – provides the context to the proliferating talk of postmodernism. Let me, before continuing, make one point clear. I do not claim that, say, Foucault's philosophy or Rushdie's fiction is in any very direct sense to be derived from the economic and political developments discussed above. I am rather concerned to explain here the *acceptance* by quite large numbers of people of certain ideas.[145]

The main themes of postmodernism become intelligible, I believe, against the background of the historical conjuncture of the late 1970s and the 1980s. For example, a principal feature of poststructuralism is its Aestheticism, inherited from Nietzsche and reinforced by the attempts of Derrida, Foucault et al. to articulate the philosophical implications of Modernism (see section 3.2 above). Richard Shusterman notes the emergence of 'an intriguing and increasingly salient current in contemporary Anglo-American moral philosophy (and culture) toward the aestheticization of the ethical. The idea here . . . is that aesthetic considerations are or should be crucial and ultimately perhaps be paramount in determining how we choose to lead or shape our lives and how we assess what a good life is.'[146] The main example he gives is that of Rorty, whose prominence in the 1980s reflected his role in translating poststructuralist themes into an analytical idiom. Perhaps the most interesting instance of this tendency is provided by the Nietzschean notion of an 'aesthetics of existence' developed by Foucault in his last books (see section 3.5 above). What is striking about the philosophical drift towards Aestheticism is how well it accords with the cultural mood of the 1980s. It has become a truism is to say that this was a decade obsessed with style. Theorists of post-Fordism were right to note a certain differentiation of markets and the proliferation of designer brands crucial to whose appeal was the suggestion that in buying, say, Levi 501s one was gaining access to a certain lifestyle, although they greatly exaggerated the scale of these developments. In various aspects of life one could detect a similar association of certain kinds of consumption with forming oneself into a particular kind of person; among the most important was a narcissistic obsession with the body, both male and female, less as an object of desire than – when disciplined by diet and exercise into a certain shape – as an index of youth, health, energy, mobility. This stylization of existence (to borrow Foucault's phrase) is surely best understood against the background, not of New Times, but of good times for the new middle class, a class which found itself in the 1980s with more money in its pocket and easier access to credit, without the pressure to save to which the old petty bourgeoisie was subject.

A further striking feature of talk about postmodernism is its apocalyptic tone, which is perhaps most strident in the writings of Baudrillard and his followers, such as Arthur Kroker. Now there is quite a strong sense in which an expectation of imminent disaster has been an endemic feature of Western culture for much of this century, and certainly since Auschwitz and Hiroshima. But I think something more involved here that this 'routinized apocalypse', as Frank Kermode calls it.[147] For what has been the experience of the generation of 1968? They lived through a period, in the late 1960s and early 1970s, when great historical transformations seemed on the agenda, and when many believed that the immediate future was finely balanced between Utopia and distopia, between socialist advance and reactionary tyranny (a belief which events like the Chilean coup of September 1973 did nothing to undermine). The hope of revolution has gone, but it has not generally been replaced, I think, by positive belief in the virtues of capitalist democracy. Apart from anything else, even for those who mistakenly believe that capitalism has overcome its economic contradictions, there are so many other potential catastrophes hovering on the horizon – nuclear war, and ecological collapse, for example. For those holding such views, it is plausible to believe that we are entering a phase of development to which classical Marxism, with its orientation on class struggle, is irrelevant, but which by no means fulfils the promises of liberalism.

_The success enjoyed by Lyotard and Baudrillard, quite out of proportion with any slight intellectual merit their work might have, thus becomes comprehensible. Both were strongly identified with 1968. Baudrillard, for example, says: 'My work really started with the movements of the 1960s.'[148] Both offer lengthy philosophical commentaries on the present – unlike Derrida, who has concentrated on the deconstruction of theoretical texts, or Foucault, whose main preoccupation was with the geneaology of modernity. Both have followed a trajectory since the late 1960s and early 1970s which has taken away from an explicitly political stance – on the spontaneist, anti-Leninist wing of the post-1968 far left (with which Deleuze and Guattari have been much more enduringly identified) – towards the adoption of what amounts as an aesthetic pose based on the refusal to seek either to comprehend or to transform existing social reality. What could be more reassuring for a generation, drawn first towards and then away from Marxism by the political ups and downs of the past two decades, than to be told – in a style decked out with the apparent profundity and genuine obscurity of the sub-Modernist rhetoric cultivated by '68 thought' – that there is nothing that they can do to change the world? 'Resistance' is reduced to the knowing consumption of cultural products – perhaps the 'Postmodern' works of art whose authors have often sought to embody in them this kind of thinking, but if not any old soap opera will do just as well, since, as Susan Sontag has often emphasized, Aestheticism involves 'an attitude which is neutral with respect to content'.[149] The kind of ironic distance from the world which was so important feature of the great works of Modernism has become routinized, even trivialized, as it becomes a way of negotiating a still unreconciled reality which one no longer believes can be changed.

As I have argued elsewhere:

The discourse of postmodernism is best seen as the product of a socially mobile intelligentsia in a climate dominated by the retreat of the Western labour movement and the 'overconsumptionist' dynamic of capitalism in the Reagan-Thatcher era. From this perspective the term 'postmodern' would seem to be a floating signifier by means of which this intelligentsia has sought to articulate its political disillusionment and its aspiration to a consumption-oriented lifestyle. The difficulties involved in identifying a referent for this term are therefore beside the point, since talk about postmodernism turns out to be less about the world than the expression of a particular generation's sense of an ending.[150]

There is nothing new about such *trahison des clercs*. One striking case in point is the brilliant group of American intellectuals won to the Trotskyist movement in the 1930s and 1940s, but who mostly backslid disillusioned into liberalism during the Cold War and often into neo-conservatism in the 1970s.[151] Similar stories could be told about every period in which radicals have found themselves isolated politically since Restoration times.[152] In this book I have sought to analyse the pathology of this latest 'experience of defeat', and in particular the attempt to explain it in terms of the emergence of a postmodern age to which the Enlightenment project − even when radicalized by Marxism − is irrelevant. This attempt fails, as I have tried to show, whether as philosophy, aesthetics and social theory. Postmodernism must be understood largely as a response to failure of the great upturn of 1968–76 to fulfil the revolutionary hopes it raised. During this upturn themes which had been marginalized for half a century enjoyed a brief revival − not simply the idea of socialist revolution, conceived as a democratic irruption from below rather than the imposition of change from above, whether by a social democratic administration or a Stalinist party, but also the avant-garde project of overcoming the separation of art and life.[153]

These aspirations have once again been largely sidelined. But to believe that this will permanently remain the case supposes that there will be no more explosions in the advanced countries comparable to those of 1968 and after. The fragile and unstable character of the 1980s' pathological prosperity suggests otherwise. World capitalism has not escaped from the period of crises which began in the early 1970s, nor has it somehow magically abolished the working class: on the contrary, the 1980s were marked by the rise of new labour movements based on proletariats created by recent industrialization − *Solidarność* in Poland, the Workers' Party in Brazil, the Congress of South African Trade Unions, the new South Korean labour movement.[154] The project of 'radicalized Enlightenment' first outlined by Marx, for whom the contradictions of modernity could be resolved only by socialist revolution, still awaits realization.

# AFTERWORD

Man is dead, but his spirit lives.
*Slogan of black strikers*
*Durban, South Africa, January 1973*

Marx and Freud are the two great heroes of the radicalized Enlightenment. Both discovered the dark underside of the *philosophes'* empire
of reason. Marx uncovered the exploitation and oppression without
which the progress of bourgeois society would have been impossible.
Freud dissolved the transparency of reason itself, exposing the
conscious self as the product of a history of desire and repression
whose effects are still stored in the unconscious. After their intervention, theory could no longer be conceived as simply the disinterested
contemplation of eternal truths, as it had been since Plato.[1] But
neither Marx nor Freud took the further step – Nietzsche's step – of
reducing reason simply to the expression of interests, to merely one
form of the will to power. Both still used reason as an instrument of
liberation. Marx did so more emphatically: theory, when integrated
by means of socialist organization in the struggle for working-class
self-emancipation, was an indispensable means of what he called
'human emancipation'. But, for Freud too, the patient's development
of a rational understanding of the history – the process of her own
formation as a person – which was the source of her suffering was an
essential feature of his therapy. It is true that Freud tended to conceive
this understanding as a stoic acceptance of the necessity of unhappi-
ness. Deleuze and Guattari compare him to Ricardo. Just as Ricardo
was the first to formulate a rigorous version of the labour theory of
value, but did not relate this discovery to the historically specific
nature of capitalist production relations, so Freud sought to contain
the unconscious drives and desires he had brought to light within the
eternal family sanctified by myth and tragedy.[2] Marx's greater
optimism about the scope for human emancipation rested on his

deeper historical understanding of the transitory nature of the social structures that have shaped our existence for the past few millenia – the family, private property and the state.

It is in any case this orientation, that of the radicalized Enlightenment, of using reason to understand, to control and to change the forces of which the *Aufklärer* had not dreamt, that provides the only appropriate guide through modernity – in which we still find ourselves, despite the postmodernists' proclamations of New Times. There are, of course, political issues at stake in all this. One of the most powerful statements of the appropriate stance to adopt towards modernity comes towards the end of Benjamin's *The Origins of German Tragic Drama*. Although the subject of this book – arguably one of the greatest, and certainly among the oddest philosophical works of the century – is the Baroque *Trauerspiel*, this form of drama's central technique – the allegory, which treats the world as fragmented, devoid of sense or of hope – bears a strong resemblance to the Modernist use of montage as a response to what Eliot called 'the immense panorama of futility and anarchy that is contemporary history'.

The Baroque, involves a moment beyond this melancholic surveying of a fallen world. This is the moment of redemption:

> In God's world the allegorist awakens . . . This solves the riddle of the most fragmented, the most defunct, the most dispersed. Allegory, of course, thereby loses everything that was most peculiar to it: the secret privileged knowledge, the arbitrary rule in the realm of dead objects, the supposed infinity of a world without hope. All this vanishes with this *one* about-turn, in which the immersion of allegory has to clear away the final phantasmagoria of the objective, and, left entirely to its own devices, rediscovers itself, not playfully in the earthly world of things, but seriously under the eyes of heaven.[3]

When he wrote these words, in the mid-1920s, Benjamin was poised between Jewish Messianism, from which he drew his concept of redemption, and revolutionary socialism. As his commitment to albeit an idiosyncratic variant of Marxism strengthened, Benjamin came to see redemption more and more as a secular event – socialist revolution, although the concept never quite lost its original religious meaning. The resulting perspective was most eloquently stated in the 'Theses on the philosophy of history', written in a desperate political conjuncture after the Hitler-Stalin pact seemed to promise a world partitioned between two monstrous despotisms. Here revolution is conceived as a violent irruption in the linear unfolding of events, redeeming a past dominated by exploitation and oppression.[4] If we understand redemption in these terms, then the passage quoted above provides an orientation on the present, on 'the supposed infinity of a world without hope', a world to which are added to the exploitation and anarchy of which Marx wrote, the repression with which Freud grappled, the fragmented consciousness which Horkheimer and Adorno traced to the workings of the culture industry and commodity fetishism, new horrors – for example, that of a nature slowly being destroyed by the consequences of competitive capital accumulation. To such a world Baroque melancholy and Romantic irony – cultivated by Modernism, reduced to the merest pastiche by the prophets of postmodernity – seem the only appropriate response, so long as we leave out of out account the possibility of a global social transformation which could impose a new set of priorities, based upon the collective and democratic control of the resources of the planet. Once we admit this possibility, then, 'with this one about-turn', everything changes: we see both sides of Marx's perspective on capitalism – not simply the destruction it wreaks, but the potential expansion of human capacities it involves. Unless we work towards the kind of revolutionary change which would allow the realization of this potential in a transformed world, there is little left for us to do, except, like Lyotard and Baudrillard, to fiddle while Rome burns.

# NOTES

## Abbreviations

FT    *Financial Times*
IS    *International Socialism*
MH    A. Callinicos, *Making History* (Cambridge, 1987)
MIC    C. Nelson and L. Grossberg, eds, *Marxism and the Interpretation of Culture* (Houndmills, 1988)
MR    P. Anderson, 'Modernity and revolution', in *MIC*
NGC    *New German Critique*
NLR    *New Left Review*
PDM    J. Habermas, *The Philosophical Discourse of Modernity* (Cambridge, 1987)
PMC    J.-F. Lyotard, *The Postmodern Condition* (Manchester, 1984)
TCA    J. Habermas, *The Theory of Communicative Action*, I (London, 1984), II (Cambridge, 1987)
TCS    *Theory Culture & Society*

## Introduction

1. I. Hassan, *The Postmodern Turn* (1987), p. xi.
2. Indeed, it seems that the first relatively systematic usage of the term 'Postmodern' was in order to characterize some experimental fiction at the end of the 1950s and in the 1960s: see Hassan, *Postmodern Turn*, pp. 85–6, and F. Kermode, *History and Value* (Oxford, 1988), pp. 129–30.
3. *PMC*, pp. xxiii–iv, 5 and *passim*.
4. Ibid., p. 66.
5. E. Laclau and C. Mouffe, *Hegemony and Socialist Strategy* (London, 1985). See the critique of this whole trend in E. M. Wood, *The Retreat from Class* (London, 1986).
6. *Marxism Today*, Introduction to special issue on 'New Times', October 1988.
7. M. Foucault, 'Structuralism and post-structuralism', *Telos* 55 (1983), p. 204.
8. Compare, for example, T. Eagleton, 'Capitalism, modernism and postmodernism', *NLR* 152 (1985), and L. Hutcheon, *A Poetics of Postmodernism* (London, 1988).

## CHAPTER 1  The Jargon of Postmodernity

1. J.-F. Lyotard, 'Defining the postmodern', *ICA Documents* 4 (1985), p. 6.
2. See R. Sayre and M. Löwy, 'Figures of romantic anti-capitalism', *NGC* 32 (1984).
3. T. S. Eliot, *Selected Prose*, ed. F. Kermode (London, 1975), p. 177.
4. F. Kermode, *The Sense of an Ending* (Oxford, 1968), p. 98.
5. A. Kroker and D. Cooke, *The Postmodern Scene*, 2nd edn (Houndmills, 1988), p. 8.
6. See Kermode, *Sense*, esp. ch. I.
7. L. Hutcheon, *A Poetics of Postmodernism* (London, 1988), p. 28.
8. R. A. Berman, 'Modern art and desublimation', *Telos* 62 (1984–5), pp. 33–4.
9. S. Gablik, 'The aesthetics of duplicity', *Art & Design* 3, 7/8 (1987), p. 36.
10. Quoted in C. Schorske, *Fin-de-Siècle Vienna* (New York, 1981), p. 19.
11. See E. Lunn, *Marxism and Modernism* (London, 1985), pp. 34–7.
12. MR, p. 332.
13. Compare F. Kermode, *History and Value* (Oxford, 1988), ch. 6.
14. F. Moretti, 'The spell of indecision' (discussion), in *MIC*, p. 346.
15. Lunn, *Marxism*, p. 58; see generally pp. 33–71.
16. C. Jencks, *What is Postmodernism?* (London, 1986), p. 14.
17. See, for example, ibid., pp. 3–7.
18. P. Ackroyd, *T. S. Eliot* (London, 1985), pp. 118–19.
19. Jencks, *Postmodernism?*, p. 43.
20. Eliot, *Selected Prose*, p. 38.
21. Hutcheon, *Poetics*, p. 41.
22. Ibid., p. 32.
23. A. Huyssen, 'Mapping the postmodern', *NGC* 33 (1984), p. 16.
24. Ackroyd, *Eliot*, pp. 105, 145–8.
25. Lyotard, 'Defining', p. 6.
26. PMC, p. 79.
27. I. Kant, *Critique of Judgement* (Oxford, 1973), I, pp. 90, 92, 127.
28. PMC, pp. 79, 81. As Huyssen observes, Lyotard's 'turn to Kant's sublime forgets that the 18th-century fascination with the sublime of the universe, the cosmos, expresses precisely the very desire of totality and representation which Lyotard so abhors and persistently criticizes in Habermas's own work', 'Mapping', p. 46. See also my discussion of the sublime in 'Reactionary postmodernism?', in R. Boyne and A. Rattansi, eds, *Postmodernism and Social Theory* (Houndmills, forthcoming).
29. Eliot, *Selected Prose*, pp. 63–4. Jencks apparently believes that Eliot 'located [the dissociation of sensibility] in the nineteenth century' (!), *Postmodernism?*, p. 33.
30. PMC, pp. 79–80.

31. F. Jameson, Foreword to *PMC*, p. xvi.
32. Jencks, *Postmodernism?*, p. 42.
33. *PMC*, p. 80.
34. G. Deleuze and F. Guattari, *Mille plateaux* (Paris, 1980), p. 12.
35. F. Jameson, *Fables of Aggression* (Berkeley and Los Angeles, 1979), pp. 2, 81, 2, 14.
36. Kermode, *History*, pp. 98ff. Perhaps the most elaborated account of the 'discrepancy theory' is P. Macherey, *A Theory of Literary Production* (London, 1978), esp. part I.
37. Jameson, *Fables*, ch. 7.
38. J. Frank, 'Spatial form in modern literature', in *The Widening Gyre* (New Brunswick, 1963).
39. Eliot, *Selected Prose*, p. 43.
40. Ibid., pp. 176–7; W. Lewis, *Blasting & Bombardiering* (London, 1967), p. 250.
41. See J. Berger, *The Success and Failure of Picasso* (Harmondsworth, 1965), pp. 47ff.
42. See J. Willett, *The New Sobriety 1917–1933* (London, 1978).
43. G. Deleuze and F. Guattari, *L'Anti-Oedipe* (Paris, 1973), ch. 2.
44. See Schorske, *Fin-de-Siècle Vienna*, chs 5 and 8.
45. S. Lash, 'Discourse or figure?', *TCS* 5, 2/3, pp. 320, 331–2.
46. J. Berger, 'Defending Picasso's late work', *IS* 2, 40 (1988), p. 113.
47. Quoted in N. Zach, 'Imagism and vorticism', in M. Bradbury and J. McFarlane, eds, *Modernism 1890–1930* (Harmondsworth, 1976), p. 234.
48. M. Nadeau, *A History of Surrealism* (Harmondsworth, 1973), p. 212 n. 5. See also W. Benjamin, 'Surrealism', in *One-Way Street and Other Writings* (London, 1979). Rimbaud defined the task of the poet in his letter to Paul Demeny of 15 May 1871, translated by Oliver Bernard in *Collected Poems* (Harmondsworth, 1969), p. 10.
49. *PMC*, p. 82.
50. F. Jameson, 'Postmodernism, or the cultural logic of late capitalism', *NLR* 146 (1984), p. 45.
51. W. Benjamin, *Illuminations* (London, 1970), pp. 226, 241.
52. S. Lash and J. Urry, *The End of Organized Capitalism* (Cambridge, 1987), pp. 286–7.
53. Benjamin, *Illuminations*, pp. 239–40.
54. Ibid., pp. 226, 242–3.
55. E. Bloch et al., *Aesthetics and Politics* (London, 1977), pp. 100–41, with a Presentation by Perry Anderson.
56. Quoted in C. Russell, *Poets, Prophets and Revolutionaries* (New York, 1985), p. 117. See more generally ibid., pp. 114–18, and H. Richter, *Dada* (London, 1965), ch. 3.
57. G. Grosz, *A Small Yes and a Big No* (London, 1982), pp. 91–2. See also Count Harry Kessler's report of his meeting with Grosz on 5 February 1919: 'Grosz argued that art as such is unnatural, a disease, and the artist a man possessed . . . He [Grosz] is a really a Bolshevist in

the guise of a painter', *The Diaries of a Cosmopolitan 1918–1937* (London, 1971), p. 64.

58. W. Benjamin, *Understanding Brecht* (London, 1977), pp. 6, 18.
59. See, for example, Hutcheon, *Poetics*, p. 35.
60. See J. Willett, ed., *Brecht on Theatre* (London, 1964): the emphasis laid by Brecht in later writings – for example, in 'A short organum for the theatre' – on the role of pleasure as well as instruction in epic theatre involves a modification rather than the abandonment of his earlier views.
61. Huyssen, 'Mapping', p. 42.
62. Kermode, *History*, p. 132.
63. D. Bell, *The Coming of Post-Industrial Society* (London, 1974), pp. 51–4.
64. J. Silverman and D. Welton, editors' introduction to *Postmodernism and Continental Philosophy* (Albany, 1988), p. 2.
65. Kroker and Cooke, *Postmodern Scene*, pp. 8, 76, 127, 129, 169.
66. *PDM*, esp. Lecture IV.
67. H. Blumenberg, *The Legitimacy of the Modern Age* (Cambridge, Mass., 1983), pp. 28, 30, 32, 182, 346, 423. Compare K. Löwith, *Meaning in History* (Chicago, 1949).
68. Blumenberg, *Legitimacy*, p. 115. Jean Baudrillard provides a good example of this style of thinking: he tells us that political economy, within whose categories Marxism is trapped, is 'only a kind of actualization' of 'the great Judaeo-Christian dissociation of the soul and Nature', *The Mirror of Production* (St Louis, 1975), pp. 63, 65.

### CHAPTER 2 Modernism and Capitalism

1. C. Baudelaire, *My Heart Laid Bare and Other Prose Writings* (London, 1986), p. 37.
2. D. Frisby, *Fragments of Modernity* (Cambridge, 1985), p. 16.
3. K. Marx and F. Engels, *Collected Works* (50 vols published or in preparation, London, 1975–), VI, p. 487.
4. Quoted in J. Rawson, 'Italian futurism', in M. Bradbury and J. McFarlane, eds, *Modernism* (Harmondsworth, 1976), p. 245.
5. G. M. Hyde, 'The poetry of the city', in Bradbury and McFarlane, eds, *Modernism*.
6. K. Wolff, ed., *The Sociology of Georg Simmel* (New York, 1950), pp. 409–10, 415, 420–1. As Simmel observes (ibid., p. 424, n. 11), 'The metropolis and mental life' is a compressed statement of some of the principal themes of his *magnum opus*, *The Philosophy of Money* (London, 1978). See Frisby, *Fragments*, ch. 2, and, for some criticisms of 'The metropolis and mental life', D. Smith, *The City and Social Theory* (Oxford, 1980), pp. 187ff.
7. Quoted in R. Cork, *David Bomberg* (New Haven, 1987), p. 78. See also, for example, T. J. Clark's fascinating study of the urban context of Manet's art, *The Painting of Modern Life* (London, 1984).

8. M. Berman, *All that is Solid Melts into Air* (London, 1983), p. 15.
9. *PDM*, p. 5.
10. H. Blumenberg, *The Legitimacy of the Modern Age* (Cambridge, Mass., 1983), p. 423.
11. *PDM*, p. 7.
12. See esp. K. Kumar, *Prophecy and Progress* (Harmondsworth, 1978), chs 1–3.
13. *TCA*, I, pp. 166, 168; and see generally pp. 143–271. While I follow in the text Habermas's account of Weber's theory of rationalization, it should be noted that his reading is hotly contested: see, for example, W. Hennis, 'Max Weber's "Central Question" ', *Economy and Society* 12 (1983).
14. *PDM*, p. 2.
15. T. Parsons, *The Social System* (London, 1951), pp. 481ff.
16. T. Parsons, *The System of Modern Societies* (Englewood Cliffs, 1971), p. 119.
17. *TCA*, II, pp. 291–2; and see generally pp. 199–299.
18. J. Taylor, *From Modernization to Modes of Production* (London, 1979), p. 31; and see generally the critiques of Parsonian modernization theory in ibid., ch. 1, and S. P. Savage, *The Theories of Talcott Parsons* (London, 1981), chs 5 and 6.
19. This account of historical materialism focuses on the theory's logical commitments rather than on the actual views of many Marxists. Recent discussion has been dominated by L. Althusser and E. Balibar, *Reading Capital* (London, 1970), and G. A. Cohen, *Karl Marx's Theory of History – a Defence* (Oxford, 1978). I give my own version in *MH*, esp. ch. 2.
20. See the interesting discussion of these changes in A. Giddens, *A Contemporary Critique of Historical Materialism* (London, 1981), ch. 6. Giddens's views on the aesthetic consequences of these changes are given in 'Modernism and post-modernism', *NGC* 22 (1981).
21. F. Braudel, *The Structures of Everyday Life* (London, 1981), pp. 560–1.
22. The work of Robert Brenner has highlighted the importance of these features of capitalism: see T. E. Aston and C. H. E. Philpin, eds, *The Brenner Debate* (Cambridge, 1985), and R. Brenner, 'The social basis of economic development', in J. Roemer, ed., *Analytical Marxism* (Cambridge, 1986).
23. Marx and Engels, *Collected Works*, VI, p. 487.
24. Ibid., XII, p. 222.
25. Marx, *Grundrisse* (Harmondsworth, 1973), pp. 409–10.
26. Ibid., pp. 487–8.
27. Ibid., pp. 162, 488.
28. *MR*, pp. 321–2.
29. Ibid., p. 323; compare M. Bradbury and J. McFarlane, 'The name and nature of modernism', in *Modernism*.
30. *MR*, pp. 324–5.

31. Ibid., pp. 325–6.
32. Ibid., p. 324. The influence may have been reciprocal: Mayer lists Anderson among those who read drafts of the crucial first four chapters; A. J. Mayer, *The Persistence of the Old Regime* (New York, 1981), p. x.
33. Mayer, *Persistence*, p. 17.
34. Ibid., p. 189.
35. Ibid., pp. 3, 4, 292, 301, 314, 329.
36. See P. Anderson, 'Origins of the present crisis', in P. Anderson and R. Blackburn, eds, *Towards Socialism* (London, 1965), and 'The figures of descent', *NLR* 161 (1987), and, in criticism, E. P. Thompson, 'The peculiarities of the English', in *The Poverty of Theory and Other Essays* (London, 1978), M. Barratt Brown, 'Away with all great arches', *NLR* 167 (1988), A. Callinicos, 'Exception or symptom?', *NLR* 169 (1988) and C. Barker and D. Nicholls, eds, *The Development of British Society* (Manchester, 1988).
37. D. Blackbourn and G. Eley, *The Peculiarities of German History* (Oxford, 1984).
38. E. J. Hobsbawm, *The Age of Empire 1875–1914* (London, 1987), pp. 8–9, 168, 176–7.
39. Mayer, *Persistence*, pp. 253ff.
40. See Hobsbawm, *Empire*, esp. pp. 56–73. I criticize the idea that military competition between states is autonomous of the dialectic of the forces and relations of production in *MH*, ch. 4.
41. N. Stone, *Europe 1878–1919* (London, 1983), ch. 2. Surprisingly, this New Right historian offers an analysis of *fin-de-siècle* Europe more in the spirit of Lenin and Trotsky than that of the *marxisant* Mayer and Marxist Anderson. A detailed portrait of Europe *circa* 1900 which conveys a powerful sense of the contradictory unity of old and new is provided by the *magnum opus* of the Dutch Marxist historian Jan Romein, *The Watershed of Two Eras* (Middletown, 1978).
42. See, for example, L. D. Trotsky, *1905* (Harmondsworth, 1973).
43. Quoted in Stone, *Europe*, p. 152. Mayer argues that '[w]ithin a decade and a half [of 1900] the labour movement and the subject nationalities suffered even greater setbacks that exposed their own intrinsic weaknesses and made plain the strength and resolve of governments to contain them. Even the great popular upheaval in Russia in 1905–1906 followed this pattern', *Persistence*, p. 301. But compare Stone: 'After 1910, in most countries, industrial unrest resulted in many more strikes than before, and in some places – Barcelona in 1909, Ancona and St Petersburg in 1914 – general strikes almost resulted in a takeover of whole towns by "the Reds"', *Europe*, p. 144. In Russia, the revival of working-class militancy after the Lena goldfields massacre of 1912 culminated in a general strike and street barricades in St Petersburg in July 1914: see T. Cliff, *Lenin*, I (London, 1975), chs 18–20.
44. MR, p. 323.

45. An indispensable source on *fin-de-siècle* Vienna is the superb catalogue of the 1986 exhibition at the Pompidou Centre in Paris, *Vienne 1880–1938: L'Apocalypse joyeuse* (Paris, 1986).
46. C. Magris, 'Le flambeau d'ewald', in *Vienne 1880–1938*, p. 22.
47. J. Clair, 'Une modernité sceptique', in *Vienne 1880–1938*, p. 50.
48. E. Nagel, 'Impressions and appraisals of analytical philosophy in Europe', I, *Journal of Philosophy* XXXIII (1936), p. 9. See also P. Jacob, *L'Empirisme logique* (Paris, 1980), pp. 95–101, and D. Lecourt, *L'Ordre et les jeux* (Paris, 1981), ch. 1.
49. See Schorske, *Fin-de-Siècle Vienna* (New York, 1981), ch. 3, R. Rosdolsky, 'La situation révolutionnaire en autriche en 1918 et la politique des sociaux-démocrates', *Critique Communiste* 7/8 (1976), and R. Loew, 'The politics of Austro-Marxism', *NLR* 118 (1979). Ernst Fischer paints a vivid picture of Vienna's postwar crisis in *An Opposing Man* (London, 1974).
50. D. J. Olson, *The City as a Work of Art* (New Haven, 1986), p. 64.
51. Schorske, *Fin-de-Siècle Vienna*, p. 7.
52. Mayer, *Persistence*, pp. 114ff. Vienna's contrasts are somehow summed up by the fact that in 1903–4 both Adolf Hitler and Ludwig Wittgenstein – born within a few days of one another – attended the same school: B. McGuinness, *Wittgenstein: A Life. Young Ludwig (1889–1921)* (London, 1988), p. 51. For a rather unsatisfactory attempt to relate Wittgenstein's thought to the broader Viennese culture see A. Janik and S. Toulmin, *Wittgenstein's Vienna* (New York, 1973).
53. Schorske, *Fin-de-Siècle Vienna*, pp. 7, 8–9, 10. Bankers and industrialists such as Karl Wittgenstein, August Lederer and Otto Primavesi financed Klimt and other members of the Vienna Secession: see B. Michel, 'Les mécènes de la secession', in *Vienne 1880–1938*.
54. Schorske, *Fin-de-Siècle Vienna*, ch. 4.
55. F. Moretti, 'The spell of indecision', *MIC*, pp. 339, 341.
56. C. Schmitt, *Political Romanticism* (Cambridge, Mass., 1986), pp. 17, 71–2, 75–6.
57. Ibid., p. 20.
58. Moretti, 'Spell', p. 342. Stephen Spender also stresses the continuities between Romanticism and literary Modernism: see *The Struggle of the Modern* (London, 1963), pp. 47–55.
59. C. McCabe, *James Joyce and the Revolution of the Word* (London, 1979), chs 6 and 7. McCabe strongly challenged Moretti's application of his general thesis to Joyce: 'Spell' (discussion), p. 345.
60. F. Jameson, *The Political Unconscious* (London, 1981), pp. 19–20.
61. Schorske, *Fin-de-Siècle Vienna*, pp. 250, 254, 258–9, 263.
62. R. A. Maguire and J. E. Malmstad, translators' introduction to A. Bely, *Petersburg* (Harmondsworth, 1983), p. vii.
63. Berman, *All that is Solid*, pp. 255–70.
64. J. Herf, *Reactionary Modernism* (Cambridge, 1984), p. 2; all quotations from ibid., pp. 83, 84, 94, 104; see generally ch. 4.

65. W. Benjamin, *Illuminations* (London, 1970), pp. 243–4; see also Benjamin, 'Theories of German fascism', *NGC* 17 (1979).
66. P. Bürger, *Theory of the Avant Garde* (Manchester, 1984), pp. 27, 49.
67. Benjamin, *Illuminations*, p. 226.
68. Baudelaire, *My Heart Laid Bare*, pp. 55, 56, 57.
69. M. Foucault, 'What is enlightenment?' in P. Rabinow, ed., *A Foucault Reader* (Harmondsworth, 1986), p. 42.
70. W. Benjamin, *Charles Baudelaire* (London, 1973), p. 172.
71. R. Sennett, *The Fall of Public Man* (London, 1986). See, on Benjamin, Frisby, *Fragments*, ch. 4.
72. G. Lukács, *The Meaning of Contemporary Realism* (London, 1972), p. 69.
73. MR, p. 324; see also ibid. (discussion), p. 337. What Lukács says about the distinctive character of Modern art is often very shrewd. It is, however, vitiated by his insistence on seeing Modernism as a degeneration from classical Realism and on deducing it from what he regards as the reactionary nature of the bourgeoisie in the imperialist epoch. The same strengths and weaknesses are to be found in Lukács's critique of post-Hegelian German philosophy in *The Destruction of Reason* (London, 1980). Adorno called this book the destruction of Lukács's own reason, but – to adapt Lenin's remark about Paul Levi – at least he had a head to lose.
74. B. Brecht, 'Against Georg Lukács', in E. Bloch et al., *Aesthetics and Politics* (London, 1977).
75. T. W. Adorno, *Aesthetic Theory* (London, 1984), pp. 31–2.
76. Bürger, *Theory*, p. 49.
77. W. Benjamin, *The Origin of German Tragic Drama* (London, 1977), pp. 54, 187, 198. One could indeed find other precursors of Modernism. Thus Mikhail Bakhtin argues that '[t]he language of the novel is a *system* of languages that mutually and ideologically interanimate each other.' (*The Dialogic Imagination*, Austin, 1981, p. 47) Having first argued that Dostoevsky was the author of 'polyphonic' novels, he later developed the idea that the employment, and indeed parodying of other genres is the specific feature of novelist discourse. Bakhtin uses Rabelais as his main example of what he calls heteroglossia, but one can think of others – *Don Quixote*, for one, *Tristram Shandy* for another. One can argue that Modernism is nevertheless distinctive in self-consciously and systematically developing the conception of language implicit in these earlier writers.
78. Bürger, *Theory*, p. 72.
79. Ibid., pp. 73, 74, 78.
80. Richard Wolin argues that Surrealism's continued commitment to 'the principle of aesthetic autonomy' was 'affirmed by Breton's decision to preserve the sovereign powers of the imagination over against Aragon's willingness to place them at the beck and call of Stalin', 'Modernism vs. postmodernism', *Telos* 62 (1984–5), p. 15. Wolin dates this decision to 1929: in fact the crisis of that year involved the

expulsion from the Surrealist movement of a group *opposed* to its identification with socialist revolution. Breton's break with Aragon came in 1931, after the latter had championed Third Period Stalinism in the poem 'Front rouge'. Breton defended Aragon against the prosecution to which the poem's calls to 'Kill the cops' and 'Fire on Léon Blum' led, but criticized 'Front rouge' as 'poetically regressive' and insisted that the rejection of *l'art pour l'art* and the demand 'that the writer, the artist participate actively in the social struggle' did not imply that 'the goal of poetry and of art' should become 'one of instruction or of revolutionary propaganda', 'The poverty of poetry', appendix to M. Nadeau, *The History of Surrealism* (Harmondsworth, 1973), p. 331. Breton's enduring commitment to an anti-Stalinist version of Marxism is shown by his opposition to the Comintern's Popular-Front policies and his association with Trotsky in the later 1930s: see Nadeau, *History*, part 4, and F. Rosemont, *André Breton and the First Principles of Surrealism* (London, 1978).

81. C. Gray, *The Russian Experiment in Art 1863–1922* (revised edn, London, 1986), p. 116.
82. Quoted, ibid., p. 219.
83. Quotations from K. Frampton, *Modern Architecture: A Critical History* (revised edn, London, 1985), pp. 117–18; see also ibid., ch. 14.
84. J. Willett, *The New Sobriety 1917–1933* (London, 1978), p. 11.
85. J. Willett, ed., *Brecht on Theatre* (London, 1964), p. 20.
86. See C. Harman, *The Lost Revolution* (London, 1982).
87. See S. Fitzpatrick, ed., *Cultural Revolution in Russia, 1928–1931* (Bloomington, 1978).
88. F. Moretti, *Signs Taken for Wonders* (revised edn, London, 1988), p. 209.
89. W. Lewis, *Blasting & Bombardiering* (London, 1967), pp. 256, 260.
90. MR, pp. 326–8.

## CHAPTER 3 The Aporias of Poststructuralism

1. See H. Barth, *Truth and Ideology* (Berkeley and Los Angeles, 1976).
2. PDM, pp. 16, 18, 42, 50, 392 n. 4. On Hegel, see esp. C. Taylor, *Hegel* (Cambridge, 1975), and M. Rosen, *The Hegelian Dialectic and its Criticism* (Cambridge, 1982).
3. PDM, pp. 53, 56.
4. See ibid., pp. 71–4. Parsons himself described 'German idealism as it passed from Hegel through Marx to Weber' as '[p]erhaps the most influential' source of his view of modernity: see *The System of Modern Societies* (Englewood Cliffs, 1971), p. 1.
5. The most systematic presentation of Nietzsche's thought is perhaps R. Schacht, *Nietzsche* (London, 1983).
6. PDM, pp. 122–3.

7. A. Nehemas, *Nietzsche: Life as Literature* (Cambridge, Mass., 1985), p. 39.
8. F. Nietzsche, *The Will to Power* (New York, 1968), § 853, 796.
9. R. Schacht, *Nietzsche*, p. 203.
10. Nietsche, *The Gay Science* (New York, 1974), Preface § 4. Nietzsche goes on to ask whether 'we daredevils of the spirit ... are not ... Greeks? Adorers of forms, of tone, of words? And therefore – *artists?*'
11. Ibid., § 335.
12. Nietzsche, *Twilight of the Idols and The Antichrist* (Harmondsworth, 1968), pp. 102, 104.
13. Nietzsche, *On the Genealogy of Morals and Ecce Homo* (New York, 1969), p. 254.
14. Nehemas, *Nietzsche*, pp. 168, 191, 234.
15. R. Sayre and M. Löwy, 'Figures of romantic anti-capitalism', *NGC* 32 (1984), p. 46. Lukács, who coined the expression 'Romantic anti-capitalism', was reluctant to apply it to Nietzsche, even though he recognized the latter's 'methodological affinities with romantic anti-capitalism', *The Destruction of Reason* (London, 1980), p. 327; see also ibid., pp. 341–2.
16. Nietzsche, *Twilight*, p. 91.
17. Nietzsche, *Will*, § 94.
18. R. Rorty, *The Consequences of Pragmatism* (Brighton, 1982), p. 141.
19. M. Foucault, *Power/Knowledge* (Brighton, 1980), p. 194.
20. E. Said, *The World, the Text and the Critic* (Cambridge, Mass., 1983).
21. J. Derrida, *De la grammatologie* (Paris, 1967), p. 227; compare the English translation by Gayatri Spivak, *Of Grammatology* (Baltimore, 1976), p. 158.
22. See, for example, J. Derrida, 'The ends of man', in *Margins of Philosophy* (Brighton, 1982).
23. Quoted in L. Ferry and A. Renaut, *La Pensée 68* (Paris, 1985), p. 105. See M. Foucault, 'Nietzsche, Freud, Marx', in *Cahiers de Royaumont: Philosophie VI, Nietzsche* (Paris, 1967) and 'Nietzsche, genealogy, history', in *Language, Counter-Memory, Practice* (Oxford, 1977).
24. A. Huyssen, 'Mapping the postmodern', *NGC* 33 (1984), pp. 37–8.
25. Foucault, *The Order of Things* (London, 1970), pp. xvff.
26. Comte de Lautréamount, *Maldoror and Poems* (Harmondsworth, 1978), pp. 216–17.
27. F. Moretti, 'The spell of indecision', in *MIC*, p. 340. See the discussion of Lautréamont's image in M. Nadeau, *The History of Surrealism* (Harmondsworth, 1973), pp. 24–6.
28. Foucault, *Order*, pp. 303, 305, 382, 383, 387.
29. M. Foucault, 'Structuralism and post-structuralism', *Telos 55* (1983), p. 199.

30. C. Norris, *Deconstruction* (London, 1981), p. 21.
31. *PDM*, pp. 189, 205.
32. Ferry and Renaut, *Pensée 68*, pp. 11–12, 38–9.
33. MR, pp. 328–9.
34. V. Descombes, *La Même et l'autre* (Paris, 1979), p. 13.
35. Quoted in Ferry and Renaut, *Pensée 68*, p. 105.
36. See D. Lecourt, *La Philosophie sans feinte* (Paris, 1982), p. 62.
37. *PDM*, p. 133.
38. Foucault, 'Structuralism', pp. 197–8.
39. See also A. Callinicos, *Is there a Future for Marxism?* (London, 1982).
40. F. de Saussure, *Course in General Linguistics* (New York, 1966), pp. 117–18, 120.
41. See esp. C. Lévi-Strauss, 'Introduction à l'oeuvre de Marcel Mauss', in M. Mauss, *Sociologie et anthropologie* (Paris, 1950).
42. P. Dews, *Logics of Disintegration* (London, 1987), p. 19.
43. Callinicos, *Future*, p. 46.
44. Derrida, *Grammatology*, p. 143.
45. J. Derrida, *Writing and Difference* (London, 1978), p. 288.
46. Dews, *Logics*, p. 24; see generally pp. 19ff.
47. Ferry and Renaut, *Pensée 68*, pp. 167–8.
48. *PDM*, pp. 180–1.
49. F. Lentricchia, *After the New Criticism* (London, 1983), p. 171.
50. Ibid., *passim*.
51. C. Norris, *The Contest of Faculties* (London, 1985), p. 18.
52. J. Derrida, 'The time of a thesis: punctuations', in A. Montefiore, ed., *Philosophy in France Today* (Cambridge, 1983), pp. 45, 49.
53. *PDM*, p. 180.
54. J. Derrida, 'Racism's last word', *Critical Inquiry* 12 (1985), pp. 291, 295, 297, 298, 299. See also A. McClintock and R. Nixon, 'No names apart: the separation of work and history in Derrida's "Le Dernier mot du racisme"' and Derrida, 'But beyond . . . (Open Letter to Anne McClintock and Rob Nixon)', ibid., 13 (1986).
55. See A. Callinicos, *South Africa between Reform and Revolution* (London, 1988), chs 4 and 5.
56. Ferry and Renaut, *Pensée 68*, p. 174.
57. *PDM*, p. 183.
58. G. Scholem, *Major Trends in Jewish Mysticism* (New York, 1961), p. 12.
59. W. V. O. Quine, 'Carnap and logical truth', in P. A. Schilpp, ed, *The Philosophy of Rudolph Carnap* (La Salle, 1963), p. 406.
60. D. Davidson, *Inquiries into Truth and Interpretation* (Oxford, 1984), pp. 109, 201; see, on reference, ibid., essay 15.
61. H. Putnam, *Mind, Language and Reality* (Cambridge, 1975).
62. T. Burge, 'Individualism and the Mental', in P. A. French et al., eds, *Midwest Studies in Philosophy*, IV (Minneapolis, 1979), and 'Other bodies', in A. Woodfield, ed., *Thought and Object* (Oxford, 1982).

63. G. Evans, *The Varieties of Reference* (Oxford, 1982), p. 256. For a discussion of the implications of these theories, see P. Pettit and J. McDowell, eds, *Subject, Thought, and Context* (Oxford, 1986), esp. the editors' introduction.
64. For a recent survey, see S. Blackburn, *Spreading the Word* (Oxford, 1984).
65. *PDM*, p. 116.
66. Ibid., pp. 116, 126–7, 185.
67. These are the two strategies taken respectively by Schacht and Nehemas in their books on Nietzsche.
68. Foucault, *Power/Knowledge*, p. 114.
69. G. Deleuze and F. Guattari, *Mille plateaux* (Paris, 1980), pp. 84–129.
70. M. Foucault, *Discipline and Punish* (London, 1977), p. 27.
71. M. Foucault, *L'Usage des plaisirs* (Paris, 1984), pp. 12–13. See my discussion of this displacement in *Future*, ch. 4.
72. Foucault, *Power/Knowledge*, p. 57. Compare Deleuze and Guattari: 'May 68 in France was molecular', involving a 'micro-politics', a flux 'irreducible to the molar segmentarity of class', *Mille plateaux*, pp. 260, 264, 265.
73. See esp. M. Foucault, *La Volonte de savoir* (Paris, 1976), pp. 123–8.
74. Foucault, *Power/Knowledge*, pp. 85, 141.
75. H. Dreyfus and P. Rabinow, *Michel Foucault* (Brighton, 1982), p. 140. See also N. Poulantzas, *State, Power, Socialism* (London, 1978), pp. 146–53, and P. Dews, 'The *Nouvelle Philosophie* and Foucault', *Economy and Society* 8 (1979).
76. Foucault, *Volonté*, p. 208.
77. Dreyfus and Rabinow, *Foucault*, p. 205.
78. Foucault, 'Structuralism', p. 204.
79. Deleuze and Guattari, *Mille plateaux*, pp. 175–6, n. 36, 512. Perversely, perhaps Deleuze's clearest statement of his vitalism is *Foucault* (Paris, 1986), which might better have been called *Deleuze*, since he uses Foucault's writings to expound his own views. Thus: 'the last word of power, is that *resistance is first*' (p. 95) – a statement which contradicts the criticism of Foucault made in the first passage cited here from *Mille plateaux*. And also: 'Force comes from outside, isn't that a certain idea of Life, a certain vitalism in which Foucault's thought culminates? Isn't Life this capacity of force to resist?' (*Foucault*, p. 98), all of which captures far more accurately Deleuze's thought than Foucault's.
80. P. Patton, 'Marxism and beyond', in *MIC*, pp. 129, 132, 133, 134. The object of his criticism is Callinicos, *Future*, chs 6 and 7.
81. Dews, *Logics*, p. 188.
82. Foucault, 'La Grande colère des faits', *Le Nouvel Observateur*, 9 May 1977.
83. Patton, 'Marxism', p. 131.
84. See F. Aubral and X. Delcourt, *Contre la nouvelle philosophie* (Paris,

1977), and, on the political context, R. W. Johnson, *The Long March of the French Left* (London, 1981).

85. P. Anderson, *In the Tracks of Historical Materialism* (London, 1983), p. 32.
86. See A. Krivine and D. Bensaid, *Mai si!* (Paris, 1988), p. 158.
87. *PMC*, p. 82.
88. W. van Reijen and D. Veerman, 'An interview with Jean-François Lyotard', *TCS* 5, 2–3 (1988), pp. 299, 302.
89. J. Baudrillard, *Forget Foucault* (New York, 1987), p. 56.
90. J. Baudrillard, *In the Shadow of the Silent Majorities* (New York, 1983), pp. 39, 52. See esp. ibid., pp. 111–23 for an ineffably silly discussion of the disastrous Schleyer affair (see ch. 4 n. 8 below).
91. Baudrillard, *Forget Foucault*, p. 62.
92. I discuss this general difficulty of Nietzschean theories of domination in 'Marxism and power', in A. Leftwich, ed., *New Developments in Political Science* (Upleadon, forthcoming).
93. Foucault, *Power/Knowledge*, pp. 73–4.
94. M. Foucault, 'The subject and power', Afterword to Dreyfus and Rabinow, *Foucault*, p. 221.
95. Foucault, 'Structuralism', p. 207.
96. Foucault, *Usage*, pp. 12, 16–17. See my review of this book and the subsequent volume of the *Histoire de la sexualité*, *Le Souci de soi* (Paris, 1984), 'Foucault's third theoretical displacement', *TCS* 3, 3 (1986).
97. Foucault, *Power/Knowledge*, p. 98.
98. See, for example, C. Gordon, 'Question, ethos, event', *Economy and Society* 15 (1986), p. 85, and Deleuze, *Foucault*, pp. 103ff.
99. Ferry and Renaut, *Pensée 68*, pp. 150–1.
100. M. Foucault, 'On the genealogy of ethics', in P. Rabinow, ed., *A Foucault Reader* (Harmondsworth, 1986), p. 350.
101. Nietzsche, *Gay Science*, § 290. Compare Foucault, 'Genealogy', p. 351.
102. Nehemas, *Nietzsche*, pp. 172, 183–4, 188.
103. Nietzsche, *Genealogy*, p. 255.
104. Nehemas, *Nietzsche*, p. 181.
105. The problems involved in such a principle of individuation to which Derek Parfit draws attention – see esp. *Reasons and Persons* (Oxford, 1984) – seem to me more to highlight the roots of the modern concept of the person in a certain conception of the world, and more particularly of spatio-temporal relationships, than to demonstrate the need to abandon it. See P. F. Strawson, *Individuals* (London, 1960).
106. Nietzsche, *Gay Science*, § 90.
107. Nehemas, *Nietzsche*, p. 253, n. 17.
108. See *MH*, esp. ch. 1.

CHAPTER 4   The Limits of Communicative Reason

1. J. Habermas, 'Modernity – an incomplete project', in H. Foster, ed., *Postmodern Culture* (London, 1985), p. 9.
2. The main texts of this debate are gathered together in R. Augstein et al., '*Historikerstreit*' (Munich, 1987). See also the special issue of *NGC* 44 (1988).
3. Habermas, 'Modernity', p. 14.
4. F. Jameson, 'The politics of theory', *NGC* 33 (1984), p. 59.
5. See esp. *PMC*, pp. 18ff.
6. C. Norris, *The Contest of Faculties* (London, 1985), pp. 23–4.
7. Hubert Dreyfus and Paul Rabinow stress the similarities between Foucauldian archaeology and Heideggerian hermeneutics: see, for example, *Michel Foucault* (Brighton, 1982), p. 122.
8. J. Habermas, *Autonomy and Solidarity* (London, 1986), p. 107. In September 1987 leading German industrialist Hans-Martin Schleyer was kidnapped by the Red Army Fraction, unleashing a crisis encompassing his own death and those of RAF leaders in Stammheim Prison.
9. Ibid., p. 158.
10. *TCA* I, pp. 143, 379, 385. See also *PDM*, Lecture V.
11. *PDM*, p. 317.
12. *TCA*, I, pp. 390, 392. See also *PDM*, Lecture XI.
13. *TCA*, I, pp. 284–7, 302, 305. Habermas in fact offers a more elaborated typology of action: see ibid., pp. 85ff. His philosophy of language is developed in some detail in *Communication and the Evolution of Society* (London, 1979).
14. Habermas, *Communication*, p. 177.
15. *TCA*, I, p. 398.
16. *PDM*, p. 315.
17. *TCA*, I, p. 241.
18. *PDM*, p. 310.
19. *TCA*, II, pp. 119, 131. See generally ibid., ch. 6.
20. J. Habermas, 'A review of Gadamer's *Truth and Method*', in F. R. Dallmayr and T. A. McCarthy, eds, *Understanding and Social Inquiry* (Notre Dame, 1977), p. 356.
21. *TCA*, I, p. 70.
22. Ibid., p. 249.
23. Ibid., pp. 241, 249. See generally ibid., ch. 2.
24. *TCA*, II, pp. 150, 184, 263.
25. See, for example, T. Parsons, 'On the concept of political power', in *Politics and Social Structure* (New York, 1969), and the critical discussion of Parsons in *TCA*, II, ch. 7.
26. A. Wellmer, 'Reason, utopia, and enlightenment', in R. Bernstein, ed., *Habermas and Modernity* (Cambridge, 1985), p. 39.
27. *TCA*, II, p. 339.
28. Habermas, *Communication*, pp. 97–8, 99, 117, 120. Compare *TCA*, II, 313–14.

29. *PDM*, p. 355.
30. *TCA*, II, p. 304.
31. See J. Habermas, *Legitimation Crisis* (London, 1976).
32. *TCA*, II, pp. 392–3, 394.
33. Habermas, *Autonomy*, p. 107.
34. *PDM*, p. 364.
35. *TCA*, I, pp. 2–3.
36. See, in addition to the following discussion on Habermas's philosophy of language, the remarks in *MH*, pp. 110–14.
37. See, for example, *TCA*, I, pp. 307–8, and Habermas, *Communication*, ch. 1.
38. See, for example, L. Wittgenstein, *Philosophical Investigations* (Oxford, 1968, I, § 194.
39. *TCA*, I, pp. 287–8.
40. Ibid., p. 305.
41. J. Habermas, *Knowledge and Human Interests* (London, 1972), p. 314.
42. P. Anderson, *In the Tracks of Historical Materialism* (London, 1983), p. 64.
43. M. Dummett, 'A nice derangement of epitaphs: some comments on Davidson and Hacking', in E. LePore, ed., *Truth and Interpretation* (Oxford, 1986), p. 471.
44. Wittgenstein, *Investigations*, I, § 242.
45. See S. Kripke, *Wittgenstein on Rules and Private Language* (Oxford, 1982), and C. McGinn, *Wittgenstein on Meaning* (Oxford, 1984).
46. Wittgenstein, *Investigations*, I, §§ 242, 206.
47. McGinn, *Wittgenstein*, p. 85.
48. W. V. O. Quine, 'Carnap and logical truth', in P. A. Schilpp, ed., *Carnap and Logical Truth* (La Salle, 1963), p. 406. Quine's famous assault on the analytic–synthetic distinction is to be found in 'Two dogmas of empiricism', in *From a Logical Point of View* (revised edn, Cambridge, Mass., 1961).
49. See my discussion of Davidson's theory of interpretation in *MH*, pp. 104–10.
50. D. Davidson, *Inquiries into Truth and Interpretation* (Oxford, 1984), p. 280. Davidson has indeed taken this anti-conventionalism to the extent of denying that communication involves interlocuters sharing a language: see 'A nice derangement of epitaphs', in LePore, ed., *Truth*, to which Dummett's paper of the same name, cited in n. 43 above, is a response. The argument here seems to be one between two different forms of naturalism.
51. Quoted in *TCA*, I, pp. 72–3.
52. Habermas, *Autonomy*, pp. 160–1.
53. *TCA*, II, p. 397.
54. Habermas, *Autonomy*, p. 205.
55. See, for example, A. MacIntyre, *After Virtue* (London, 1981), S. Lovibond, *Realism and Imagination in Ethics* (Oxford, 1983) and B. Williams, *Ethics and the Limits of Philosophy* (London, 1985).

56. R. Rorty, 'Posties', *London Review of Books*, 3 September 1987, p. 12.
57. See Norris, *Contest*, ch. 6, for a critical discussion of Rorty's 'post-modernist bourgeois liberalism'.
58. R. Rorty, *The Consequences of Pragmatism* (Brighton, 1982), p. 165.
59. See Rorty, 'Pragmatism, Davidson and truth', in LePore, ed., *Truth*.
60. Davidson, *Inquiries*, p. xviii. Davidson has explored the epistemological implications of his philosophical semantics in 'A coherence theory of truth and knowledge', in LePore, ed., *Truth*.
61. See, for example, the statement (and critique) of Habermas's theory of truth in J. B. Thompson, 'Universal pragmatics', in J. B. Thompson and D. Held, ed., *Habermas: Critical Debates* (London, 1982), pp. 129–31, and also A. Giddens, 'Reason without revolution?', in Bernstein, ed., *Habermas and Modernity*, pp. 114–17.
62. I. Lakatos, *Philosophical Papers* (2 vols, Cambridge, 1978), I.
63. K. R. Popper, *Realism and the Aim of Science* (London, 1982).
64. J. Habermas, 'A reply to my critics', in Thompson and Held, eds., *Habermas*, p. 275.
65. *PDM*, pp. 64, 78–9; see generally pp. 75–82, 316–36.
66. Ibid., p. 81. See also J. Habermas, 'Labour and interaction', in *Theory and Practice* (London, 1974), and *Knowledge*, part 1.
67. See esp. V. N. Voloshinov, *Marxism and the Philosophy of Language* (New York, 1973). I discuss the implications of the work of Bakhtin and his school for Marxism in 'Postmodernism, poststructuralism, post-Marxism?', *TCS* 2, 3 (1985), and in an unpublished paper, 'The missing link?'.
68. See G. A. Cohen, 'Reconsidering historical materialism', and N. Geras, 'The controversy about Marx and justice', both reprinted in A. Callinicos, ed., *Marxist Theory* (Oxford, 1989). I discuss these matters in my Introduction to this collection, and in *MH*, ch. 1.
69. See, for example, A. Heller, 'Habermas and Marxism', in Thompson and Held, eds, *Habermas*, J. Whitebrook, 'Reason and happiness', in Bernstein, ed., *Habermas and Modernity*, and, for an essential critique of deontological ethics, see Williams, *Ethics*.
70. See *MH*, chs 3 and 5, for a discussion of the sense in which the Marxist theory of interests is not reducible to the concept of instrumental action.
71. Habermas, *Communication*, p. 144.
72. *TCA*, II, p. 168.
73. Habermas, *Communication*, p. 99; see generally ibid., chs. 2–4.
74. *PDM*, p. 359.
75. *TCA*, II, pp. 350–1.
76. See D. Held, 'Crisis tendencies, legitimation and the state', in Thompson and Held, eds, *Habermas*. Habermas himself makes the same point at times: 'In place of the positive task of meeting a certain need for interpretation by ideological means, we have the negative requirement of preventing holistic interpretations from coming into existence ... *Everyday consciousness* is robbed of its power to synthesize; it

becomes *fragmented*', *TCA*, II, p. 355. But this seems to conjure up the vision of a state of affairs (precapitalist society?) where ruling-class 'holistic interpretations' were accepted by the masses – a historically questionable view: see N. Abercrombie et al., *The Dominant Ideology Thesis* (London, 1980), and *MH*, ch. 4.

77. *TCA*, II, p. 345.
78. Habermas, *Communication*, p. 186.
79. Habermas, 'Sovereignty and the *Führerdemokratie*', *Times Literary Supplement*, 26 September 1986, p. 1054.
80. See the texts concerning Schmitt's collaboration with the Nazis, along with broader discussion of his thought, in *Telos* 72 (1987), a special issue devoted to Schmitt.
81. C. Schmitt, *Political Theology* (Cambridge, Mass., 1985), p. 5 and *passim*.
82. C. Schmitt, *The Concept of the Political* (New Brunswick, 1976), p. 29 and *passim*.
83. Schmitt, *Political Theology*, p. 59.
84. C. Schmitt, *The Crisis of Parliamentary Democracy* (Cambridge, Mass., 1985), pp. 5–6.
85. Habermas, 'Sovereignty', p. 1054.
86. Habermas, *Autonomy*, pp. 178–9.
87. See B. Hahn and P. Schöttler, 'Jürgen Habermas und "das ungetrübte Bewußtsein des Bruchs"', in H. Gerstenberger and D. Schmidt, eds, *Normalität oder Normalisierung?* (Münster, 1987).
88. Habermas, *Legitimation Crisis*, p. 117.
89. For a fascinating example of such enquiry, see E. M. Wood, *Peasant-Citizen and Slave* (London, 1988).
90. Giddens, 'Reason', p. 120. See also A. Giddens, 'Labour and interaction', in Thompson and Held, eds, *Habermas*.
91. Another example of Habermas's tendency to adopt too uncritical a stance towards modernity in his claim that the social differentiation produced by capitalist development is irreversible – or rather, that any attempt to overcome this differentiation would in fact invite social regression (see esp. section 4.2 above). This implies that one must either accept the separation of economy and polity characteristic of capitalism, or seek only to modify it, a position which has received independent support from the current vogue for market socialism: see esp. A. Nove, *The Economics of Feasible Socialism* (London, 1983). Although I believe that socialist acceptance of the market represents a disastrous retreat based in part on a misunderstanding of the economic trends discussed in section 5.3 below, the subject raises issues which cannot be dealt with here, but see, for example, E. Mandel, 'In defence of socialist planning', *NLR* 159 (1986), and C. Harman, 'The myth of market socialism', *IS* 2, 43 (1989). On the more general question of social differentiation, it seems to me perfectly possible to accept that a socialist society would be a highly complex form of social organization, as Marx came to recognize – see A. Rattansi,

*Marx and the Division of Labour* (London, 1982) – but that it would nevertheless involve a *different* form of complexity from that of capitalism. Anderson makes some interesting observations on the subject: see MR (discussion), p. 336.

### CHAPTER 5    So What Else is New?

1. D. Bell, *The Coming of Post-Industrial Society* (London, 1974), pp. 212, 284, 297–8 and *passim*.
2. See ibid., pp. 33–40, on the history of the expression 'postindustrial society': Bell apparently shares with David Riesman the dubious honour of having invented the phrase at the end of the 1950s.
3. See, for example, R. Heilbroner, *Business Civilization in Decline* (Harmondsworth, 1977), ch. 3, and K. Kumar, *Prophecy and Progress* (Harmondsworth, 1978), chs 6 and 7.
4. M. Prowse, 'The need to bolster confidence', *FT*, 30 November 1987.
5. See my discussion of Gorz in *MH*, pp. 184–9.
6. A. Kaletsky and G. de Jonquieres, 'Why a service economy is no panacea', *FT*, 22 May 1987.
7. M. Prowse, 'Why services may be no substitute for manufacturing', *FT*, 25 October 1985.
8. Ibid.
9. See, for example, in addition to Prowse, 'Services', Kaletsky and Jonquieres, 'Service economy', and the special report 'Can America compete?', *Business Week*, 27 April 1987.
10. See A. Callinicos and C. Harman, *The Changing Working Class* (London, 1987), ch. 1.
11. Kaletsky and Jonquieres, 'Service economy'.
12. Information on California in this paragraph drawn from P. Stephens, 'Uneasy realities behind a post-industrial dream', *FT*, 15 October 1986.
13. M. Davis with S. Buddick, 'Los Angeles: civil liberties between the hammer and the rock', *NLR* 170 (1988), p. 48. The expression 'Bloody Taylorism' was coined by Alain Lipietz to denote Third World industries devoted to the unskilled, repetitive and highly exploited assembly of manufactured exports, especially textiles and electronics: see *Mirages and Miracles* (London, 1987), pp. 73ff.
14. Stephens, 'Uneasy realities'.
15. See esp. N. Harris, *The End of the Third World* (London, 1986).
16. P. Kellogg, 'Goodbye to the working class?', *IS* 2, 36 (1987), pp. 108–10.
17. C. Owens, 'Feminists and postmodernists', in H. Foster, ed., *Postmodern Culture* (London, 1985), p. 63.
18. See, for example, M. Poster, *Critical Theory of the Family* (London, 1978).

19. See, for example, A. Rogers, 'Women at work', *IS* 2, 32 (1986), and the much more extended analysis in Lindsey German's forthcoming book on women and class.
20. J. Baudrillard, *The Mirror of Production* (St Louis, 1975), p. 80.
21. MR (discussion), p. 337. See, on 'primitive' societies, *inter alia*, M. Godelier, *Rationality and Irrationality in Economics* (London, 1972), and M. Sahlins, *Stone Age Economics* (London, 1974).
22. PDM, p. 79. See also, for example, J. Habermas, *Autonomy and Solidarity* (London, 1986), pp. 140ff.
23. F. Jameson, 'The politics of theory', *NGC* 33 (1984), p. 53.
24. F. Jameson, *Marxism and Form* (Princeton, 1971), pp. 103–4, 105. Jameson's discussion of Surrealism (ibid., pp. 95–106) seems to have influenced Anderson's views on Modernism: see MR, 327.
25. F. Jameson, 'Postmodernism, or the cultural logic of late capitalism', *NLR* 146 (1984), pp. 78 and *passim*.
26. Ibid., pp. 83, 85, 86, 88.
27. W. Benjamin, *Understanding Brecht* (London, 1973), p. 121.
28. F. Jameson, *The Political Unconscious* (London, 1981), pp. 35, 41, 57, 52–3, 75, 98.
29. L. Althusser and E. Balibar, *Reading Capital* (London, 1970), p. 94.
30. See, for example, G. Stedman-Jones, 'The Marxism of the early Lukács', *NLR* 70 (1971).
31. For a similar criticism of the 'Postmodernism' article, see M. Davis, 'Urban renaissance and the spirit of postmodernism', *NLR* 151 (1985), pp. 106–7. See more generally on Jameson, T. Eagleton, 'The idealism of American criticism', *NLR* 127 (1981), pp. 62–4, E. Said, 'Opponents, audiences, constituencies and community', in Foster, ed., *Postmodern Culture*, pp. 146–8, and D. Kellner, 'Postmodernism as social theory', *TCS* 5, 2/3 (1988), pp. 258–62.
32. Jameson, 'Postmodernism', p. 80.
33. See A. Callinicos, 'Reactionary postmodernism?', in R. Boyne and A. Rattansi, eds, *Postmodernism and Social Theory* (Houndmills, forthcoming).
34. Jameson, *Political Unconscious*, p. 53.
35. See esp. Jameson, 'Cognitive mapping', in *MIC*.
36. See D. Latimer, 'Jameson and post-modernism', *NLR* 148 (1984), and, on Marxism and ethics, *MH*, ch. 1.
37. Althusser and Balibar, *Reading*, pp. 99, 104; see generally pp. 91–105, and P. Anderson, *Arguments within English Marxism* (London, 1980), pp. 73–7.
38. See Callinicos, 'Reactionary postmodernism'.
39. Jameson, *Marxism*, pp. xvii–xviii, 36n., 105.
40. Jameson, 'Postmodernism', pp. 53, 55.
41. Davis, 'Urban renaissance', pp. 106–7. See E. Mandel, *Late Capitalism* (London, 1975), and *The Second Slump* (London, 1980).
42. S. Lash and J. Urry, *The End of Organized Capitalism* (Cambridge, 1987).

43. See esp. M. Aglietta, *A Theory of Capitalist Regulation* (London, 1979).
44. See, for example, R. Murray, 'Life after Henry (Ford)', *Marxism Today*, October 1988.
45. S. Hall, 'Brave new world', ibid., pp. 24, 27.
46. K. Williams et al., 'The end of mass production?', *Economy and Society* 16 (1987). I am grateful to Lindsey German for drawing my attention to this article.
47. Callinicos and Harman, *Changing Working Class*, pp. 62–7. For a general critique of the 'post-Fordism' thesis, see J. Robertson, 'Consuming passions', *Socialist Worker Review*, December 1988.
48. Though it should be noted that Lash and Urry do detect a trend towards 'flexible specialization': see *End*, p. 199.
49. Ibid., pp. 208–9.
50. N. Harris, *Of Bread and Guns* (Harmondsworth, 1983), esp. chs 2, 4, 7, and *End of the Third World, passim*.
51. D. M. Gordon, 'The global economy: new edifice or crumbling foundations?', *NLR* 168 (1988), pp. 54, 63–4, and *passim*.
52. See A. Callinicos, 'Imperialism, capitalism, and the state today', *IS* 2, 35 (1987).
53. *FT*, 21 October 1987.
54. For an analysis of Black Monday and its immediate aftermath, see C. Lapavitas, 'Financial crisis and the stock exchange crash', *IS* 2, 38 (1988).
55. M. Wolf, 'The need to look to the long term', *FT*, 16 November 1987.
56. H. Belloc, *The Servile State* (Indianapolis, 1977). For a general summary of *fin-de-siècle* economic trends, see E. J. Hobsbawm, *The Age of Empire 1875–1914* (London, 1987), pp. 50–73.
57. See N. I. Bukharin, *Imperialism and World Economy* (London, 1972), and, for an analysis of the interwar crisis along these lines, C. Harman, *Explaining the Crisis* (London, 1984), ch. 2.
58. Harris, *Of Bread*, ch. 2 provides the best general survey of these changes.
59. See, for example, D. Filtzer, *Soviet Workers and Stalinist Industrialization* (London, 1986), p. 91, and M. Ellman, 'Did the agricultural surplus provide the resources for the increase in investment in the USSR during the First Five-Year Plan?', *Economic Journal* 85 (1975).
60. J. M. Keynes, *The General Theory of Employment Interest and Money* (London, 1970), p. 313.
61. See esp. Harman, *Explaining*, ch. 3.
62. A. Kaletsky, 'The triumph of John Maynard Reagan', *FT*, 3 May 1986.
63. P. Green, 'Contradictions of the American boom', *IS* 2, 26 (1985). Another remarkable form of economic intervention by the American state is the rescue of bankrupt savings and loan associations by the

Federal Home Loan Bank Board in co-operation with corporations like Ford and Revlon at an estimated eventual cost to the US government of $38.6 billion: see *New York Times*, 31 December 1988.

64. For a general survey, see P. Green, 'British capitalism and the Thatcher years', *IS* 2, 35 (1987). Not every major Western capitalist state has followed the pattern set by the US; the chief exception is West Germany, which, under the direction of the Bundesbank, has pursued tight-money policies. On the different trajectories of the Western economies, see M. Aglietta, 'World capitalism in the eighties', *NLR* 136 (1982).

65. M. Davis, *Prisoners of the American Dream* (London, 1986), p. 233; see ibid., ch. 6 *passim*.

66. Quoted in R. Brenner, 'The roots of US economic decline', *Against the Current* 2 (1986), p. 27.

67. *FT*, 18 April 1987.

68. Ibid., 13 August 1988.

69. F. Nietzsche, *The Gay Science* (New York, 1974), § 383.

70. C. Lasch, *The Culture of Narcissim* (London, 1980), p. xvi.

71. D. Bell, *The Cultural Contradictions of Capitalism* (London, 1979).

72. S. Bellow and M. Amis, 'The moronic inferno', in B. Brooks et al., eds, *Modernity and its Discontents* (Nottingham, 1987), the transcript of a discussion moderated by Michael Ignatieff on Channel 4 TV's now defunct series *Voices*, shown in the spring of 1986.

73. G. Lipovetsky, *L'Ère du vide* (Paris, 1983). See also Bell, *Contradictions*, ch. 3.

74. J. Baudrillard, *Simulations* (New York, 1983), pp. 12, 48, 53–4, 143, 146.

75. J. Baudrillard, *In the Shadow of the Silent Minorities* (New York, 1983).

76. J. Baudrillard, *Simulations*, p. 115.

77. J. Baudrillard, *Mirror*, p. 122.

78. Baudrillard, *Simulations*, pp. 99, 150–2.

79. Baudrillard, *Amérique* (Paris, 1986), pp. 21, 32, 143, 150, 151, 178, 194–5, 150, 195.

80. J. Baudrillard, *Shadow*, pp. 83–4.

81. J. Bouveresse, 'Why I am so very unFrench', in A. Montefiore, ed., *Philosophy in France Today* (Cambridge, 1983), p. 15.

82. *PDM*, p. 188; see generally ibid., pp. 185–210.

83. R. Sennett, *The Fall of Public Man* (London, 1986), pp. 19, 21, 23, 261–2.

84. K. Marx, *Capital*, I (Harmondsworth, 1976), p. 165.

85. Quoted in D. Frisby, Introduction to G. Simmel, *The Philosophy of Money* (London, 1978), p. 11; see, on Simmel, Kracauer, and Benjamin, D. Frisby, *Fragments of Modernity* (Cambridge, 1985). Simmel was an important influence on both Lukács and Benjamin.

86. See, for example, Simmel, *Philosophy*, pp. 472ff.

87. W. Benjamin, *Charles Baudelaire* (London, 1973), p. 172. Compare

his definition of modernity as 'the new in the context of what has always been there', quoted and discussed in Frisby, *Fragments* pp. 207ff.

88. G. Debord, *The Society of the Spectacle* (Detroit, 1970), § 1, 4, 6, 36.
89. Baudrillard, *Simulations*, p. 54. See, on the Situationists' influence, Baudrillard, 'Lost in the hypermarket', *City Limits*, 8 December 1988, p. 88.
90. Debord, *Society*, § 7, 9.
91. See A. Callinicos, *Marxism and Philosophy* (Oxford, 1983), pp. 127–36.
92. See Harman, *Explaining*, pp. 143–7 and M. Glick and R. Brenner, 'The regulation approach to the history of capitalism', forthcoming in *NLR*; his reliance on the regulation school's theory of crises is the major flaw in Davis's writings on American capitalism.
93. Aglietta, *Theory*, pp. 158–61.
94. Bell, *Coming*, p. 318, n. 30.
95. Lipovetsky, *Ère*, pp. 7, 14, 47–8, 142–3.
96. Hobsbawm, *Empire*, pp. 220, 237–8.
97. MR, 329.
98. T. W. Adorno, *Aesthetic Theory* (London, 1984), pp. 83–4.
99. C. Greenberg, 'Avant garde and kitsch', *Partisan Review* VI: 5 (1939), p. 49.
100. See S. Guilbaut, *How New York Stole the Idea of Modern Art* (Chicago, 1983), and J. D. Herbert, 'The political origins of Abstract-Expressionist art criticism', *Telos* 62 (1984–5).
101. Adorno, *Aesthetic Theory*, p. 44.
102. R. A. Berman, 'Modern art and desublimation', *Telos* 62 (1984/5), p. 41.
103. P. Bürger, *Theory of the Avant Garde* (Manchester, 1984), pp. 17, 80, 81.
104. Quoted in C. Ratcliff, 'The marriage of art and money', *Art in America*, July 1988, p. 78.
105. Quoted in E. Hartney, 'Art vs. Market', ibid., p. 31.
106. C. Schorske, *Fin-de-Siècle Vienna* (New York, 1981), p. 36; see generally ibid., ch. 2.
107. K. Frampton, *Modern Architecture: A Critical History* (revised edn, London, 1985), pp. 231, 237.
108. Berman, 'Modern art', p. 43.
109. Ibid., pp. 45–6. Bürger argues that this 'false sublation' of art and life is a danger inherent in the avant-garde project since 'the (relative) freedom of art *vis-à-vis* the praxis of life is at the same time the condition that must be fulfilled if there is to be a critical cognition of reality. An art no longer distinct from the praxis of life but wholly absorbed in it will lose the capacity to criticize it.' (*Theory*, p. 50) But surely much depends on the conditions under which the integration of art and life occurs. The avant-garde movements aspired to

reintegrate art into a *transformed* social life; in the absence of such transformation, their members could only carry on as *artists*, on the terms of bourgeois society, with all the contradictions entailed, some of which are outlined in the text. An attempt to reaestheticize social life on the basis of the collective and democratic control of resources by the direct producers would not entail the suppression of the critical role historically played by art in bourgeois society, since the exercise of such control would require constant discussion of alternatives. Trotsky's exploration of these questions in *Literature and Revolution* (Ann Arbor, 1971) retains its relevance. In the meantime, the avant-garde project seems unfulfilled rather than misconceived. See Habermas's rather ambiguous remarks in *Autonomy*, p. 173.

110. P. Bürger, 'The decline of the modern age', *Telos* 62 (1984–5), pp. 117–18.
111. Ibid., pp. 120–1.
112. Greenberg, 'Avant-Garde', p. 37; see also Greenberg, 'Towards a newer Lacoon', *Partisan Review* VII, 4 (1940).
113. See J. Willett, *The New Sobriety 1917–1933* (London, 1978).
114. Greenberg, 'Avant-Garde', p. 37.
115. See, for example, C. Jencks, 'The Prince versus the architects', *Observer*, 12 June 1988.
116. For a summary of these trends, see Lash and Urry, *End*, pp. 99ff.; on the US, see, for example, D. Smith, *Social Theory and the City* (Oxford, 1980), pp. 236ff., and, on Britain, D. Massey, *Spatial Divisions of Labour* (London, 1984).
117. D. Harvey, *The Urbanization of Capital* (Oxford, 1985), pp. 205–6, 207, 215.
118. Ibid., pp. 215–17.
119. Davis, 'Urban renaissance', pp. 109–10, 111–12. See also the critical comments on Jameson's discussion of the Bonaventure Hotel in R. Jacoby, *The Last Intellectuals* (New York, 1987), pp. 168–72.
120. P. Townsend et al., *Poverty and Labour in London* (London, 1987).
121. D. Davis, 'Late postmodern: the end of style', *Art in America*, July 1987. I am grateful to Margie Robertson for drawing my attention to this article.
122. D. Ghirardo, 'Past or post modern in architectural fashion', *Telos* 62 (1984–5), p. 190.
123. See S. Zukin, 'The postmodern debate on urban form', *TCS* 5, 2–3 (1988), pp. 437–8.
124. Frampton, *Modern Architecture*, p. 306.
125. MR, p. 329.
126. PMC, p. 76.
127. J. Goldthorpe, 'On the service class, its formation and future', in A. Giddens and G. Mackenzie, eds, *Social Class and the Division of Labour* (Cambridge, 1982), p. 172.
128. E. O. Wright, *Class, Crisis and the State* (London, 1978), ch. 2, and

Callinicos and Harman, *Changing Working Class.*

129. Although Lash and Urry in my view greatly exaggerate the importance of the 'new middle class', treating it as the main initiator of first
the organization and then the disorganization of twentieth-century,
especially US, capitalism: see *End*, pp. 163ff.
130. R. Samuel, 'The SDP and the new political class', *New Society*, 22
April 1982.
131. For an attempt to do so which seems to me largely a wasted
opportunity, see F. Pfeil, 'Postmodernism as a "structure of feeling"', in *MIC*.
132. See Callinicos and Harman, *Changing Working Class*, pp. 37–49.
133. Davis, *Prisoners*, pp. 211, 212, 218, 234.
134. See, on the collapse of the French intellectual left, A. Callinicos, *Is
there a Future for Marxism?* (London, 1982), and P. Anderson, *In
the Tracks of Historical Materialism* (London, 1983). Chris Harman
analyses the general crisis of the European far left in *The Fire Last
Time* (London, 1988), ch. 16.
135. Harman, *Fire*, p. viii.
136. For a survey of the French debate on 1968, see L. Ferry and
A. Renaut, *La Pensée 68* (Paris, 1985), ch. 2.
137. R. Debray, 'A modest contribution to the rites and ceremonies of the
tenth anniversary', *NLR* 115 (1979), p. 47.
138. Lipovetsky, *Ère*, pp. 119, 143.
139. Debray, 'Modest contribution', p. 48.
140. See H. Weber, 'Reply to Debray', *NLR* 115 (1979).
141. A. Krivine and D. Bensaid, *Mai Si!* (Paris, 1988), p. 59.
142. H. Weber, *Vingt ans après* (Paris, 1988), pp. 166, 177; see generally
ibid., ch. 6. See Krivine and Bensaid, *Mai Si!*, pp. 59–61 for a critical
discussion by his former comrades of Weber's own analysis of 1968.
143. Harman, *Fire*, p. 339. See ibid., *passim*, for the analysis which
follows.
144. *Business Week*, 27 April 1987.
145. More generally, I think that the Marxist theory of ideology is best
concerned with explaining why certain beliefs are accepted, not how
they originated: see *MH*, p. 139.
146. R. Shusterman, 'Postmodernist aesthetics: a new moral philosophy',
*TCS* 5, 2–3 (1988), p. 337.
147. See F. Kermode, *History and Value* (Oxford, 1988).
148. Baudrillard, 'Lost', p. 88.
149. S. Sontag, 'Notes on camp', in *A Susan Sontag Reader* (Harmondsworth, 1983), p. 107.
150. Callinicos, 'Reactionary postmodernism'.
151. See A. Bloom, *Prodigal Sons* (New York, 1986), and A. Wald, *The
New York Intellectuals* (Chapel Hill, 1987).
152. See C. Hill, *The Experience of Defeat* (London, 1984).
153. See, for example, on the American avant garde of the 1960s,
A. Huyssen, 'Mapping the postmodern', *NGC* 33 (1984), pp. 20ff.

154. For a case-study with some general reflections, see A. Callinicos, *South Africa between Reform and Revolution* (London, 1988), Introduction and chs 4 and 5.

### Afterword

1. See J. Habermas, *Knowledge and Human Interests* (London, 1972), pp. 301–7.
2. G. Deleuze and F. Guattari, *L'Anti-Oedipe* (Paris, 1973), pp. 356ff.
3. W. Benjamin, *The Origins of German Tragic Drama* (London, 1977), p. 232.
4. Benjamin, 'Theses on the philosophy of history', in *Illuminations* (London, 1970); see R. Wolin, *Walter Benjamin: an Aesthetic of Redemption* (New York, 1982). I discuss the 'Theses' in *MH*, ch. 5.

# INDEX